# URBAN MARATHONS

This original social science text approaches marathon running as an everyday practice and a designed event, to draw upon and contribute to the literature on practice theory, urban events, rhythmanalysis and mobility. It bridges sport studies and discussions within sociology and geography about practice, movement and the city.

Inspired by theoretical debates about embodied and multi-sensuous mobilities, social and material practices, and urban rhythms, this book explores the characteristics of marathon running as a bodily practice on the one hand and, on the other, marathon training grounds and events as unique places. This account takes marathon running seriously, using sociological and geographical theory to understand the practice in and of itself. Based on original empirical research and accessible to readers, taking them to training sessions in Copenhagen and to marathons in Tokyo, Kyoto, Berlin, Frankfurt, Valencia and Copenhagen, it draws out the globalised, codified and generic nature of marathon practices and design, yet also brings out the significant local differences. The book examines in ethnographic detail how marathon practices and places are *produced* by various materialities, cultural scripts, experts, runners and spectators, and *practiced* in embodied, multi-sensuous and 'emplaced' ways by ordinary runners. It develops a sociological practice approach to marathon running and geographical understanding of marathon places and rhythms. It demonstrates that marathon running is of broad interest because it calls for and allows lively and expressive ways of conducting and writing research and understanding the becoming of bodies, the intertwining of biological and mechanical rhythms and the eventful potential of streets.

It will appeal to postgraduate students and scholars in sport studies, geography and sociology interested in running, active mobility and ethnography, as well as tourism and urban events. The book will also appeal to general readers with an interest in marathon running.

**Jonas Larsen** is an internationally recognised professor of mobility and urban studies at Roskilde University, Denmark. He has published extensively about tourist photography, tourism, cycling, running and mobility more broadly.

# URBAN MARATHONS

## Rhythms, Places, Mobilities

*Jonas Larsen*

Routledge
Taylor & Francis Group

LONDON AND NEW YORK

First published 2022
by Routledge
2 Park Square, Milton Park, Abingdon, Oxon OX14 4RN

and by Routledge
605 Third Avenue, New York, NY 10158

*Routledge is an imprint of the Taylor & Francis Group, an informa business*

Front cover. The start at the Valencia Marathon. Photo credit: The Valencia Marathon.

DOI: 10.4324/9781003125068

*British Library Cataloguing-in-Publication Data*
A catalogue record for this book is available from the British Library

*Library of Congress Cataloging-in-Publication Data*
Names: Larsen, Jonas, author.
Title: Urban marathons : rhythms, places, mobilities / Jonas Larsen.
Description: Abingdon, Oxon ; New York, NY : Routledge, 2022. |
Includes bibliographical references and index.
Identifiers: LCCN 2021020111 (print) | LCCN 2021020112 (ebook) |
ISBN 9780367642822 (hardback) | ISBN 9780367645519 (paperback) |
ISBN 9781003125068 (ebook)
Subjects: LCSH: Marathon running. | Marathon running--Training. |
Running--Social aspects. | Human geography. |
Sports--Anthropological aspects.
Classification: LCC GV1065 .L37 2022 (print) |
LCC GV1065 (ebook) | DDC 796.42/52--dc23
LC record available at https://lccn.loc.gov/2021020111
LC ebook record available at https://lccn.loc.gov/2021020112

ISBN: 978-0-367-64282-2 (hbk)
ISBN: 978-0-367-64551-9 (pbk)
ISBN: 978-1-003-12506-8 (ebk)

DOI: 10.4324/9781003125068

Typeset in Bembo
by Taylor & Francis Books

# CONTENTS

# ILLUSTRATIONS

**Figures**

# PREFACE

This book has finally made it to the finish line. A number of good people helped me along. This book draws on some of the ideas that I have developed with Tim Edensor, Jørgen Ole Bærenholdt and Ole B. Jensen in three different publications. It has been rewarding and a pleasure to work with each of you.

I'm very grateful to David Pinder, Mikkel Bille, Tim Edensor and Ole B. Jensen for giving excellent feedback on various chapters. It was much appreciated.

I would also like to thank Professor Hideki Endo for generously inviting me to Ritsumeikan University, Japan, on three occasions. These visits have made it possible to do research at the Kyoto Marathon and the Tokyo Marathon.

A huge thank you to Henrik Thorn, Sofie Riisgaard and the Valencia Marathon for giving me permission to print their photographs in this book. A special thank you to the Valencia Marathon for allowing me to use their super cool photograph of their amazing marathon as the front cover of this book.

A big kudo goes to the NBRO community and all the people that I have been running with over the years. This book would not have happened without you.

Lastly, thanks to all the runners who participated in the interviews. I hope my interpretations of your words make sense and that you will enjoy this book. And many thanks to my production editor Megan Hiatt at Routledge for the amazing and kind support.

This book is dedicated to Pernille, Wilson and Elliot. I might run too much. But I will never run away from you.

Parts of this book draw on and extend the following publications:

Edensor, T. & Larsen, J. (2018). Rhythmanalysing marathon running: 'A drama of rhythms'. *Environment and Planning A: Economy and Space*, 50(3), 730–746.

Larsen, J. (2018b). Autoetnografi: kropslig mobilitet og sport. In M. Jacobsen & H. L. Jensen (eds), *Etnografier*. København: Hans Rietzels, pp. 151–170.

Larsen, J. (2019a). Running and tourism: A practice approach. In L. James, C. Ren & H. Halkier (eds), *Theories of Practice in Tourism*. London: Routledge, pp. 41–57.

Larsen, J. (2019b). 'Running on sandcastles': energising the rhythmanalyst through non-representational ethnography of a running event. *Mobilities*, 14(5), 561–577.

Larsen, J. (2021). *Marathon mobilities*. In H. Endo (ed.). *Understanding Tourism Mobilities in Japan*. London: Routledge, pp. 124–137.

Larsen, J. & Jensen, O. B. (2021). Marathon running in the 'weather'. In K. Barry, M. Borovnik & T. Edensor (eds), *Weather: Spaces, Mobilities and Affect*. London: Routledge, pp. 67–80.

# 1

# INTRODUCTION

I was soaking wet and freezing, and my legs were cramping. 'Never again, no way!' I said to my partner. I'd hit the 'marathon wall' really badly during my marathon debut – and to make things worse, ice-cold rain began to pour down. Throughout the last 14 kilometres, I experienced arrhythmical torture, where my speed gradually dropped and every straight felt harder than the last. While I managed the run in under four hours, I could not mobilise much joy as I passed the finishing line. I felt that I had cheated somehow because my body was not 'marathon ready'. I had not trained enough and the marathon had punished me for taking it too lightly. I have changed my mind. I will train hard for a marathon later in the year; I need to experience what it feels like to run a good and well-prepared-for race. I raised my glass and said, 'Next time'. Endorphins and beer had lifted my mood.

*(Field notes)*

As a complete novice, I did not know that thousands of other runners were having the same experience, or that I was in the process of developing a practical and intellectual obsession with marathons:

At the finish of every London Marathon, one of the great ritual statements is: 'Never again'! The runners say it, but it's not true. They come back because this time they think they won't end up hitting the wall. You always believe that next time you can beat it. You can run around it, over it, past it, some-how. You'll get fitter, you'll drink more, you'll get the pace right, the shoes right. You will always think that this time you will be the hero you were meant to be – so you come back, year after year if you can get in. You come back because you know that you can do better. You're like a surfer searching for the perfect wave.

*(Bryant, 2006, p. 18)*

DOI: 10.4324/9781003125068-1

Today's cities are full of runners 'searching for the perfect wave' in popular road races. Running is one of the most popular forms of sport and exercise in many western and some Asian societies (Cook et al., 2016; Latham, 2015; Laub, 2011; Scheerder et al., 2015). The increasing popularity of running is somewhat paradoxical. Running is good for public health and the quality of urban life; public agencies promote it to combat obesity, improve public health and make cities green and sustainable (Latham, 2015). However, urban planners and municipalities have done little to encourage running, and the social sciences have largely ignored this leisure practice. Urban runners 'inhabit' an urban infrastructure that is not designed or regulated to suit their needs or rhythms. They are forced to run on car-clogged streets and pavements, and on paths that are dominated by and designed for walkers; this can cause conflicts and deter some people from running. Runners fight for space with pedestrians on pavements and with cyclists and cars on streets. They often run in parks and along canals to avoid stoplights, dangerous situations, car fumes and too many pedestrians.

Now and then this order changes. At weekends, road races often interrupt normal traffic, as one aspect of the broader festivalisation and eventalisation of cities. On these days only, runners rule the streets. They are allowed to run on streets that have no motorised traffic, traffic lights, or pedestrians to get in their way. These streets belong to them, and they are frequently cheered on by thousands of spectators. This is particularly true in the case of urban marathons, the most popular and spectacular type of race, which attract many runners and spectators from near and far.

There are now more than 4,000 marathons that take place around the world. Some are tiny events, while others – especially those staged in major cities – are massive events with 50,000 runners and up to a couple of million spectators along the route. They are increasingly run by private companies rather than local athletics clubs, and they are often renamed to include the names of their sponsors, as the BMW Berlin Marathon, Virgin Money London Marathon, TCS New York Marathon, and Telenor Copenhagen Marathon have done. Marathons are no longer considered extreme events reserved for the super fit. Instead, they attract a wide demographic, including people with very different fitness levels and running biographies. Once, marathons were considered a men's sport and women were banned from running. This has changed dramatically over the years; women now account for around 30 percent of all worldwide marathon runners. However, there are striking national differences, and marathon running remains resolutely male in some European countries (e.g. Spain and Portugal) and in Asia (Andersen 2021). While many younger adults (aged 20–29) and older adults (50+) run marathons, most participants are adults in their thirties and forties; this explains why marathon running is sometimes referred to as a sport for soon-to-be middle-aged people and a symptom of a mid-life crisis.

The world's best marathon runners continue to run faster and to set new records. The current world record for men is 2:01:39 (Eliud Kipchoge of Kenya at the 2018 Berlin Marathon) and 2:14:04 for women (Brigid Kosgei of Kenya at the 2019 Chicago Marathon). By contrast, the average marathon runner – in Berlin, Chicago and elsewhere – has become slower over the years, although how much slower is unclear. Based on a study of 34 million individual race results between 1996 and

2016, the Danish website RunRepeat claims that the average American marathon time has slowed by 14 minutes over a 20-year period: from four hours and 15 minutes to four hours and 29 minutes. The fact that marathons now attract less serious runners, including older people and novices, probably explains this slower average time. In this sense, marathons have become more inclusive (Andersen, 2021).

It can be difficult to secure a start number in one of the major marathons, which are notoriously oversubscribed. In the 2019 marathon lottery ballots, 350,000 people applied to run in the 40,000-capacity Tokyo Marathon, and a world record of 414,168 people applied for the 50,000-capacity London Marathon (McQuire, 2018). Other extremely popular marathons include Berlin, New York and Chicago, which all also turn down many applications annually. This makes it very difficult – in fact, almost impossible – to plan for such events. In 2018, for example, I was (not for the first time) among the 90 per cent of applicants who did not win a start number in the Tokyo Marathon Lottery:

> Thank you for registering to the Tokyo Marathon 2019.
> We regret to inform you that you were not selected for the Tokyo Marathon 2019 entries.
> We look forward to your application for our future events.

In addition to being notoriously oversubscribed, urban marathons can be costly affairs, especially in the US. The New York Marathon, in particular, is phenomenally expensive. The entrance fee for the 2019 event was $358 for non-US residents and $295 for US residents. On top of the entrance fee, many runners incur significant transport and accommodation expenses; in 2018, only 13,635 of the 53,315 starters lived in the state of New York. Of these, 14,675 of the American starters lived in other states and 24,503 of the finishers came from countries outside the US, including tens of thousands of runners from Europe and Asia. For these participants, the event must have been extremely costly, given the need for long-haul flights and at least one extended weekend in a hotel.[1] Other marathons produce similar figures. For instance, the finishers at the 2013 Berlin Marathon came from 122 countries; only 25 per cent of the 40,000 participants lived in Berlin (Munch, 2013). As a general rule, urban marathons attract many international runners and their supporting families (Scheerder et al., 2015).

Marathons have become part of the international staging of places; as events for cultural consumption and tourism, they draw many well-paid professionals and generate significant revenue: 'The ability to host sport-related mega-events is increasingly an essential capacity for cities to strategically claim status as a global city' (Carter, 2011, p. 133). Under the economic imperatives of neoliberalist 'place competition', municipalities increasingly endorse and sponsor marathons and other events in public spaces (as opposed to specifically designed venues or stadiums) to animate public spaces, make cities more liveable, attract tourists, and promote urban transformation more broadly (Gratton & Henry, 2002; Smith, 2015).

## An overlooked phenomenon

Despite the popularity of marathon running in many parts of the world, relatively few social scientists have written about this phenomenon. There are no previous social science monographs on urban marathons, although sport historians and journalists have written histories of specific marathons, including those in Chicago (Suozzo, 2006) and London (Bryant, 2006), and monographs on marathon cultures in particular countries, such as Kenya (Finn, 2012), the US (Cooper, 1998), Japan (Finn, 2015; Havens, 2015) and Denmark (Vorm, 2017). Although these are full of interesting facts and anecdotes, few are theoretical; they do not reference theoretical or empirical discussions within the social sciences. They also tend to be overly concerned with elite runners, paying little attention to the fact that marathons now cater for and are experienced by non-elite runners.

Several interesting articles have considered urban marathons from sociological and anthropological perspectives. Berking and Neckel (1993, p. 68) interpret the urban marathon as emblematic of an individualised society in which fitness and physical virtue are valued: 'In short, the urban marathon, almost bursting with normative significance, is the staging of the individualised society as a spectacle, a symbolic and real experience, which narrates directly the role casting and character qualities in demand today.' They argue that (middle class) people are drawn to marathons because they allow participants to develop and express a desirable characteristic valued in contemporary society. The anthropologist Reischer (2001) has also pointed out – in a less critical tone – that marathon runners are motivated by the desire for self-transformation. According to the sociologists Nettleton and Hardey (2006), the opportunity to support a health charity offers marathon runners another way to develop a desirable character. Most London Marathon participants collect money for charitable organisations (it is almost impossible to get in otherwise), suggesting that marathon running is a philanthropic enterprise, through which 'active citizens' can ostentatiously enact their rights and fulfil their responsibilities by raising money for those 'in need' (Nettleton & Hardey, 2006, p. 441). Other researchers have investigated the links between marathons and leisure travel and tourism consumption (Green & Jones, 2005; McGehee et al., 2003; Sheehan, 2006; Shipway & Jones, 2007; Wicker et al., 2012). Race organisers touristify their marathons by bundling them with suitable tourism organisations and products in specific destinations (Axelsen & Robinson, 2009; Chalip & McGuirty, 2004). Moreover, several leisure researchers have explored marathon running as a form of 'serious leisure' (Stebbins, 1992) that involves the development of specific competences and 'social identities' (for instance, Robinson et al., 2014; Shipway & Jones, 2007, 2008; Shipway et al., 2013).

Marathons have been similarly overlooked in the subfields of 'sport geography' (Bale, 2000; Koch, 2017) and 'mega-event studies' (Klauser, 2012), where the focus is typically on much larger events, such as the World Cup in football or the Olympics (Chalkley & Essex, 1999). For example, sport-tourism studies (Weed, 2009) generally highlight the economic impact of large sporting events, rather than how tourists experience the events as spectators or participants. In sport geography, 'the key debates ... are focusing on the political economy of sport and the role of sport mega-events in urban planning agendas. Attention has been focused on the role of sport as a development strategy due to the increasing scope and scale of the World Cup and the Olympics' (Gaffney, 2014, p. 128; see also Gratton & Henry, 2002; Koch, 2017, 2018). Another example of the way in which sport, ironically, almost disappears in sport geography is Koch's (2017) article, in which sport is framed within and researched in relation to debates around exclusion, inclusion and political economy, at the expense of analysing the visceral sensations of sport.

Compared to mega-events, which involve public investment in new infrastructure and sport facilities, urban marathons – even the major ones – are minor events; they use existing roads and interrupt city life for a single day. Another difference between mega-events and marathons can be seen in how people participate. People participate in mega-events as spectators and fans; by contrast, in urban marathons, they participate as *runners* or as supporters of friends and family members.

Thus, the literature on marathons is limited, reflecting the fact that relatively few sociologists or geographers have studied running. As the geographer John Bale wrote in 2004:

> The sensory effect of running is different from that of walking, and from movement by vehicular-aided transport. Yet as a body-cultural phenomenon running has eluded serious study in the humanities and social sciences. Of course, this is not to deny a substantial number of publications that have been written on the techniques of running, on the history of running and on the biographies of runners. Running also features in novels and movies. But interpretative studies of running remain limited.
>
> *(2004, p. 1)*

This interpretative knowledge gap is unfortunate as social scientists have an obligation to scrutinise the emblematic leisure practices of their own times. However, this is changing, as now discussed.

## Ordinary running

There has recently been an upsurge in writings about running as a more or less ordinary form of sport and exercise. While some sport scholars approach running as a training-intensive, competitive and club-based sport (Bale, 2004; Bridel et al., 2016; Smith, 2002), others focus on the runners themselves, investigating how they learn new skills, perform physically and sense the environment. Such studies include phenomenological and sensory ethnographies that explore how people develop the skills they need to run (Allen-Collinson, 2003, 2009; Bridel et al., 2016; Hockey, 2006, 2013; Whelan, 2012).

Sociologists and geographers (Barnfield, 2016; Cook et al., 2016; Hitchings & Latham, 2016, 2017a, b; Latham, 2015; Nettleton, 2015; Qvistström, 2013, 2017) are beginning to research 'ordinary' running as a distinct form of mobility that requires as much attention as walking or cycling. This literature includes studies of ordinary runners on streets (Cook et al., 2016), in parks and forests (Qvistrӧm, 2013, 2017), on fitness-centre treadmills (Hitchings & Latham, 2016) and at small low-key events (Hindley, 2020; Larsen & Bærenholdt, 2019), as well as providing historical accounts of how running coaches invented 'jogging' (Latham, 2015).

## Research questions: ordinary runners, extraordinary events and rhythmic dramas

The literature review above highlights the fact that running is a growing, yet relatively undeveloped, research field. The existing literature focuses on everyday running while barely discussing the excitement of running *events*. This is particularly the case when it comes to ordinary runners and extraordinary events designed for ordinary runners, such as urban marathons (exceptions include Masters & Ogles, 1995, Shipway & Jones, 2007, 2008, amongst others). From a social science perspective, we know relatively little about why or how people participate in marathons, or what sort of places and experiences are involved. Moreover, sports geography/sociology is not a large sub-field; few urban scholars or mobilities researchers have any knowledge of sport, except in relation to the political economy of urban events.

To fill this gap, I will explain how and why marathons are highly exciting (social science) events. This social science account takes marathon running seriously, using sociological and geographical theory to understand the practice in and of itself – not just as a symptom of a particular time or society. Without losing sight of the discourses and forces that condition it, this book presents a sympathetic, rather than critical, account of marathon running. In doing so, it is driven by a non-representational life-affirming 'ethos' that commemorates and rejoices in the bodily sensations of running, as well as in the social life, conviviality, energy and vitalism that running and marathons generate (Larsen, 2019b; Latham & McCormack, 2017). In subtle ways, this book also provides content to think *with*. It demonstrates that marathon running is of broad interest because it calls for and allows lively and expressive ways of conducting and writing research and understanding the becoming and potential of bodies, the intertwining of biological and mechanical rhythms, and the eventful potential of streets.

In redressing such lacunae while inspired by theoretical debates about embodied and multi-sensuous mobilities, social and material practices, and urban rhythms, this book explores both empirically and analytically the characteristics of marathon running as a *bodily practice* on the one hand and, on the other, marathon training and events as unique *places*. It examines in ethnographic and historical detail how marathon practices and places are materially, culturally and socially *produced* by various materialities, cultural scripts, experts, runners and spectators, and *practised* in embodied, multi-sensuous and 'emplaced' ways by ordinary runners. I explore how and why aspiring runners learn, perform or defect from this practice, and how we can understand the significance of the meanings, competences, objects, environments and 'communities' they encounter during this process. How are marathon courses designed and experienced – and how do they transform the usual rhythms and atmosphere of cities?

These questions will be answered and developed through theory-informed ethnographic description and theorising. Although several previous studies have conducted *auto*-ethnographical research on *endurance* running (for instance, Allen-Collinson & Hockey, 2007; Fisette, 2015; Stone, 2009; Sutton, 2016; Whelan, 2012), relative few have expanded this perspective or carried out ethnographic research with a larger population of 'serious' ordinary runners (exceptions include Green & Jones, 2005; Shipway & Jones, 2007, 2008). Based on original empirical research, this book takes readers to training sessions in Copenhagen and marathons in Tokyo, Kyoto, Berlin, Frankfurt, Valencia and Copenhagen. The multi-ethnographic element allows me to discuss the globalised, codified and generic nature of marathon practices and design while also highlighting significant local differences and unique experiences, reflecting the fact that marathons are staged on streets in many different cities, each with its own unique topography, weather, architecture and infrastructure. The reader will learn how marathon training is scripted and carried out as an everyday practice, how marathons are designed, and how runners experience racecourse affordances, various types of atmosphere and the marathons and cities they run in. This book will explain how an activity as strange and strenuous as marathon running has become so popular, and how this 'boom' reflects societal trends.

Along the way it will develop a sociological practice approach to marathon running and geographical understanding of marathon places, rhythms and spatial practices. As few running theories currently exist, these will be of interest to running researchers and mobilities scholars more broadly, advancing and offering new insights into how a corporeal practice, such as marathon running, is designed and experienced. While this book focuses on marathon running, these arguments are exemplary and can be used to inform other research on corporeal mobilities or spaces of embodied movement.

The four main arguments in this book will unfold empirically, analytically and theoretically. First, I will argue that marathon running is a *rhythmic embodied practice* that enables able-bodied people to understand, use, appreciate, re-shape and energise their otherwise decaying and immobile bodies. They learn to appreciate self-generated movement in order to 'feel alive', develop bodily competences and 'stop the ageing process'. I will also show that the pleasures and competences of marathon running are highly scripted; essentially, they involve adhering to and appreciating long-established temporal rhythms associated with particular ways of running. These rhythmic scripts and competences involve specific embodied skills of flow and listening to one's body. They also involve using various training programmes, timing technologies and specialised objects to monitor, mediate and afford bodily rhythms. This co-existence of different ways of assessing rhythms is sometimes aligned and sometimes in conflict. To become a competent marathon runner, one must also synchronise running with one's own ecology of everyday practice, social relations, work arrangements and tourist leisure practices in order to find the requisite time and places in which to train and race. Marathon running becomes 'a way of life', not just a passive leisure activity. It gives meaning to people's lives.

Second, I will argue that running is a distinct *spatial practice* and that marathons are truly distinctive *mobile places*, which I will call 'course-places'. Running provides a unique form of movement and new understandings and sensuous experiences of streets and cities: their surfaces, topographies, traffic rules, weather conditions, types of atmosphere and sights. I suggest that marathon running provides distinctive ways of using, being in and comparing cities during training and events. Marathons fascinate runners and spectators because they afford novel experiences of places and take place in exciting cities. I will show how they powerfully reconfigure streets and cities, transforming their usual affordances, rhythms and types of atmosphere into highly affective, atmospheric environments that create excitement, sociability and 'tourist gazing', as well as fast running. Marathons prove that streets can be something other than 'transport corridors'; we can therefore understand them as 'experimental urban mobility labs'. Runners do not simply run city marathons; they run *in* exciting cities. They are given access to unique stages and wrapped in a mesmerising atmosphere.

Third, I will argue that marathons constitute a fascinating 'drama of rhythms'. On the one hand, marathons are painstakingly planned and designed to be smooth and ordered events. Runners undertake much systematised and specialised training to become competent rhythm-makers, who can execute a well-paced race in a short time or, alternatively, take longer and enjoy the atmosphere. While this script is sometimes enacted with success and according to plan, marathon running also constitutes a drama of rhythms because marathons can be ruined by poor planning and adverse weather, while individual runners can be injured or exhausted, encountering that physical and emotional painful 'marathon wall' that puts a stop to their anticipated rhythms and shatters their ambitions.

Fourth, in order to craft the above accounts, I will develop new theoretical and methodological constellations and methods. Drawing upon and bringing together a diverse literature (the mobilities paradigm, practice theory, non-representational theory and carnal sociology), I will propose notions such as corporeal mobile practices, course-places, and drama of rhythms. These allow me to understand places as constituted through material affordances, the regular and intermittent flows of humans and non-humans, and immersive weather worlds. They also allow me to approach bodies as mobile, social and active; always engaged with things; 'emplaced' in specific places, temporalities and weather worlds; and comprising biological, mental, social and cultural processes. From a methodological point of view, I coin the notion of 'energising the rhythm analyst' and develop – in dialogue with non-representational and carnal ethnographers – a lively and engaging ethnographic position that accounts for the corporeal sensations and the types of atmosphere that marathons comprise.

## Book outline

The book is divided into eight chapters. Chapters 2 and 3 mainly address an academic audience and may be skipped by the general reader. While chapters 4–8 are informed by my theoretical and empirical approach, they are relatively light on theory and are intended to present interesting and lively discussions of marathons. They are written to appeal to both scholars and general readers.

The second chapter, 'Theorizing running: corporeal mobile practices and mobile places' follows this introductory chapter. It outlines my own theoretical approaches to marathon running, as rhythmic embodied practice, spatial practices and rhythmic places. In doing so, it draws upon, critiques and expands the mobilities paradigm, practice theory, rhythmanalysis, non-representational theory and carnal sociology. Informed by and expanding the mobilities paradigm and practice theory, this book presents a way of understanding marathon running as an embodied and emplaced practice that is systematised by experts and mediated by various discourses, meanings, materials and skills. By modifying the rhythmanalysis of Lefebvre (2004) and others, I develop an analytical position and language that allow me to understand running as a temporal rhythmic practice and marathons as a drama of rhythms. Lastly, drawing on non-representational theory and carnal sociology, I critique rhythmanalysis for not being corporeal or lively enough. Non-representational theory and carnal sociology allow me to bring out the multi-sensuous and embodied character and sheer physicality of running and marathon environments, as well as the raw liveness of marathon running.

In chapter 3, 'Running methods: lively ethnographies and energising the rhythm analyst', I discuss and expand upon various qualitative methods that can be used to research running as a rhythmic practice and an embodied mobile life more generally. I argue that current approaches to rhythmanalysis are insufficiently somatic and energise the rhythm analyst by researching internal biological and physiological rhythms, as well as external place rhythms. From my perspective, the rhythm analyst uses his or her own heartbeat and internal rhythms as research tools. This links rhythmanalysis more closely to ethnographical participant observation, auto-ethnography, non-representational ethnography and carnal sociology. I also describe the specific marathons at which I conducted research and developed my ethnographic research strategies.

Drawing on practice theory's focus on meanings, chapter 4, 'Innovating new aspirations: the birth of ordinary marathon practices and extraordinary marathons', examines the changing cultural and social meanings of marathon rhythms and places over time. The first section explores the significance of time and temporal rhythms in elite running; it discusses the fact that traditional marathons were tiny events for elite runners, so-called 'achievement runners'. Against this backdrop, I analyse later innovations: ordinary running and the slower rhythms introduced by the jogging movement; the extraordinary and experience-rich street marathons designed for ordinary runners; and international marathons, which combine the rhythms of sport, international tourism and cosmopolitanism. I coin the term 'experience runner' to contrast with 'achievement runner'. The second section explores the aspirations of my interviewees, establishing that they are attracted and adhere to different rhythms of running (both competitive and non-competitive). I show that they run marathons partly to 'feel alive and improve themselves' and partly to explore exciting places.

Chapter 5, 'Materialities of marathon running: Designing practices and places', analyses the material mediation of marathon bodies and their rhythms, as well as racecourse design. First, I explore the material design of what I call 'course-places', showing how 'event assemblages' of managers, volunteers, timing devices, objects and technologies come together to create smooth and atmospheric spatial practices and place rhythms. I discuss how managers and volunteers design and erect safe 'course-places', offering generic *courses* for smooth running, *places* of local significance for 'tourist gazing', and a vibrant atmosphere on an otherwise lazy Sunday morning. Second, I discuss how specialised consumer objects (especially shoes) and data-tracking devices (particularly watches and social-media sites) recast, enable and innovate specific corporeal rhythms, creating a second opinion on felt sensations, as runners become data-assemblages, beating in harmony with their (anticipated) 'live data' as well as their hearts. This processed data produces a route that may, over time, become studded with significant places, as indiscriminate roads converge into a recorded, measured, mapped and communicated training ground.

Chapter 6, 'Preparatory rhythms: everyday running and training grounds', examines marathon *training* as a codified, lived and routinised set of rhythmic practices that reorganise everyday activity and convert roads and parks into habitual training grounds. This chapter begins by exploring how experts and training programmes prescribe rational and linear rhythms of calculated time, distance and repetition. The second section is a lively and fleshy ethnographic exploration of how, and to what extent, novices and experienced runners (learn to) use prescribed rhythms and programmes. It explores how local spaces become significant training grounds and the dramatic high and lows of marathon training, and shows how people either fail to make their bodies marathon fit or succeed in doing so, becoming skilled rhythm- and route-makers.

Chapter 7, 'Dramatic race rhythms', also draws on Lefebvre's terminology, again with a distinct non-representational injection of 'liveliness', corporeal sensibility and, importantly, 'drama'. It provides a lively, dramatised ethnographic rhythmanalysis of the embodied ups and downs of marathon racing with and against the clock. It brings out the embodied, sensuous and emotional sensations of pre-race nerves, how the weather can ruin a planned pace, the sheer physical strain, the psychological stress involved in running fast, and the challenge of maintaining a prescribed, even-paced rhythm over such a long and gruelling distance. The focus is on racing fast and runners' *internal* rhythms during the different stages of the race. Overall, this chapter highlights the significance of time and pacing and the reality that marathons assault the mind and body.

Chapter 8, 'Atmospheric sensations and places', explores the significance and production of various types of atmosphere and the wider visual environment of marathons. This chapter is concerned with documenting and analysing the dramatic and energising atmospheric qualities of 'course-*places*' and the *external* atmospheric rhythms that resonate between the bodies of supporters and runners, or come into being when runners pass stunning buildings and sights. I explore how runners' senses are affected by, and make sense of, cheering and support at various points along the course. I argue that the vibrant (or dead) atmosphere at a marathon is co-produced by supporters on the streets. Overall, I discuss how the internal rhythms of runners are affected by, and potentially aligned with, external rhythms. This chapter brings out the excitement of running in a gorgeous city in a sea of likeminded people, on broad boulevards with no stoplights, dangerous cars or obstructing pedestrians – only thousands of noisy people cheering you on.

Chapter 9 concludes the book's empirical and theoretical contribution and discusses how this study can inform other running studies, studies of corporeal mobilities practices and the literature on sport more broadly.

## Note

1  www.tcsnycmarathon.org/about-the-race/results/finisher-demographics.

# 2

# THEORISING RUNNING

## Corporeal mobile practices and mobile places

## Introduction

This chapter discusses the theories that inform this book and to which it contributes. The first section is devoted to the 'mobilities paradigm', which 'coaches' sociologists and geographers to take movement and travel seriously. This paradigm has informed much of my academic thinking. My initial interest in running stemmed from the curious neglect of running (and sport more generally) amongst mobilities scholars (Newman and Falcous, 2012). The paradigm has been largely confined to the study of motorised movement (Urry, 2007). This chapter suggests the need for a new theoretical focus on *corporeal* mobile practices. The first section takes the first steps towards understanding marathon running and events as a specific mode of mobility and 'mobile' place. The second section discusses practice theory, arguing that this approach makes it possible to approach marathon running as a socialised, material and emplaced practice, tied up with specific materials, competences and meanings over time. This chapter advances practice theory by actively integrating places and weather, a theme that is currently underdeveloped in the theory. Third, it discusses Lefebvre's rhythmanalysis (2004), arguing that aspects of his thinking and language allow us to think about running as a rhythmic and temporal practice (Edensor & Larsen, 2018). Finally, to analyse and communicate the sheer physicality and embodied sensations of marathons, I push on from rhythmanalysis to discuss the lively, vitalist work of non-representational scholars and carnal sociologists. They bring to fore the truly corporeal – biological, physiological and social elements – emphasising the lively and moving body that is more or less absent from other theories. They constitute the final cog, enabling the theorisation of 'corporeal mobile practices'.

## The mobilities paradigm

Over the last decade, mobility has become a key feature of global modernity and social theory. The 'mobilities paradigm' (Sheller & Urry, 2006; Urry, 2000) explores

DOI: 10.4324/9781003125068-2

the way in which public and private agents produce infrastructures and mobile cities – and how, in turn, car drivers, pedestrians, cyclists and tourists inhabit urban infrastructures and move about within their everyday and leisure lives. Urry has argued that social scientists have long overlooked the significance of mobility in modern life, mistakenly theorising the urban and everyday as static and a-mobile – and roads as 'non-places' (Augé, 2008). He has persuaded scholars to explore cities and events as constructed and experienced through the spatial and temporal mobilities of mobile things, technologies, information and mobile people, facilitated by extensive infrastructures (or 'moorings'). This paradigm takes movement seriously and does not reduce it to a purely rational or technical means of getting from A to B. It understands mobility as socially meaningful and embedded in wider everyday practices and social norms. It is known for analysing social and sensuous experiences of being on the move and for exploring how 'mobilities skills' are learned and become habitual (Ehn & Löfgren, 2010). As Cresswell notes, mobility is socially produced and made meaningful within broader conventions, discourses and institutions. He argues that mobility is made up of time and space; it includes sheer physical movement, representational practices (or shared meanings) and experienced, embodied practices (2006, 2010).

This paradigm also analyses the *system* of mobilities (Urry, 2007), since all forms of mobility are socio-technical systems that involve complex networks of people, competences, regulations, laws, designs, technologies, energy, infrastructures, cultural norms and many other factors. Cars, for example, cannot be understood without appreciating their dependence on oil, aluminium, roads, traffic laws, suburbs, out-of-town shopping and extended families. The mobilities paradigm aims to understand how various material worlds, including design, technologies and environments, 'afford' (on affordance, see Gibson, 1977; Jensen, 2013, p. 49) the mobilities of certain people and not those of others. Indeed, bodies and voices cannot travel far on their own. This material approach is evident in writing on 'mobilities affordances' (Jensen, 2016; Jensen et al., 2016) and 'staging mobilities' (Jensen, 2013), which explores the relational staging of specific mobilities. According to Jensen, mobility designs are always staged 'from above' (by engineers, planners, and politicians) and from 'below' (by everyday users). They are 'acted out, performed and lived from below, individually and especially in social interactions' (2013, p. 14). This suggests that cities are produced by mobile flows and the specific infrastructures that afford such movements. From this perspective, a marathon is 'an assemblage of mobile body – subjects, material conditions and social interactions' (Jensen et al., 2016, p. 28).

Mobilities scholars have generally studied motorised mobility, sedentary practices and experiences of being transported, focusing on 'comfortable bodies' and 'sedentary affects' (Bissell, 2008). Cars and trains shield mobile people from inclement weather and other people in traffic and physical work (Larsen, 2014; Sheller & Urry, 2000, p. 747). By requiring minimal energy, fitness and kinaesthetic movement from users, they have caused obesity and many illnesses (see health scholars: Agger 2011; Freund & Martin, 2004; Roberts, 2010; Sallis et al., 2004). Although recent studies have focused on active mobility, including walking (Edensor, 2010; Middleton 2010), cycling (P. Jones, 2017; Larsen, 2014, 2017) and running (Cidell, 2014, 2016; Cook , 2016), they rarely dialogue explicitly with sport studies, even though many sports, such as running and cycling, are essentially about mobility.

Discussions about active transport, exercise and corporeality have become more central to this paradigm, as part of a wider focus on public health and sustainable transport. For instance, several studies have discussed the unique features that distinguish cycling from motorised mobility with regard to embodiment and perceptions of the urban landscape and changing weather conditions (for the latter, see Larsen, 2020). Such studies follow calls to investigate how 'the material, "elementary", molecular and physical aspects' of movement influence the affective and experiential qualities of being on the move' (Merriman, cited in Simpson, 2019, p. 4). Cycling is different from motorised travel, since cycling technology is energised by bodies, not motors, and therefore requires significant physical work. While bicycles enable humans to move faster, more easily and for longer distances than they could on foot, cycling resembles walking and especially running because it brings embodiment to the forefront. Cycling is experienced in the joints, muscles and tendons; it can on occasion be uncomfortable and feel like hard work (Larsen, 2014, p. 62; Simpson, 2019; Spinney, 2006). Cycling can raise the pulse and cause fatigue because cyclists are not protected from hills, rain, wind or distance. *Ceteris paribus*, weathered cyclists ride faster and longer than novice or unfit cyclists; people can lose their cycling fitness. From the perspective of bodily exercise, active (walking, running or cycling) travel and inactive (motorised) travel are worlds apart; different bodies have more or less capacity to manage such demands.

Mobility is mediated not only by surfaces and topographies but also by the material sensations of weather worlds (Larsen & Jensen, 2021). People move in and through the air, sunshine, heat, rain, wind, snow and fog and on icy, wet or dry roads. Despite this, the weather is rarely an analytic focus in mobility studies (or the social sciences, but see Barry et al., 2021; Vannini et al., 2012) because cars, planes, and trains are designed to isolate people from direct sensuous exposure to the weather. Unless conditions are terrible, car drivers and train passengers do not pay much attention to the weather outside, which does not touch or affect them (Ingold & Kurttila, 2000), since wind direction and small gradients rarely interfere with their rhythmic movement (Nixon, 2012). By contrast, cyclists are seldom *unaware* of the environment: 'the nature of cycling means that spaces otherwise rendered homogenous when travelling by car have widely varying characteristics' (Spinney, 2008, pp. 29–30). They feel and experience weather as a 'taskscape', requiring energy use, (Nixon, 2012) because it affects their pace, rhythm and comfort.

The mobilities paradigm is also relevant here because it concerns tourist travel and the way in which certain places and events become 'must-see' (Urry, 2007) or (in the case of marathons) 'must-do' events in must-see cities, such as London, Berlin, New York, and Tokyo. This paradigm accounts for the multi-sensuous experiences of tourists and their performances of places (Urry & Larsen, 2011). I will explore the sensuous way that runners experience places when running marathons in foreign countries. Various experts, discourses and technologies are constructing our gaze and senses as tourists; they are teaching us to see certain things and places and not others. Gazing is not merely seeing, but also a socially patterned learned activity or practice. In Cresswell's terminology, gazing is socially produced (Urry & Larsen, 2011) by experts and discourses. This book adopts a similar focus on marathon running as a socially learned way of moving.

As discussed below, mobilities scholars are increasingly using 'practice theory' as a lens through which to study the trajectory of specific embodied practices, how they come into being or die out, and how they attract practitioners and inform doings. I find this approach useful for investigating how marathon running has become so widespread. Below, I introduce some key features of practice theory which are particularly useful when analysing marathon running.

## Practice theory

Practice theory investigates the rise, endurance or fall of specific practices over time. It makes it possible to understand how people become, or fail to become, devoted runners – it also makes it possible to explores the meanings, knowledge, aspirations, material worlds and bodily transformations associated with running that enable ordinary people to become marathon runners (see Larsen, 2019a, for the following section).

Practice theories have certain common features. They examine the routinised and taught nature of specific practices, investigating how such practices attract and deflect practitioners, and how such practitioners learn to become competent performers who co-produce and re-innovate the practice by 'playing it out' in multiple ways. They explore social practices rather than individual mindsets or the characteristics of social groups. Reckwitz (2002) defines practices as 'routines' and 'sets of routinized bodily performances'. When investigating the trajectory of a specific practice and how it attracts practitioners and their demands, we must understand that the practice encompasses various related elements. Reckwitz defines them as 'forms of bodily activities, forms of mental activities, "things" and their use, a background knowledge in the form of understanding, know-how, states of emotion and motivational knowledge'; they also include 'sayings' and texts as much as doings (Reckwitz, 2002, p. 249). Shove et al. have condensed this to: 'meanings', 'competences' and 'materials'. 'Meanings' refer to 'symbolic meanings, ideas and aspirations'; 'competences' include 'skill, know-how, and technique'; and 'materials' are 'things, technologies, tangible physical entities, and the stuff of which objects are made' (Shove et al., 2012, p. 14).

Practice theory highlights the recursive nature of 'elements', arguing that they persist across individual moments of activity, performed by many more or less knowledgeable and capable actors. Such elements must be reproduced and normalised; they distinguish between 'practice-as-entity' and 'practice-as-performance' (Schatzki, 2001; Shove et al., 2012, p. 7; Warde, 2005, p. 133). 'Practice-as-entity' frames the possibility of doing, learning or speaking about a specific practice (Shove et al., 2012, p. 7). 'Elements' are enacted by attracting people who 'feature as the *carriers* or hosts of a practice' (Shove et al., 2012, p. 7). Practitioners and their skills and motivations are composed of elements and practices (Larsen 2019a, p. 44). Thus:

> in practice theory, agents are body/minds who 'carry' and 'carry out' social practices. Thus, the social world is first and foremost populated by diverse social practices which are carried by agents. Agents, so to speak, 'consist in' the performance of practices to norms ... They understand the world and themselves, and use know-how and motivational knowledge, according to the particular practice.
>
> *(Reckwitz, 2002, p. 256)*

However, practices must be reproduced through sedimented performances, a process known as 'practice-as-performance' (Shove et al., 2012, p. 7). While it is fair to say that practice theory, historically, has said relatively little about people as practice participants, it does discuss the individual. For example, 'football is constituted through participation and will only exist for as long as people play the game. While performances such as football are scripted through rules and established ways of playing, they are not performed by passive and preformed practitioners; improvisation and novelty are always possible. Practitioners are *co*-producers of practices-as-entities' (Larsen, 2018a, p. 44; Pantzar & Shove, 2010; Shove & Pantzar, 2007, pp. 155, 448). As Warde writes:

> Social practices do not present uniform planes upon which agents participate in identical ways but are instead internally differentiated on many dimensions. Considered simply, from the point of view of the individual person, the performance of driving will depend on past experience, technological knowledge, learning, opportunities, available resources, previous encouragement by others ... . From the point of view of practice as a whole, we can think of a dedicated domain comprising many different competencies and capabilities.
>
> *(2005, p. 138)*

Increasingly, empirical researchers investigate how people become participants in specific practices and how practitioners transform practices. For example, Shove and Pantzar (2007) have explained how new practitioners changed the spirit of floorball and Nordic walking, while seasoned practitioners defected from the practice or insisted on playing their usual game. Different practices may exist simultaneously within a given sport and can be performed in different ways. The research also shows that people have and move through practice careers, although this is rarely discussed within practice theory. Within their individual biographies, people are likely to have periods in which their commitment and results peak and times when they have injuries, poor health or reduced commitment due to other obligations, as this book will demonstrate.

While practices are often stable, they can change from time to time, as new meanings, competences, or materials are introduced, or old connections between elements are reworked. Such changes reconfigure the factors involved in participation and change requirements over time (Shove & Pantzar, 2007, p. 15). This is happening in London and New York, where municipalities and activists are trying to make urban cycling *less* sporty and more inclusive by 'bundling' it with everyday commuting, rather than allowing it to remain the domain of road racers and bike messengers (Larsen, 2017, 2000). A similar innovation has occurred in the case of Nordic walking, where walking sticks were associated with frailty and disability, not brisk walking in nature, which was the desired association. A practice can also die out because of competition from a new and more attractive practice; practices 'compete with each other for recruits and carriers' (Shove et al., 2012, p. 87). In this sense, practice theory is a theory of change. It is relevant to this book because (marathon) running has changed dramatically over the last four decades, becoming both doable and meaningful for ordinary runners (chapter 4).

### 'Meanings', 'competences' and 'materials'

The section above explains that practices are made up of 'meanings', 'competences' and 'materials'. We can only understand a practice if we analyse its discursive elements, discovering how practitioners find meaningful ways to fulfil certain ideas and aspirations within their wider everyday lives. This pattern resembles the way in which tourists learn to gaze at the world, although the focus on embodied skills is more prevalent in practice theory. Moreover, practices are tied up with cognitive and embodied competences, performed by people who have acquired these skills via words and especially through use.

This focus on meanings and competences allows us to discuss how marathon practices slowly became desirable and legitimate. Training programmes, road races and running communities passed on know-how to ordinary people, enabling them to develop their bodies through marathon training. This sits with Reckwitz's argument that 'a social practice is the product of training the body in a certain way: when we learn a practice, we learn to be bodies in a certain way'. In other words, 'a practice can be understood as the regular, skilful "performance" of (human) bodies' (2002, p. 251). Thus, 'bodies are not static. People generally need to train to learn to perform a specific practice in a skilful manner. This focus on training and bodily change implies that potential practitioners lack the corporeal and mental competences needed to carry out specific practices. It also suggests that such skills and aspirations can be learned if the social practice is both well established and attractive' (Larsen, 2018a, p. 44). In this book, inspired in part by 'carnal sociology' (discussed below), I develop an approach to embodied competences that allows us to discuss physiological and biological aspects of bodily competences, which are rarely included in practice theory. Here, I draw on Pink (2011), who describes how bodies change physically when people develop sporting habits, arguing that practice researchers, as Ingold also insists, should understand bodies as an aspect of the material world:

> Thus, we might start thinking of the body as part of a total environment, and recognise that the body provides us not simply with embodied knowing and

skills that we use to act on or in that environment, but that the body itself is simultaneously physically transformed as part of this process.

*(Pink, 2011, p. 347)*

This physical transformation involves weight loss, injuries, and muscular development. Our bodies are indispensable resources when running or playing football (see below). Without relatively fit bodies, capable of running, tackling, and hitting a ball, football would, for instance, never be played or reproduced as a practice. Football players also get scratches, sore legs, and injuries.

## Materiality

Practice theorists' focus on 'materials' allows me to discuss the significance of specialised objects, infrastructures, environments and the weather-world in relation to marathon running. Objects are necessary components of many practices. They convey specific symbolic meanings to experienced practitioners; importantly, for ANT-inspired practice scholars, they afford agencies, competences and actions (Shove et al., 2012, p. 9; Warde, 2005). *Material* practice theorists are critical of early practice-theory approaches and studies, which reduce consumer objects and materials to symbolic worlds and means of power, overlooking the role they play in enabling things and materials in everyday practices (Warde, 2005). As Reckwitz argues, 'Carrying out a practice very often means using particular things in a certain way. It might sound trivial to stress that in order to play football we need a ball and goals as indispensable "resources"' (2002, pp. 252–253).

However, Reckwitz's approach to materiality is somewhat reductionist. Practice theorists focus predominantly on objects and infrastructures, ignoring the materiality of bodies, environments and places. For instance, a ball and goals cannot create a game of football; to play football, fit-enough bodies (as argued above) and a suitable place are needed, whether that place is a lawn, street, beach or designated infrastructure, such as a well-maintained football pitch. Few practice theorists have asked how practices are 'emplaced' or why routinised activities tend to take place at specific locations. Clearly, a practice theory of football must account for the fact that some places are better suited to football than others; it is likewise illegal, impossible or dangerous to play football in places that would otherwise be perfect (for instance, roads and immaculate park lawns). Worldwide, there are designated football infrastructures: locations designed specifically for football. In other words, football requires as many places as objects because it is an emplaced practice (Larsen, 2018a, 2019a). While shoes and watches are part of the material culture of running, running requires tracks, parks, paths, pavements and streets.

Since both football and running are normally practised outdoors, they are also immersed in, and affected by, what the anthropologist Tim Ingold calls the 'weather-world' (heat, wind, rain, etc.) and the topography of the natural and built world (as discussed in the mobilities-paradigm section). Ingold argues that 'the experience of weather lies at the root of our moods and motivations' (2010, p. 131). The weather is something we perceive, perceive in, and inhabit as part of our everyday practices and lives in the open world (Ingold, 2007, p. 20). Weather is also part of the material world. In relation to air, Ingold writes:

> To draw the limits of materiality around the surfaces of the landscape and artefacts would be to leave the inhabitants of the landscape and the users of artefacts in a vacuum. They would be unable to breathe. ... Let us, then, readmit the air as an essential material constituent of the inhabited world. This is easily done, yet is not without consequences for the way we think about our relations with the environment. One consequence is that we can no longer imagine that all such relations take the form of interactions between persons and things, or that they necessarily arise from the conjoint action of persons and things assembled in hybrid networks. For the air is not a person or a thing, or indeed an entity of any kind, and cannot therefore comprise part of any networked assembly. It is rather, quite simply, a medium which, as Gibson pointed out, affords locomotion, respiration, and perception.
>
> *(2010, p. 132)*

Weather is a contingent *medium* that shapes – with different intensities and forces – how people can move and experience it (Larsen & Jensen, 2021; Rantala et al., 2011). It also colours the atmosphere of places (Hauge & Bille, forthcoming).

Places, the weather world and *material* environments require further attention in practice theory. Pink's work on the sensoriality and affordances of sport environments can be helpful here (Larsen, 2018a). She develops a notion of 'emplacement', which defines places as (temporal) mobile events, comprising 'geological forms, the weather, human socialities, material objects, buildings, animals, and much more' (Pink, 2011, p. 348). Practice studies must explore 'social, material, and technological' environments 'charged with energy, emotion, shifting with the weather, and contingent on the activity of non-human organisms too' (Pink, 2012, p. 23).

Places are always somewhat atmospheric – cosy, noisy, vibrant or boring – and experienced as atmospheric entities as people engage practically with them. According to Pink et al. (2015, 355): 'we suggest seeing atmosphere as likewise part of the environment – as much as we and other things and processes are. That is, it is something that we live through, as much as being something that we make.' Bille et al. have suggested that atmosphere reflects how people experience the material environment; atmospheres 'have something to do with spaces and temporality, something to do with the intrinsic qualities of materials, and something to do with experience ... in essence it must be understood as a spatial experience of being attuned in and by a material world' (2015, p. 35). In a similar vein, Edensor (2015, p. 2) writes that 'atmosphere folds together affect, emotion and sensation in space', highlighting the importance of the lived body, senses and perception. This ties into Böhme's founding idea that atmospheres are simultaneously objective and subjective, partly existing in the always shifting environment and partly depending on how they are sensed and made sense of (Bille et al., 2015). Atmospheres are co-produced between the practices and dispositions of designers and users, that is, from 'below' as well as 'above'. While materially and culturally designed, atmospheres (Edensor & Sumartojo, 2015) are subjectively felt and 'not set in stone' (Hauge & Bille, forthcoming). I support the scholars who have developed a practical approach to atmosphere. They refuse to separate affects, feelings and emotions and insist on understanding 'atmospheres' as partly designed through practices (both professional and everyday) and always 'attuned' to peoples' practical engagement with the world, practice-at-hand and emotional sensibility (Bille & Simonsen, 2019; Edensor, 2015; Edensor & Sumartojo, 2015).

This 'approach enables a material understanding of running as a mobile place event with a complex ecology of diverse things, corporeal bodies, places and environments' (Larsen, 2019a, p. 42). Such an approach is evident in Maller et al.'s study of the way in which 'materials' such as trees, parks, weather, seasons, lights, roads, paths and play equipment (2016, p. 56) contribute to how, when and where people run in parks. The need to spatialise practice theory is essential; running is an 'emplaced' mobile practice in and across different environments, in which surfaces, topography, the weather, atmosphere, people, objects and animals condition its rhythms and the way people experience it.

## *Everyday practices*

Finally, a key argument for practice theorists is that practices only attract practitioners if they can be synchronised with everyday practices. For instance, I argue that long-distance bicycle commuting makes sense to practitioners who want to bundle exercise and transport so as to become fit in a time-effective way (Larsen, 2018a). The importance of synchronising different practices is also demonstrated by the sociologist Blue's (2017) ethnography, detailing the way in which participation in the sport MMA (mixed martial arts) ebbs and flows. He shows that everyday life practices, such as socialising, working and eating, influence exercise practices. According to Blue, the ability to maintain sport practices depends on the ability to synchronise with broader practices that make up people's everyday lives (2017, p. 344). Thus, while time is essential, it is not enough simply to have the time to exercise. His respondents gave up training when they gave in to other practices (such as partying or eating junk food) that did not support a strict training regime. Blue suggests that the break in his subject Johnny's training did not result from a lack of time to practice MMA every day. Instead, Johnny abandoned his training when crucial supporting practices, including dieting, strength and conditioning, became desynchronised (2017, p. 348). This example shows that 'physical exercise routines are not maintained in isolation, but in combination with other practices' (Blue, 2017, p. 347) and the rhythms of everyday life. Following this, I will discuss how marathon running is a time-demanding practice that must be synchronised with other practices. This, as we will see, is not easy. The demands of marathon training often clash with, and even undermine, other practices and their demands and rhythms. When people insert six to ten hours of training into their weekly routines, there are obvious consequences for other practices.

Blue's focus on rhythms leads to my third theoretical inspiration, Henri Lefebvre's book on rhythmanalysis (2004).

## Rhythmanalysis

> All human rhythms are rooted in co-ordinated physiological processes. We are affected too, by the rhythms of the natural environment. These include seasonal, lunar and circadian rhythms of the day/night cycle which relate to the cyclical nature of ecological processes too, all dominated by our primary energy source, the sun.
>
> *(Goodridge, 1999, pp. 27–28)*

Crucially, embodied rhythms link diverse temporal and spatial scales. According to Lefebvre, 'everywhere there is interaction between a place, a time, and an expenditure of energy, there is *rhythm*' (2004, p. 8). For Lefebvre, a key feature of places is the fact that they are mobile and dynamic, being constantly (re)produced and identified by the daily, seasonal and annual flows of people and things, together with the non-human effects of plants, animals and the weather, which moves from, to and across them. Places are composed of a medley of human rhythms, including commuting, shopping, work hours, the night-time economy, seasonality and tourist seasons. Although they are fluid entities, places are normally typified by a polyrhythmic ensemble (Crang, 2001), with some master rhythms that ensure repetitions, regularities and ordered flows. Places and mobile practices are shaped by – and always in the process of becoming as a consequence of – (changing) cyclical and linear rhythms. Urban rhythm analysts study and attend to the regular and occasionally dissonant rhythms of the city, including traffic lights, vehicles, pedestrians, animals, trees, rain and sun, as well as the coordinated routines of individuals aligning their daily and weekly work, leisure and family practices. Lefebvre and later rhythm scholars emphasise the way in which politicians, bureaucrats, entrepreneurs and event makers exercise power by using and manipulating 'time, dates and time-tables' (2004, p. 68; Adam, 1995). Those in power create cities by synchronising repetitions and regularities, that is, rhythmic and temporal norms determining where, when, for how long and at what speed social practices should occur. Lefebvre calls these hierarchically synchronised rhythms 'isorhythmia'.

From a mobilities perspective, it is clear that the rhythms of cars have long ruled streetscapes, while sidewalks are normally dominated by the rhythms of pedestrians, rather than runners. This implies that plural rhythms coexist in the city; streets have different rhythms on a weekday during rush hour than they do on a Friday night when people are 'going out', or on an idle Sunday morning. Rhythmanalysis is particularly useful for describing and analysing urban marathons as unique temporal and temporary urban events that reconfigure the regular order of the streets (Edensor & Larsen, 2018).

However, rhythmanalysis also provides a language for understanding bodily rhythms and the intersection between mechanical and recorded time and timing technologies, both of which are central to running. According to Lefebvre, bodies and rhythms are connected, and rhythmanalysis highlights the role of the body: 'at no moment has the analysis of rhythms and the rhythmical project lost sight of the body', since 'the theory of rhythms is founded on the experience and knowledge [connaissance] of the body' (Lefebvre, 2004, p. 77). Lefebvre also argues that embodied rhythms are always measured, simultaneously natural and rational. They reunite qualitative and quantitative elements:

> Rhythm appears as regulated time, governed by rational laws, but in contact with what is least rational in human being: the lived, the carnal, the body. Rational, numerical, quantitative and qualitative rhythms superimpose themselves on the multiple natural rhythms of the body... .
>
> *(Lefebvre, 2004, pp. 18–19)*

This plants the seeds for what I call the 'drama of rhythms', when difference and unpredictable outcomes strike back and disrupt the ordering and 'dressage'.

Lefebvre also distinguishes between cyclical (nature, seasonality and biology) and linear rhythms (socially ordered human practices, measurement, clock time and timetables), bemoaning the fact that linear rhythms have come to dominate modern everyday rhythms. Today, 'everyday life is modelled on abstract, quantitative time, the time of watches and clocks' (Lefebvre 2004, p. 82). This also ties into his notion of 'dressage', a term that he uses to describe how people in power use biopolitical power relations to discipline other bodies into docility and to impose disciplined rhythms of work and leisure, as if training domesticated animals to submit to their owners' demands ('dressage' is a French word for training). Dressage is a form of repetition that eventually breaks people down, forcing them to become effective and skilful workers, schoolchildren or soldiers who perform certain drills effectively and habitually, without conflict or very much thought. Dressage teaches people to follow and master specific gestures and rhythms that are more or less beyond their control and will (Edensor & Larsen, 2018; Lefebvre, 2004, pp. 47–54). More broadly, dressage focuses attention on the socially produced nature of specific human gestures and movements, such as walking. He writes: 'These gestures, these manners, are acquired, are learned' (2004, p. 47).

Rhythm scholars also discuss how different linear rhythms can be plaited together without dissention and still fall apart because the rhythms are not mechanical. This is especially true when the rhythms are produced, as noted above, by 'what is least rational in human being: the lived, the carnal, the body' (Lefebvre, 2004, p. 18). The significance of the 'irrational' body is clear in his notions of 'eurhythmia' and 'arrhythmia': 'Whereas eurhythmia refers to a body in flow and harmony, or bodies that rhythmically align, arrhythmia describes pain, friction and a body out of flow' (Larsen, 2019b, p. 563; Lefebvre, 2004, p. 78).

Lefebvre's book has inspired sociologists and geographers to think about the polyrhythmic nature of events, the differently scaled rhythms of cities, and how various forms of mobility contribute to the temporal nature of places and the way in which different people experience such place rhythms. In line with the work discussed above, this research emphasises the non-human effects of weather, pollution, plants and many other elements within the changing nature of place rhythms. Mobilities scholars have explored the rhythmicity of situated and embodied walking (Middleton, 2010; Vergunst, 2010; Wunderlich, 2008), cycling (Spinney, 2006), everyday running (Edensor et al., 2018), and marathon running, as discussed in the present book (Edensor & Larsen, 2018). Building upon the insight that rhythms are experienced and partly constituted through the body, this literature reveals that embodied human movement is rhythmic. As Wunderlich writes in relation to walking:

Walking as both an experienced and observed activity in urban space involves regularity and routine. It is performed rhythmically step after step, after step, after step, after step … . The rhythms closely relate to our internal biological and psychological rhythms … following a regular pace, in synchrony with our breathing, heartbeat and the degree to which we are relaxed, nervous, anxious or determined. The rhythm of walking is influenced by the interaction with other external rhythmical events that we come across in urban environments, such as other walking practices, or other bodily movements or activities that contrast in pace or rhythm.

*(2008, p. 133)*

Edensor (2010) uses Lefebvre's concept of dressage to refute the idea that walking is a natural practice, arguing instead that walking is 'styled' and produced by social and cultural forces that change over time. Rhythmanalysis has also inspired Edensor et al. (2018) to investigate how non-competitive running interacts with the rhythms of walkers, dog owners and cyclists in a large park in central Malmö, Sweden. The popularity of urban running has changed the park's character, transforming it into yet another landscape in which mobile rhythms clash and users must align their rhythms with those of others to avoid disruptions and conflicts (for conflicts between runners and other mobile figures, see Cook, 2016; and chapter 5). According to Edensor et al. (2018), rhythmic harmony resonates in the park as people achieve accord in their movements.

This book critically analyses the way in which specific relations between place, time and energy constitute marathons as corporeal rhythmic practices and mobile places. Given that rhythms are closely linked to *time* and repetition, I explore how event managers design marathons as carefully managed rhythmic events, and also how various human and non-events can cause 'arrhythmia'. I am drawn to Lefebvre because he highlights the role of the body and insists that bodies and rhythms are connected. However, although rhythmanalysis sometimes touches on the 'internal biological and psychological rhythms' enmeshed in the human body, it primarily focuses on sensing *external* place rhythms (Crang, 2001; Duffy et al., 2011; Edensor, 2012). I extend this perspective by discussing the internal and somatic rhythms of running, which is always 'emplaced'. Despite its shortcomings (see below) and the fact that Lefebvre neither wrote about sport nor was adopted by sport scholars, this perspective may offer a rich and suggestive language (for instance, 'eurhythmia' and 'arrhythmia') for analysing both the rhythmic organisation of marathon places and the embodied rhythmic drill and sensations of running and training for a marathon. Running is essentially a 'rhythmic spatio-temporal practice' (Larsen, 2019b, p. 562; Edensor et al., 2018) centred around pace and pacing. According to two mobility scholars:

Pace is a concept that helps us understand the dynamic relationships between people, space, and time. Paying analytical attention to pace is a way to remediate what has been considered a failure to 'adequately explore and theorise mobility itself'. … In employing the terms 'pacing' and 'pace', we are placing a deliberate emphasis on interrogating the momentum for and temporal composition of mobility.

(Amit & Salazar, 2020, p. 2)

Building on the temporal 'pacing' of mobilities, Lefebvre's rhythm terminology can provide new insights into the established significance of time, timing, and training in marathon running. This is particularly relevant because some argue that running occurs in 'a prison of measured times' (Brohm, 1978; Bale, 2004), under the supervision of authoritarian coaches (Denison & Mills, 2014). While Lefebvre associated dressage and time-keeping with a biopolitical technique imposed on people to coerce them and render their bodies docile, this book focuses on active, knowledgeable people who are willing to adopt this form of dressage to become competent runners and achieve something meaningful (Edensor & Larsen, 2018). It also argues that rhythms dictated by clock-time and repetitive training can be meaningful and pleasurable.

This book shows that marathon dressage involves learning to run specific distances in a specific time (sometimes slow, sometimes very fast), while sustaining an even pace throughout. Such rhythmic training is typically measured using a GPS watch to ensure accurate quantitative data (see chapters 5–8). Clearly, this approach sits well with Foucault-inspired sport studies of the power relations involved in sport training (Denison & Mills, 2014; Markula & Pringle, 2006). So the otherwise free and self-generated training undertaken by marathon runners captures some elements of the physical training introduced by Lefebvre, which emphasised experts, discipline, standardised procedures and recorded time. As noted, however, I show that such linear rhythms and dressage can be experienced as liberating and desirable.

Although embodied rhythms imply 'repetition' and 'dressage', Lefebvre stressed their unpredictability, which can occur when people run out of energy. Due to the somatic rhythms of running, marathons constitute 'a drama of rhythms', with long periods of desired harmonious eurhythmia and painful periods of 'arrhythmic interruption', especially at the end (chapters 7 and 8). The form of rhythmanalysis presented here explores how bodies experience polyrhythmic situations with diverse rhythms, including harmonic periods of eurhythmia and painful moments of arrhythmia, when rhythms break apart, causing friction and pain.

Thus, the social and biological body is central to how people experience rhythms as part of everyday life. In reality, I agree with those researchers who argue that Lefebvre is too concerned with the social disciplining of the body, rather than its 'visceral, elusory nature' (Simpson, 2008, p. 824). The next chapter argues that rhythmanalysis is insufficiently concerned with visceral rhythms. Below, I discuss how aspects of non-representational theory and carnal sociology can enliven rhythmanalysis by making physical landscapes and the visceral body more visible, as well as by conducting 'live' studies of ongoing events.

## Non-representational theory

Non-representational scholars disapprove of geography's fixation with representations, cognition, gazing and visual landscapes (see Larsen, 2019b, pp. 544–546, for the following). They focus instead on multi-sensuous encounters, physical landscapes, 'a more grounded' and performative sense of perception and lively interactions with physical landscapes (Ingold, 2004; Thrift, 2008; Waitt, 2017; Waterton, 2013). Non-representational theory

> encourages scholars to engage with the material world using all the senses including bodily movement (kinaesthetic) and … highlights that landscapes that we may take for granted as places for nature are made and remade through what bodies 'do'. We sense, and make sense of landscapes as natural through the frictions and rhythms of our movement and how we orientate ourselves towards the world. Attention is drawn to how landscapes are formed in terms of the body's position and orientation in relation to the tensions between material, cultural, social and physiological processes that intertwine together the body and world.
>
> *(Waitt, 2017, p. 325)*

Non-representational theorists investigate and analyse the expressive liveliness of emplaced encounters and body-centred activities and events. They acknowledge that skills and practices can be hard to communicate with words (Lorimer, 2005; Vannini, 2015a, 2015b). They are concerned with the 'lived now'. As Thrift puts it, their research advances 'towards a poetics of encounter which both conveys a sense of life in which meaning shows itself only in the living, and which … recognizes that the unsayable has genuine value and can be "felt on our pulses"' (cited in Thorpe & Rinehart, 2010, p. 1269).

Before outlining the ways in which this book is inspired by non-representational theory, I would like to make a few cautious remarks. Nigel Thrift's discussion of dance as pre-representational and pre-choreographed overlooks that dance is always 'twice-behaved behaviour' (to use the lingo of performance theory), mediated by dressage and choreographed using rules and norms (Cresswell, 2006; Larsen, 2008). Thus, practices also involve choreographies and cultural constructions, a fact downplayed by Thrift and non-representational theorists. As Classen writes:

> Sensory perception, in fact, is not simply one aspect of bodily experience, but the basis for bodily experience. We experience our bodies – and the world – through our senses. Thus the cultural construction of sensory perception conditions our experience and understanding of our bodies and the world at a fundamental level.
>
> *(1997, p. 402)*

We must not occlude the effects of power relationships, ideological forces and social structures on the performative practices of individuals. This book, as previously noted, does discuss the ways in which marathon running is representational and choreographed. We do not have to accept every argument to find inspiration in non-representational theory.

First, this book's focus on the 'liveliness' of marathon running is inspired by non-representational theory. Most sport scholars disregard the immediate and active details of what is 'taking place' and instead promote 'static images of sporting landscapes … the field fails to get to grips with the raw performance of sport; sport as a material, embodied, expressed, and sensed physical act happening in space and time' (Andrews, 2017, p. 669). Andrews argues that we should move beyond conventional 'post-game interrogation' to animate the energy and physicality of sporting landscapes and bodies through 'lively "play-by-play" running commentary' (2017, p. 772; see also Thorpe & Rinehart, 2010; Vannini, 2017). Such research requires a full material understanding of places and the ability to analyse how emplaced people experience running on the ground, in the weather and with specific objects. Moreover, as the next chapter will discuss, this type of running commentary requires an 'exercising researcher' and imaginative, poetic prose.

Second, non-representational theory provides a richer and more sensuous language than the theories discussed above, including sensations of movement (kinaesthesia), pain (nocioception), muscles and organs (proprioception), balance (equilibrioception) and body temperature (thermoception). In addition to taking the classical senses seriously, non-representational theory argues that the haptic extends beyond cutaneous contact with the material world; it accepts the view that aspects of biology and physiology must inform discussions of embodiment, which work with a body that is simultaneously biological, material and social (Vannini, 2015a, 2015b). This perspective is crucial for the present argument; internal somatic sensations are central to running, which involves 'intense embodiment' and a heightened awareness of how the body feels during and after running (Allen-Collinson & Owton, 2015; Larsen, 2019b; Sparkes, 2017; Vannini et al., 2013). Groth and Krahn have highlighted the multiple and culturally mediated significance of the senses in running:

> the importance of the senses stretches from material aspects (the comfort of apparel, the quality of running shoes …) to practices of self-measuring (perceived efforts versus measured efforts) and self-presentation (beauty standards and appearances). Moreover, proprioception (perceiving one's own body and movements in space), the self-diagnosis of injuries or fitness levels, and knowledge of biomechanics and physical capabilities are all related to the senses. For recreational athletes, knowledge of the senses and emotions in sport as circulated in magazines, podcasts or online fora, cultural perceptions about landscape and nature, conceptions of immersion, ideal or desired leisure activities, the role of atmospheres (in general and specifically for bigger sporting events), and sensory biographies are important sensory dimensions which need to be considered when researching sport and the senses.

*(2017, p. 5)*

Lastly, as discussed in the Introduction, non-representational theory is driven by a life-affirming and engaged 'ethos', which celebrates the social life, conviviality, energy, and vitalism generated by marathons and other events (Larsen, 2019b; Latham & McCormack, 2017). According to Latham and McCormack, this ethos helps one to:

> avoid the common academic tendency to incorporate them [events] within a narrative of critical disenchantment, as evidence of how contemporary urban life and the bodies that inhabit them are becoming alternately too fast, too slow, too sedentary, too active, too individualized, too competitive, or too unthinking.
>
> *(2017, p. 374)*

With this life-affirming ethos in mind, this book offers a largely upbeat analysis of the embodied and affective sensations of marathon training and racing. This brings us to 'carnal sociology', the final theoretical inspiration for this book. Carnal sociology complements the non-representational perspective; it is also essential, as we cannot understand the running body as a socio-biological entity without fleshing out a carnal rhythmanalysis of marathon running.

## Carnal sociology

Like non-representational theorists, carnal sociologists are concerned with developing corporal or fleshy sociology. This contrasts with many other types of 'sociology of the body', which are informed by social constructivism and Foucault. Carnal sociologists rightly blame sociologists of the body for offering disembodied and overly theoretical accounts of embodiment, failing to carry out empirical research, bracketing out the individual, and ignoring practical experiences of embodiment. In short, they reduce the body to a discursive entity without flesh or organs (Wainwright & Turner, 2006, p. 238). Sentient bodies and practical experiences are lacking in these accounts. As the sport scholar Sparkes writes:

> disembodiment was soon identified as a general feature of an approach that came to be known as the 'sociology of the body' which was informed by a strand of social constructionist thinking that focussed predominantly on the cultural at the expense of the corporeal dynamics of being.
>
> *(2017, p. 2)*

By contrast, various writers have drawn on the work of the existentialist phenomen-ologist, Maurice Merleau-Ponty, outlining a form of carnal sociology that analyses what active bodies do and sense by theorising 'from' lived bodies (Crossley, 1995). In 2007, the two running scholars Allen-Collinson and Hockey made the case that the sociology-of-sport literature lacked a 'carnal-sociology' perspective; they promoted a phenomenology of the body that focused on the sensuous and sensing sporting body (Allen-Collinson & Hockey, 2015; Hockey & Allen-Collinson, 2007). They called for research into 'the carnal, "fleshy", lived, richly textured realities of the moving, sweating, sensuous sporting body' (Allen-Collinson, 2009, p. 292). Since then, they have (alone, together and with other scholars) produced numerous articles on the phenomenology of the sensuous running body (and other sporting bodies) and running as an outdoor weathered practice (Allen-Collinson & Leledaki, 2015). Mainly drawing on their own living, running bodies, they analyse the ways in which runners sense and navigate the environments they run in (Hockey, 2006, 2013); they also explore their own bodies, as they train hard, become injured and lose the kinaesthetic sense and strength of running (Allen-Collinson, 2003). In addition, they discuss runners' visual practices and sense of heat (Allen-Collinson & Owton, 2015; Allen-Collinson et al., 2019; Hockey & Allen-Collinson, 2017).

The most famous carnal sociologist is Wacquant (2004, 2015). His work 'takes seriously the fact that people are motile, sensate, sensual, suffering, skilled, sedimented, and situated creatures of flesh, blood, nerves and sinews that are doomed to death, who know it, and make their world through and with their enskilled and exposed "mindful bodies"' (Sparkes, 2017, p. 4). During the early 2000s, Wacquant (2004) conducted fieldwork in an American boxing club to study ghetto life. He became so fascinated with boxing that he began to practise and study it instead. Because he took up boxing and eventually became a very competent boxer, he was able to carry out a carnal sociological study of boxing. Boxing competences are first and foremost acquired in action, through repetitive gestures – what Lefebvre would call 'being broken in'. Aspiring boxers must put in many hours of hard training, become fit, and learn the boxer's gestures, moves and punches, mediated by a coach (Wacquant, 2004).

Lastly, carnal sociologists rethink the relationship between sociology and biology in their discussions of the active body. Thorpe reflects on the way in which the 'biological body' is missing in her otherwise embodied analysis of snowboarding:

> I also sought to engage with recent theoretical developments on embodiment and dedicated a chapter to exploring the lived, sensuous and affective boarding body. But the messy insides of the snowboarding body 'the bones, blood, muscles, nerves and hormones' remain hidden in this text. I do not apologize for this absence; I am a sociologist, not a scientist, and understanding what was going on inside the biological snowboarding body was not the intent of this project. But, following the publication of this book, my own body rudely reminded me of the importance of the biological. As some readers may attest, there is nothing quite like surgery or time in a hospital ward to remind us of the complex processes operating inside our bodies, beyond our sociological gaze. As is often the case, my personal experiences prompted me to ask new questions about the body, and particularly the tendency in the sociology of sport and physical culture to ignore the biological dimensions of moving bodies.
>
> *(2014, p. 669)*

Thorpe is inspired by feminist scholars who engage in biology in non-reductionist and non-determinist ways. They pay attention to the way in which 'social and cultural forces do indeed write upon the body as surface', and consider how these forces 'communicate with the body's inside' (Birke, cited in Thorpe, 2014, p. 670). More recently, Thorpe (2015) has explored experiences of exercise and hormones, with particular reference to the amenorrhea caused by intensive daily exercise (not elite training). Drawing on her own running body and kinesiology studies, she shows how daily running interferes with hormones, explaining that menstrual disturbance, or amenorrhea, is relatively common among serious female runners.

Carnal sociology is relevant to the present book for at least four reasons. First, running can only be fully understood by the runner (chapter 3). Second, although punching and running may be seen as 'natural' movements of the body, marathon running – like boxing – is an artform, a learned practice (chapter 6). Both practices – perhaps running even more than boxing – are taught through 'instructions', which only make sense during and through training. Third, most people probably picture dramatic fights when they think of boxing; however, Wacquant notes that such events are rare (in part because they damage the boxer's health). The 'life of a boxer' mainly consists of training. As this book details, the same is true for marathon running. Finally, there is a dark biological side to running: the 'inevitable' injuries that plague most marathon runners. Ironically, injuries are often caused by the fact that most practitioners lack a physiological understanding of how their bodies work and respond to training.

## Conclusion

This chapter has discussed the theories that inform my methods and understanding of marathon running and events, as corporeal mobile practices and mobile places. Inspired by the 'mobilities paradigm', which focuses on mobility and experiences of being on move, this book moves the paradigm forward by discussing the characteristics of running as a *corporeal* practice; in doing so, it takes the temporal and spatial dimensions of movement and places seriously. It also moves the mobilities paradigm forward by linking it with sport studies and more fully with practice theory, rhythmanalysis and non-representational and carnal sociology.

Informed by practice theory, this book discusses various materials (including environments), meanings, and competences that organise, systematise and enable (various) running *practices* and *places*. This resonates with sport research, which explores how sporting bodies are always coached and trained (chapter 6). Marathon practices are contextualised; the book explores how runners learn and perform this practice, identifying the types of practices that marathon running is bundled with. An analysis of the way in which racecourses are designed and bodies are equipped to afford rhythmic order is inspired by discussions about affordances, 'emplacement' and rhythmanalysis (see chapter 5).

In this book, I argue that running is a rhythmic (emplaced) practice, influenced by biological rhythms, external place rhythms and material environments. In doing so, I use, stretch and develop Lefebvre's intriguing, but rather sketchy, rhythm concepts, including arrhythmia and eurhythmia, and relate them to running.

However, I am not fully committed to Lefebvre's project; I diverge from his critical project and critique of linear, rational and timed rhythms because they imply the premature conclusion that rational and coached marathon training is alienating – and that marathon running is trapped within a prison of time.

To avoid this, I draw on the life-affirming 'ethos' of carnal sociology and non-representational theory and insist on seeing bodies as lively and expressive, and places as enacted. Injecting a large dose of non-representational theory and carnality into rhythmanalysis makes it possible to write evocative, atmospheric and lively accounts of the streetscapes, corporeal mobile practices and drama of rhythms that comprise urban marathons. Moreover, the fact that non-representational theory insists on understanding the physical, energising, and truly embodied nature of urban landscapes allows me to explore training rhythms and training grounds (chapter 6), corporeal race rhythms (chapter 7), and atmospheric place rhythms (chapter 8). These are conditioned by and also intermittently reconfigure infrastructures, surfaces, gradients, sounds, objects, people, weather worlds and atmospheres.

# 3

# RUNNING METHODS

## Lively ethnographies and energising the rhythm analyst

## Introduction

In the last chapter, I discussed my theoretical approach to marathon running as a corporeal practice and marathon courses as mobile places. This chapter explores why such theories call for ethnographic approaches that particularly emphasise participation and lively forms of representation. First, I argue that in practice, rhythmanalysis neglects internal biological rhythms and is insufficiently corporeal and sensuous. To compensate, I propose a method of instructing the rhythm analyst to listen to his or her heartbeat and internal rhythms as well as to external location rhythms. This section 'energises the rhythm analyst' (Larsen, 2019b), leading me to coin the term 'energetic rhythm analyst'. Second, I address the lack of sensuosity in rhythm studies by linking this topic to non-representational ethnography (Andrews, 2017; Vannini, 2015a, b; Waterton, 2013), sensory ethnography (Pink, 2009), and the carnal sociology of sport bodies (Allen-Collinson & Owton, 2015; Pink, 2011; Sparkes, 2017), all fields that focus on the lively and enacted nature of movement and sport. Third, I discuss what is characteristic of auto-ethnography, as this method plays a relative prominent role within the academic field of running studies. While this book has a light auto-ethnographic sensibility, I will argue that the running literature also needs to move beyond (although not to dispense with) the researcher, engaging with other runners, so as to create a fuller ethnographic picture. In other words, running researchers should engage more with other runners. In this work, I combine ethnography with a moderate dose of auto-ethnography and speak of '(auto)ethnographies' (Larsen, 2014). Fourth, in dialogue with the above discussions, I outline in detail how the research for this book was conducted, analysed, and represented in photographs and words; I also reflect on my positionality as a particular 'research-runner'.

DOI: 10.4324/9781003125068-3

## Doing rhythmanalysis

Bodies are central not only to the way in which people experience rhythms but also how researchers in rhythmanalysis must study them. Prefiguring the 'sensory turn' (Vannini et al., 2012), Lefebvre argued:

> The rhythm analyst calls on all his senses. He draws on his breathing, the circulation of his blood, the beatings of his heart and the delivery of his speech as landmarks. ... He thinks with his body, not in the abstract, but in lived temporality. ... He listens – and first to his body; he learns rhythm from it, in order consequently to appreciate external rhythms.
>
> *(2004, pp. 31, 29)*

Scholars are instructed to sense rhythms through their bodies by observing and listening to urban rhythms, as well as to the rhythms of their own bodies: their 'respirations, pulses, circulations, assimilations – durations and phases of durations'; these can be used as a 'metronome' (Lefebvre, 2004). In his own writing, however, Lefebvre focused on socially disciplined bodies; his book includes very few breathing and moving bodies. We read little about Lefebvre's rhythms, respiration, pulse or movement in the city. Elsewhere, I have made the argument that his chosen perspective is 'the balcony-gaze', which

> privileges the visual sense and some detachment from beating hearts and somatic sensations below ... He was standing apart from them and experienced them from a safe distance, at rest, and with a low pulse, while his feet never met the pavement. He literally set himself apart from the mobile crowd and embodied practices below him ... The balcony exemplifies the sort of 'groundlessness' and immobility that many have identified as characterising landscape studies and western ocularcentric sensory hierarchies ... .
>
> *(Larsen, 2019b, p. 564)*

Most importantly, this aloof gaze 'is too distant and discordant to account for the somatic sensations of running a marathon' (Larsen, 2019b, p. 564).

The American geographer Tuan noted the limitations of observing – especially from afar – from a balcony, or in this case, high up in the stands of a stadium:

> The athletes looked beautiful to me from a distance, but if I could see their faces I would no doubt see them twisted and ugly. But then the same could be said of ballet – how elegant the dancers look from a distance, how ugly from up close. And how close this elegance is to violence! At the end of a performance, the ballet slippers are stained by blood.
>
> *(Tuan, cited in Bale, 2004, p. 3)*

Moreover, a distant viewing position not only precludes a close-up look at bloodstained slippers but also avoids touching or smelling them. There are similar limits to relying on distant observations when accounting for embodied rhythms. As the performance-and-rhythm scholar Goodridge writes:

> Some physiological features of rhythm can be observed easily with the naked eye; others, referred to as innate or inner rhythms, are less accessible or readily discernible. These require the use of technological equipment for their observation. For instance, it was easy for me to see the outward bodily action of the child on the pavement, transferring her weight from one foot to the other. ... But I could not observe her pulse rate, breathing pattern or the movements of her internal organs which were occurring instinctively and involuntarily.
>
> *(1999, pp. 26–27)*

However, this position is only partially true. If one were very close to that child (walking with her, for example), one might be able to hear her 'breathing patterns' without any 'technological' aid. While observation is important, the rhythm analyst must find some way to combine observation and full-blown participation.

Overall, I argue that rhythmanalysis is too observation-based and insufficiently concerned with visceral rhythms and does not fully follow the methodological principle 'of listening to and appreciating external rhythms, through one's own body and internal rhythms' (Larsen, 2019b, p. 574). I suggest that non-representational and carnal ethnography can energise and enliven rhythmanalysis, contributing to a revised form of rhythmanalysis in which 'the rhythm analyst literally thinks with his or her active, mobile body and by attending directly to his or her breathing, blood circulation, heartbeat, muscles and visceral rhythms' (Larsen, 2019b, p. 575). Rhythms are appreciated in the midst of the action and not solely from a balcony.

## Carnal, sensuous and non-representational ethnography

Ethnography values thick descriptions of practices, events, rituals and places. Ethnographers interview people *in situ*, observe their doings, and participate in the practice being studied. The extent to which an ethnographer ought to participate is fiercely debated. I will argue that serious participation is crucial when studying corporeal practices such as running. I agree with Laurier's claim that researchers tend to be 'commentators' and not 'players', and this is a problem because the best ethnographic studies are generally done by those who have been playing (2010). I concur with non-representational geographers and carnal sociologists (chapter 2), who argue that embodied and emplaced analyses of sport and movement require sustained participation in, and development of, the specific embodied skills of that sport or movement in its natural habitat. Wacquant speaks of 'enactive ethnography', urging sociologists to put their 'own organism, sensibility, and incarnate intelligence at the epicentre of the array of material and symbolic forces that [they] intend to dissect' (Wacquant, 2004, p. viii). Wacquant insists that anyone who wants to study boxing must put on boxing gloves and become a boxer:

To understand the universe of boxing requires one to immerse oneself in it firsthand, to learn it and experience its constitutive moments from the inside. Native understanding of the object is here the necessary condition of an adequate knowledge of the object.

*(2004, p. 59)*

He explains that 'few practices may be said to be more "practical" than boxing. For the rules of the pugilistic art boil down to bodily moves that can be fully apprehended only in action and place it at the very edge of that which can be intellectually grasped and communicated' (Wacquant, 2004, pp. 58–59).

As non-representational ethnography begins with the researcher's body, researchers are encouraged to activate the sensations and emotions of movement and to 'get moving'. As Vannini writes:

Our presence in the world is embodied. Non-representational ethnographic research begins from the researcher's body as the key instrument for knowing, sensing, feeling, and relating to others and self. … From fatigue to enthusiasm, melancholia to keenness, pain to enchantment, non-representational ethnographic research is affected by bodies' capacity to affect the world and their capacity to be affected by it.

*(2015a, p. 321)*

This perspective requires an energised scholarly body. Elsewhere he writes:

The sensuality of non-representational ethnographies depends on a re-awakened scholarly body: a body 'stiffened from long sleep in the background of scholarly life' that now 'yearns to exercise its muscles', and 'aches to restore its sensibilities' by opposing the dullness of overly analytic, formal, anonymous, and unimaginative scholarship.

*(2015a, p. 322)*

Such awakened bodies and elegiac accounts are present in ethnographies of exercising and mobile bodies, where researchers in part base theories about bodies and movement on their own moving bodies and write imaginative, evocative and vitalist accounts of embodied and emplaced experiences (Andrews, 2017; Vannini, 2015a, 2017). They report on how movement and bodies affect and are affected by contingent arrangements of people and dogs on the pavement, urban infrastructures, vehicles, materials, surfaces, weather conditions, atmospheres and the topography they walk, run or cycle in (Barnfield, 2016; Edensor & Larsen, 2018; Lorimer, 2012; Spinney, 2006). For example, this sensibility informs Spinney's non-representational study of amateur cycling on Mount Ventoux, which interrogates the 'less representational – those fleeting, ephemeral and often embodied and sensory aspects of movement' (2011, p. 161). Interestingly, to be able to conduct this research, Spinney had to train (often with other cyclists) for months prior to the event, otherwise he would have lacked the skills and endurance needed to climb the mountain and maintain the pace. As he writes: 'physical training was equally important to the research and methodology as both a means and object of insight' (2006, p. 716). By actively participating in the cycle rides with others, Spinney gained a much better understanding of the meanings and sensuous sensations of descending this mountain. Such embodied studies of sport and movement are attuned to the senses and more or less informed by the forms of sensuous scholarship discussed below.

## Senses

Wacquant, Vannini, and Pink explore the sensuality of everyday practices and argue that ethnographic participation requires a multi-sensuous approach that 'accounts for how this multisensoriality is integral both to the lives of people who participate in our research and to how we ethnographers practice our craft' (Pink, 2009, p. 1). Researchers must learn to use all of their senses and to 'participate in *their* worlds, on the terms of their embodied understandings' (Pink, 2009, p. 72). The sensuous scholar must develop 'sensory intelligence'

> that involves all our senses and the reflexive cultivation of our sensations. … It is the skilled use of sensibility to approach life situations. It is the ability to utilize one's senses as skills to manipulate and adapt to one's environment. It is the combined emotional, visceral, and cognitive ability to engage in somatic work. Without sensory intelligence there can be no sensuous scholarship. Indeed, we will go further and suggest that all sensuous scholarship is a form of sensory intelligence.
>
> *(Vannini et al., 2013, p. 67)*

This work is more difficult than it sounds; it requires training to develop such intelligence. Sociologists and geographers are primarily trained to describe and analyse places, objects and practices in visual terms, based on observations. They are not trained to describe sensuous sensations, such as touch, smell, heat or pain.

To sum up, running researchers need to lace up their running shoes and spend many hours running with competent practitioners. They must learn from runners by mimicking their routines and observing and talking with them (including through informal and formal interviews) about how they practise this activity and what it means to them. Non-representational scholars argue that practices are difficult to talk about and interviews are typically not in their toolboxes. While even competent sportspeople sometimes struggle to explain fully how they do their sports, I concur with practice scholars, who argue that 'people can talk about their practices' (Hitchings cited in Blue, 2017, p. 346) and 'sayings, after all, are a part of any doings' (Blue, 2017, p. 346). However, in order to understand such 'sayings', it is necessary for ethnographers to master the sport in practice. As Blue writes: 'I emphasise that to better decode participants' "sayings", to interpret their meanings, and to be able to contextualise the cues and signs of this practice, it is entirely necessary to have had one's body disciplined through the training of MMA' (2017, p. 346). Informal conversations and formal interviews with different runners (of very different levels of ability) will play a key role in this book, as they have played a crucial role in my own participation in the field. In combination with my training and observations, they have given me the knowledge to become a competent marathon runner and analytical insight into various marathon meanings and aspirations. Accordingly, the preceding chapters include and discuss many interesting 'citations' derived from my interviews (discussed below).

Thus, while this book is grounded in my participation in the field and includes some auto-ethnographic elements, I seek a healthy balance between reporting on my own body and those of others. In this book, the voices of others largely prevail, partly in response to the popularity of auto-ethnography in running and sport literature. For this reason, the book includes a discussion of auto-ethnography.

## Auto-ethnography[1]

The argument that full-blown participation is crucial is seen in the running literature, where many studies are conducted by keen runners, and such scholars often – in the tradition of *auto*-ethnography – write about their own experiences (for instance, Allen-Collinson & Hockey, 2015; Allen-Collinson et al., 2018; Denison, 2006; Hockey, 2009; Hockey & Allen-Collinson, 2006, 2017; Sparkes, 1996). It is striking that this otherwise inferior method is so prevailing in running studies.

There is significant overlap between auto-ethnography and the type of participatory ethnography discussed above. For example, both fields have an epistemological focus on the researcher's body and presence in the text,[2] although auto-ethnography is more radical in this respect than non-representational and carnal sociology. Auto-ethnographers fully embrace and accentuate the researcher's subjectivity, bodily experiences and emotions – elements that most social scientists downplay or eliminate. The researcher thus becomes the main character in the finished text. Such researchers do not worry about becoming too involved or overidentifying with the field.

The leading auto-ethnographic sociologist Carolyn Ellis (2004, p. xix) describes how this method unites the personal and biographical with a wider cultural, social and political context. The basic idea is to use one's own body and/or biographical involvement to create an interesting narrative that both reveals and exceeds the author, allowing self-reflections to merge with cultural insights that go beyond the purely personal.

One auto-ethnographic assumption is that researchers must experience certain social practices in their own bodies in order to understand them. Many researchers have written about traumatic experiences that have lingered in their bodies for a long time, such as sexual abuse or eating disorders (Spry, 2001). For example, Tillman-Healy wrote about bulimia based on her own struggle with this disease. She believes that her story contains special knowledge: 'I can give you an insight that no psychiatrist or therapist can give you, for I have had an experience of how bulimia is lived and feels' (1996, p. 80). Alongside these often heart-breaking stories of traumatised and affected bodies, auto-ethnographic studies – often phenomenologically inspired – focus on the active body and bodily knowledge. Such auto-ethnographies provide detailed and sensual portraits of particular practices, focusing on body movements and mutual interactions. Examples include research on playing the piano (Sudnow, 1993), tying ship ropes (Laurier, 1999) and jazz improvisation (Dempsey, 2008). If the researcher does not have prior experience with a given practice, he or she should try to learn it (as long as the practice is not harmful or traumatising); this may require many months of training.

Last, auto-ethnography emphasises interesting stories and passionate, literary writing styles capable of moving the reader. While all ethnographic communication involves writing in an engaging and expressive way so that the reader can sense and feel the field (Van Maanen, 1988), auto-ethnography combines science and art (Sikes 2013, p. 7). Ellis et al. argue:

> Autoethnography, as method, attempts to disrupt the binary of science and art. Auto-ethnographers believe research can be rigorous, theoretical, and analytical *and* emotional, therapeutic, and inclusive of personal and social phenomena. Auto-ethnographers also value the need to write and represent research in evocative, aesthetic ways … .
>
> *(2010)*

Auto-ethnographers are sceptical of the neutral, objective and distant writing style traditionally used in conventional ethnography, where the author is an invisible third-person narrator. They find it dead and boring, devoid of aesthetic pleasures and opportunities for identification and empathy.

So far, I have described auto-ethnography as a distinct method with a number of specific characteristics. However, Andersen (2006) argues that, in principle, there are two different auto-ethnographic methods. He refers to these as 'evocative auto-ethnography' (the dominant school, discussed in the previous section) and 'analytical auto-ethnography'. I agree with Anderson who finds the 'evocative' school too radical because it rejects established scientific quality standards; its own epistemological focus is on emotional experiences, seductive texts and aesthetic criteria. It focuses too much on the researcher's (obviously limited) experiences and perspective and not enough on those of other actors in the field (Anderson, 2006, p. 386). Anderson also argues that 'evocative auto-ethnographies' rarely dialogue with existing theories or lead to new concepts. As a counterweight, Anderson (2006) offers what he terms 'analytical auto-ethnography'. This approach is informed by the realistic school of ethnography; scholars conduct research with other practitioners who have similar experiences or passions. It is also committed to a more conventional writing style and an analytical research agenda in which research is informed by theories and contributes new analytical insights or concepts.

## Auto-ethnographies of sport

Auto-ethnography has a special focus on the body, on the scars and bumps that life inevitably inflicts on human beings. Its methods have inspired sociologists and geographers who study sports and physical mobility. Although most of these studies are 'analytical', some are noticeably 'evocative'. The auto-ethnographic method is appealing because it allows them to study sport and mobility as unique bodily activities, without having to reduce bodies to biology (as physiological sport studies do) or discourse (as in some sociological studies). This approach bypasses the dead scientific language of most sport science, allowing researchers to write evocative narratives about the physical highs and lows of doing sports (Denison & Markula, 2003; Markula, 2003; Sparkes, 2000, 2002a, b).

The auto-ethnographies of sport sociologists also explore diseased bodies and pathological practices. For instance, Sparkes (1996) writes evocatively about how he was once an elite athlete before becoming permanently affected by inflammatory back disease. Stone (2009) has written a short story about anorexia and excessive exercise, while Drummond (2010) has published a personal story about how his body eventually broke down due to a gruelling training regimen. The long description below is good example of how sport sociologists do auto-ethnography:

> I feel tired, excruciatingly lethargic. The twenty-five stairs that I negotiate every morning from the University car park have become their own mini training session unto themselves. … The extensive training regime and clear lack of food is starting to weigh heavily on my day-to-day functioning. However, the sports-related performance results are impressive despite low energy levels and more impressive are the changes to my physique. Visibly and distinguishably, I am becoming an endurance athlete. The more training I perform and the stricter I become on my dietary regime, the more people are telling me how much weight I am losing. This displays evidence of bodily control and is something that is essential in an elite endurance athlete's life, or so I have read in the popular culture triathlon magazines. I reach the top of the stairs and walk over to my peers mingling outside the auditorium prior to the physiology lecture. I am too weary to talk and too washed out to laugh and disillusioned with my immediate surroundings. Ironically, it is the training and dietary restraint that is creating this disenchantment and yet it is luring me away to perpetuate the problem. I want to be elsewhere, I want to be training and yet I find difficulty walking from one end of the campus to the other. This is not important, I know that once I start training the chemicals in my body will take over and I will be 'normal' once more. It is interesting that normalcy is now viewed in terms of training. I begin to wonder how natural all of this is. However, I do not question it for long. By questioning, I am undermining my central focus on 'being' an elite level triathlete.
>
> *(Drummond, 2010, p. 379)*

During his debut, Drummond develops the ambition to become a really talented amateur triathlon performer. In the subsequent race, he collapses. This will also be his last race. Drummond realises that his training regime is excessive and making him ill. The critical sociological point is the fact that a dedicated practitioner of a physically demanding sport, such as triathlons or marathons, risks developing an exercise addiction that is physically and mentally harmful and detrimental to his or her social life. Sport is far from always healthy. What once was characterised by desire and well-being can become an unhealthy obsession. As with other forms of abuse, the realisation is difficult to swallow and address. Drummond's auto-ethnographic account helps him to free himself from what has become an unhealthy practice.

However, dedicated running can also be therapeutic when life is most painful. I now leave sociology behind for a brief moment to discuss how two Danish journalists (one with a sociology degree) wrote 'auto-biographically' about marathon running in relation to pain, grief and redemption. Legarth Smidt's running routines began with a personal tragedy:

> About two years ago, I lost my daughter Ellen. She was six years old and died of cancer … after being ill for a long time. I have tried many times to put into words how much it hurts. But it is when running that I have found the greatest relief and the purest answers.
>
> *(Schmidt, 2015, my translation)*

In his book *I Run* [*Jeg løber*] (Schmidt, 2018), Ellen and his running body are woven together in beautiful, evocative passages. It is when he 'eats miles', or pushes his body at a high pace, that he finds 'the greatest relief and the purest answers'. *I Run* is a therapeutic space in which he processes an all-consuming grief. However, it is more than that. It gives the reader an insight into how a pained soul tries to hold on to beloved memories and move on at the same time. It can help others who have experienced a great loss – whether they are runners or not.

The second example is the memoir *Reconciliation* [*Forsoning*] by Aydin Soie (2016). The book describes Aydin's difficult upbringing in Iran, the Soviet Union and Denmark. Aydin and his mother were subjected to harassment and violence from their increasingly psychologically unstable father and husband. They ran away from him several times but never managed to escape completely. At one point, his father killed a close friend of the family. Even in prison, and later, when he was deported to Iran, he managed to terrorise them. Only when Aydin received the message that his father had died could he breathe with relief. The book is about reconciling with the past, forgiving oneself and others, and finding ways to avoid reproducing or passing on one's own negative heritage to one's child. It includes several future letters to his small son, in one of which Aydin links his own therapeutic progress with the painful euphoria of a marathon:

> 'You've used the pain to motivate you,' said the first friend I told about my father's story, and until recently I used this story as an explanation every time I did better than expected. Also, when I ran. While I ran those 42 kilometers through the Copenhagen streets, I looked around at the other runners and told myself that I could endure more than them. Thanks for that dad, I thought along the way and remembered the time he beat me in the bathroom … my fuel was rage.
>
> A few weeks ago, I ran the Berlin Marathon more than half an hour faster. This time I was thinking of you all the time. The night before I found two

pictures [of you] that I memorized. … I ran at my limit all the way, and when I started to doubt whether I could keep going, I thought of the pictures of you and found myself smiling to the audience along the route. Instead of running on pain, I thought about our future together. …

[W]hen I passed the finish line, I again thought of the picture of the two of us on the sofa. I almost broke down in tears. Why did it take me so many years to get rid of the idea that it is pain and the bitter part of the past that drives me forward? Why did I romanticize that part of life until you were born?

*(Soei, 2016, pp. 645–46, my translation)*

Some analytical auto-ethnographies of sport place more emphasis on theorising and conventional writing. Examples include studies of body regulation in elite swimming (McMahon & Thompson, 2011), women and boxing (Nash, 2017), and power and resistance in competitive rowing (Purdy et al., 2008). As previously mentioned, Allen-Collinson and Hockey have, both individually and together, written several insightful auto-ethnographic studies of running. Basing their research on their common training routines, they explore and contribute to theories and debates about identity, senses, embodiment and places (Allen-Collinson & Hockey, 2007, 2011; Hockey, 2006, 2013). When research is firmly informed by theory and uses analytical insight to make a contribution, it does not dissolve into self-absorption.

Having said that, the prominent position of auto-ethnography in running studies is a potential problem. The problem is not that researchers engage in the sport or is present in the text, but that 'other runners' are often missing. Needless to say, it cannot be taken for granted that 'others' share the researchers' experiences or practice and understand running in a similar way. For this reason, auto-ethnography should rarely stand alone if there is an opportunity to carry out a larger ethnographic study that includes interviews with different types of people. Auto-ethnography must never be a 'shorthand method' or an excuse for not undertaking time-consuming and cumbersome research about and with other people. Perhaps this is the case today, when relatively few studies convey the voices of a range of different runners. Instead, 'serious' scholars-turned-runners (or vice versa) write from and about their own bodies. There is a danger that such research can blind them to the many – often casual – runners they pass on their daily runs. This book sets out to avoid this trap. How, where and with whom this research has been conducted is discussed next.

## My approach

This monograph is based upon extensive and multifaceted ethnographic research carried out between 2015 and 2020 (prior to the COVID-19 outbreak). Most of the book was written in 2019 and especially 2020 – ironically a period when virtually all marathons were cancelled due to COVID-19 lockdowns and restrictions on public gatherings. All of us had trained in vain, and many runners ran low on energy with no races on the immediate horizon. I had signed up for the 2020 Valencia Marathon in December and planned to base parts of this book on how we trained for and performed at this event. However, staying true to the main body of material, this book does not focus on COVID-19, mentioning it sporadically only in the last two chapters.

I conducted research in many different places, talking with different runners, and using various methods from the ethnographic toolbox. While the empirical chapters are based on interviews with and observations of other runners, they simultaneously deal with my own body and relatively fast and competitive approach to running (see below), both individually and as a member of the Copenhagen-based running community, NBRO (Box 3.1).

This book is concerned with 'serious' (Stebbins, 1992) runners. Even among relatively slow runners, marathon running is a fairly 'serious leisure' activity because it requires so much training and dedication. Drawing a contrast with 'casual leisure' activities, Stebbins defines 'serious leisure' as 'the systematic pursuit of an amateur, hobbyist, or volunteer activity sufficiently interesting for the participant to find a career they are acquiring and expressing a combination of its special skills, knowledge, and experience' (Stebbins, 1992, p. 3; Elkington & Stebbins, 2014). Although many marathon runners quickly lose interest in the practice and never develop marathon careers, most runners are 'serious' during the months they spend training. The present study does not include elite or semi-elite runners (e.g. those who run the marathon in less than two hours and 30 minutes, or 'sub 2:30' in marathon lingo).

I have carried out formal interviews, made observations, and participated as a runner (often together with other NBRO runners) at the following urban marathons: the Berlin Marathon (2015), the Frankfurt Marathon (2016 and 2017), the Tokyo Marathon (2018), the Odense Marathon 2017, the Kyoto Marathon (2018 and 2020), the Copenhagen Marathon (2015–2020) and the Valencia Marathon (2018, 2019). I studied marathon training in Copenhagen as part of my NBRO training routines and training sessions. Excluding holidays and times spent recovering from injuries, I have trained with the NBRO one to three times weekly since 2014, participating in numerous marathons and other races wearing a singlet with the NBRO logo (reserved for club members with some seniority). Like Wacquant and others, my own research and embodied knowledge are based on active involvement in the sport and loosely within a particular local community. I write 'loosely' because this is not a case study of the NBRO; I am involved with the NBRO primarily as a runner, not a researcher. However, many NBRO members knew that I was a scholar (my nickname is 'the professor'), that I was writing this book about urban marathons, and that they would be mentioned in it. They all accepted and encouraged me to complete this project. I interviewed some NBRO members and chatted informally with many of them about my research during training sessions and journeys abroad. About one-fourth of the formal interviews are with NBRO members. During many training runs and journeys to foreign marathons, I overheard endless conversations – especially on our long Saturday runs – about runners' training routines, intervals, long runs, tempo runs, positive and negative splits, injuries (and how best to cure and prevent them), shoes, GPS watches, race plans, weight loss, personal records, personal bests, failed record attempts, weekly training miles, training philosophies, good and bad places to train and where (not) to run marathons. However, our conversations often go beyond running, developing into friendly chats or heated discussions about football, politics, music, work, being in love, falling out of love, fatal illnesses or buying new loudspeakers or a new property. We have fun telling jokes, talking pure nonsense and winding each other up, just killing time as we endlessly pound the Copenhagen asphalt or the gravel paths in parks and around lakes. When training hard or racing fast, I have heard runners short of breath and ragging, heard their running sounds, and seen their clenched faces and sweaty bodies, near to collapse after a tough interval. Because runners spend so much time together and share a passion, we form (sometimes close) friendships and have affectionate feelings about our community. Sometimes I wonder if we run to talk.

This book draws on my involvement in the running community to give a specific account of how people learn to become (committed) marathon runners and what (marathon) runners 'talk about'. I – like Wacquant, Spinney and Blue – am absorbed by the sport and belong to a runners' association; this insider perspective is the book's strength *and* its weakness. Inspired by the non-representational ethos, it offers an empathetic insider account of marathon running. This book is concerned with portraying, evoking and understanding, rather than criticising, the practice of marathon running (chapter 1).

As discussed, both auto-ethnography and non-representational ethnography experiment with creative and evocative writing. Although the writing in the first chapters is fairly conventional, some of the empirical chapters are more vivid, despite adhering to the analytical version of auto-ethnography. These chapters attempt to enliven the field of rhythmanalysis and sport geography by introducing evocative, vivid and lively prose into an analytical writing style. I hope that this writing will do some justice to the sheer drama and lively, raw quality of marathons and the multi-sensuous nature of marathon running. I know that some of it will escape me and that my modest writing skills will fall flat on many occasions.

---

### BOX 3.1

The NBRO is a running crew in the Copenhagen district of Nørrebro. The NBRO was created by a small group of young men who began to run regularly together from the same place. On Facebook, the NBRO describes itself as 'a non-profit, independent running crew founded on Nørrebro soil in the fall of 2010'. By describing themselves as a 'crew', they distinguish themselves from traditional running associations, which have leaders, coaches, regulations and paid membership. Although the crew has a founding figure and 'captains', its structure is looser, flatter and more inclusive than that of a traditional association. Members believe that having only a few rules and focusing on socialisation sets the group apart from traditional running associations: 'From day one, we've tried to hold on to a few core values: 1) all sessions free of charge and open for everyone; 2) as few rules as possible; 3) an equal balance between training and socializing.' The rules state that all training sessions must start from the current 'headquarters' (a meeting place more than a club house) and that members must earn the privilege of buying NBRO gear through loyalty and seniority. There are around ten weekly training sessions, each attracting between five and 100 runners of varying ability. There is no coach or leader as such, and the training sessions are largely self-organized by members who show up on a particular day. However, the training sessions are associated with certain routes and ways of training (chapter 6). Over the years, the NBRO has gradually become more serious and distanced from casual running. Many of the 'old' members have become fast and serious runners. The group now attracts many ambitious runners, who expect the NBRO to make them even faster. This focus on results and competitive running has led to many less serious members leaving the NBRO, which today attracts few inexperienced or slow runners. Indeed, the sight of super thin, NIKE-wearing young runners (often men) engaged in high-speed, extensive training sessions must intimidate novices and reluctant or casual runners.

*(www.facebook.com/groups/108900355842020/about/)*

## Interviews

Altogether, I conducted around 50 formal single and group interviews, most during the marathon weekend. To do this, I adopted an 'opportunistic approach', asking runners during registration and in the EXPO area for quick here-and-now interviews. Longer interviews with NBRO runners were carried out in airports and hotels. To account for the polyrhythmic nature of marathons, I recruited a heterogeneous group of runners of different ages, with a range of different abilities and ambitions. In the end, I interviewed more men than women, as men attend marathons more frequently than women (chapters 1 and 4). At all the marathons where I conducted research the female participation was (in some cases significantly) lower than the world average (32%). This also means that male voices dominate in this book.

The first 25 interviews took place in 2015 during the Berlin and Frankfurt marathons, with each interview lasting between ten minutes and an hour. Most were around 15 minutes long. These interviews covered each runner's preparation, training routines, race strategy, expectations and running biography. We talked in particular about the embodied rhythms and somatic sensations of marathon running, individually and as part of a collective body. However, the interviews also had a tourism dimension; we explored the significance of the tourist gaze in relation to marathon running and various other tourism practices before and after the event.

The second group of interviews took place in 2018 in Tokyo, where I carried out 18 relatively short (5–25-minute) interviews with *western* runners. While these interviews covered some of the same issues as the first group, they focused on exploring why western people came all the way to Japan to run and what they expected to gain from this event and from Tokyo and Japan more broadly.

Between 2019 and 2021 I also conducted eight protracted home interviews (lasting between one and two hours each). Three took place after the participants had run the Tokyo Marathon, and these interviews focused on their experience of running in Tokyo and the appeal of tourism travel and participating in highly prestigious international marathons. A second group was interviewed a week or two after finishing the Valencia Marathon (which I also participated in), at a time when the race was still present in their legs, heads and heart, which were either high on success or depressed by failure. These interviews set out to verbalise the rhythmic and somatic sensations experienced at various stages of the race. To achieve this, I attempted to relive the race, discussing it in the present tense and erasing all knowledge of how the race actually turned out. This was somewhat difficult since the interviewees were still digesting their success or disappointment and often spoke retrospectively, using the past tense. However, they did provide personal accounts of how they coped, both cognitively and physically, with the rhythmic ups and downs that this particular marathon 'threw at them' and how they retrospectively made sense of the experience. In addition to these issues, all of the interviewees talked about how they became keen marathon runners, their daily training routines, and how they made time for running alongside everyday practices and obligations. The names of the interviewees used in this book are *fictional* to ensure anonymity.

While these interviews provide valuable insights, some subjects found it hard to verbalise the physical sensation of running out of energy, being in the flow or even sensing a city during a marathon run. As discussed below, this is partly why I chose to observe runners as a spectator and also reported on training sessions and actual races that I participated in myself as a committed runner.

## *Observations*

At various marathons (Kyoto, 2018, 2020; Tokyo, 2018; Copenhagen, 2016, 2017; Berlin, 2015), I have been an observing multi-sensory spectator, moving along certain parts of the route and stops between the start and the finishing line as runners advanced through the course. This stance has allowed me to maintain a close, yet distant 'spectator gaze' on the course design, the collective rhythms of runners and the supporting crowd. I have observed, photographed and listened to a diverse range of rhythms and bodies. I have witnessed the polyrhythmic nature of the event: from the world's fastest African runners to the thousands of slower (and heavier) bodies that run, jog and walk by later; the varied musical bands along the route; and the spectators' clapping and exhortations, delivered in many languages. Animated and absorbed by the affective rhythms of each event, I have often found myself moving to the music, clapping vigorously and shouting in support of agonised runners. In this way, I have shifted – often unconsciously – between being a distant spectator and becoming an engaged co-producer of the visual and sonic atmosphere.

On several occasions, before or after a race, I have walked or run parts of the course; once, I even cycled the entire length to experience and photograph its affordances and to scrutinise or re-experience the course itself, taking in the distance and appreciating the everyday rhythms that were ousted and hushed on the day of the race.

## Participation as runner

While I have paid attention to *other* bodies through interviews and observations, in the tradition of (auto)ethnography, non-representational ethnography and carnal sociology, my own body has also been central to my research. This has allowed me to become an energetic rhythm analyst, attend to and write about the internally felt rhythmic sensations and experiences of marathon running, a difficult topic to approach, based solely on interviews and observations involving other runners. This book explores and reports on my own body and training routines, injuries, aspirations, and somatic race experiences. It is partly based on my participation as a runner in various marathons (the Berlin Marathon 2015; the Copenhagen Marathon 2015, 2019; the Kyoto Marathon 2018; the Frankfurt Marathon 2015, 2016, 2017 and 2018; Odense 2017 and the Valencia Marathon 2018, 2019), as well as NBRO training sessions from 2015 onwards.

I have deliberately run marathons in three different ways, each of which has produced distinct forms of embodied insight. First, I have paced (helped) NBRO runners during two marathons: Berlin 2015 and Odense 2017. Here, my task involved taking the lead, sticking to the agreed pace, carrying energy gels, and collecting water and energy drinks from nutrition stations for as long as possible. I left the races after 32 and 24 km, respectively. Although pacing is a courteous way to support a friend, it also provides a good opportunity to observe other runners. On one occasion I ran with a cap-mounted video camera; however, the recording quality was poor and did not really capture the embodied sensations or sonic excitement of running.

Second, in the 2018 Kyoto Marathon, I participated in 'tourist gazing' (Urry & Larsen, 2011), aiming to fully experience and enjoy this sightseeing-friendly course rather than achieve a fast time. I deliberately ran slowly to better appreciate the visual spectacle and atmosphere. On this occasion, I was keen to test the nature of 'marathon tourist gazing', especially while jogging, rather than racing all out. I took (tourist) photos, made short videos and recorded comments with my iPhone (chapter 8).

Last, but certainly not least, since the early days of this book, I have run nine marathons, aiming to run as fast as possible, preferably beating my own personal best record (called PR or PB). During these races, I did not care much about my fellow runners or the scenery we passed. Instead, I focused on keeping a good pace and sticking to the optimal line. Not all runners favour this competitive achievement-based approach to running or find it appealing (chapter 4). This calls for reflexivity.

## Reflexivity

Lyon (2018) has justly criticised present rhythmanalysis for neglecting positionality and reflexivity. Such research reveals little about the body that serves as the 'instrument'. To remedy this, I now discuss my running biography and how it has changed over the years. Without this knowledge, it would be difficult to fully understand this book. This book opens by 'recalling' my first marathon in Stockholm in 2013. My new partner (now wife) Pernille and I had the idea that it would be fun to run a marathon together, especially in an exciting place, turning it into an extended weekend. We were in our early thirties and forties (me), with plenty of time at our disposal as we had no children together and my seven-year-old son lived with us every other week. We settled on the Stockholm Marathon because we longed to visit this Nordic capital for the first time; it also gave us six to seven months to get in shape. Indeed, we needed all of this time. While Pernille ran sporadically, I did not (although I had previously been an on-off casual runner). However, I was lean and considered myself reasonably fit for my age, having cycled 27 km to work (each way) three times a week for the past year or so (Larsen, 2018a). I would soon learn that a fit cyclist is not necessarily a fit runner. We knew next to nothing about training principles and did the bare minimum, peaking at around 30–35 km weekly, as far I remember. Our ambitions were modest: I wanted to beat my father's 30-year-old narrow sub-four-hour time and Pernille simply wanted to finish.

Like many other hopeful marathon runners, Pernille's build-up was hampered by injuries and she did very little training during the final critical periods. On race day, she was all 'tapped up', with no realistic hope of being able to complete the marathon. Inevitably, she pulled out, in agony and dead tired at the half-marathon point, where medics inspected her. My spirit and form were better. I enjoyed the race until I reached the infamous marathon wall, at around the 28–29 km signs. This affected me very badly: my pace dropped dramatically, my legs were hurting and negative thoughts tormented my soul, causing me to run the second half 15 minutes slower than the first. I was cramping, the rain was pouring down and 'heavier' bodies drifted 'effortlessly' past me. Some people were even chatting, and I felt sure that they did this just to torture me. In the end, I managed to beat my father's old time by a minute, stumbling across the finish line in just under four hours. I crashed to the ground, grateful to be finished with this misery – and then the cramps kicked in. I was freezing wet: cramping, freezing, cramping, freezing, and promising myself: 'Never again. Never again.'

Although Pernille gave up on running, this painful experience motivated me to take revenge. Almost straight away, I signed up for the Frankfurt Marathon, six months later. I stepped up the training, and Pernille travelled with me, this time as a 'supporter'. My training paid off: I ran much faster – three hours and 28 minutes – and avoided the excruciating wall. When I crossed the finish line, I was jubilant and felt like a proper marathon runner. Half a year later, I ran 40–45 km a week and improved my 'personal record' (PR) by another ten minutes (three hours and 18 minutes). Equally important, running had a positive effect on my mental health, and I finally managed, after years of trying, to quit the nicotine gums and nerve-calming 'evening cigarettes', hanging out of the kitchen window.

That summer I also began to show up at NBRO training sessions. I was tired of always running alone and having no likeminded friends to share my evolving passion with. I grew up with *team* sports (football and handball) and missed the social aspect and affective sociality of group sport. During my first NBRO session, I immediately sensed that I was a 'novice', who trained less, ran more slowly and lacked the knowledge of many of the more experienced runners, who came across as fairly 'serious'. After 'joining' the NBRO, my training gradually increased and became social. I became more committed and faster, running my next marathon in three hours and eight minutes. My final integration into the NBRO and my transition from a 'casual' into a 'serious' runner occurred when I became part of a small NBRO group that was training for a sub-three-hour attempt at the Copenhagen Marathon in 2015. Many of us, myself included, were successful. As a sub-three-hour man, I felt like a *fast* marathon runner.

This achievement only increased my desire to train more and to run faster. I improved my time over the following years by a couple of minutes. Then a string of knee injuries undermined my training for three years, causing much self-pity, anxiety and depression, coupled with numerous visits to specialists and countless solitary nights on the cross trainer in an anonymous training gym (Allen-Collinson & Hockey, 2007). However, there were also periods when I could get some fresh air and run with my NBRO friends. Somehow, I managed to do enough training to run a few fast marathons, only narrowly missing my record. However, my knee always seemed to strike back with some type of soreness or itchy pain. I was soon back to torturing myself in the gym and doing rehabilitation exercises. I missed my social life with running friends and my vanity almost killed me. I feared that I would never be able to race again and experience the highs of another 'personal record', being too old (now in my late forties) and prone to injury. It felt like the future would be all downhill – perhaps a classic symptom of a midlife crisis? I embarked on holiday to Italy in 2018, knowing that my 'running career' was over and that it was time to find a new hobby. I panicked at this prospect, being fully addicted to running and having no idea what could possibly replace it.

Miraculously, however, my knee recovered over the course of that summer and I have been largely injury-free since then. This sustained period of good health has allowed me to escalate my training, running both faster and longer. In the final three months before a marathon, I now run between 80–110 km or 7–10 hours weekly, using up a lot (perhaps too much) of my available leisure, family and even work time. While this sort of training schedule will sound extreme to most, it is perfectly normal in the NBRO, where runners seem to train more, run faster and grow more competitive year by year, forever propelling each other forward in a never-ending race for the next record. This trend was particularly evident during the 2019 Valencia Marathon. Even though this is a highly competitive race, the NBRO was one of the fastest 'clubs', with an average time of three hours, 12 minutes and 19 seconds. I excelled, clocking a new 'personal record' at the age of 47 at two hours, 52 minutes and 20 seconds. My competitive side was flattered to read that this was approximately one hour and twenty minutes faster than the average male runner (Watson, 2021).

Despite my age, I still yearn for another PR. My secret plan was to finish 2020 with a sub 2.50 run at the Valencia Marathon, but COVID-19 made that impossible. I am one of those typical time-obsessed runners who abound in the NBRO and elsewhere. As Bauman (2001) once explained, the satisfaction of consumer desires is very brief and never long lasting. As soon as we acquire something, we want something better. The same goes for the type of runner that I and many NBRO runners have become: as soon as we achieve a new PR, we immediately want an even better one. Satisfaction is short-lived, while aspirations are all-consuming and never-ending.

I have written about running and this book on and off for the past five years. During this time I have changed from a near-novice runner who did not know much about marathons into a fairly serious and knowledgeable *insider* who knows much more about this sport, in practice and theory, as both a runner and an academic scholar. This book cannot reflect the sheer diversity of bodies – young and old, small and big, fit and unfit – or ways of running – fast and slow, for fun or competition – that constitute a marathon as polyrhythmic entities. However, I am somewhat representative of the average runner, since more men than women run marathons and the largest age group is 40–49. Being a university professor, I am also fairly representative; marathon runners tend to be erudite, well-paid people with flexible working hours (chapter 4). In other words, this book has been written by a skinny runner who has, over time, become relatively serious and fast. A less competitive or more portly jogger/scholar who did not care as much about his or her finish time or who finished in five to six hours would certainly write a different book. However, I hope that all runners and scholars will find this book interesting and relevant. After all, we share an odd fascination with marathon running, run the same streets and are carried by the sheer excitement and sensations of these events.

## Conclusion

In this chapter, inspired by non-representational, carnal ethnographers and auto-ethnography, I have made the argument that the marathon researcher must become an energetic rhythm analyst, fully engaged and passionate marathon runner, able to report on and analyse his or her moving and becoming body. However, I would advise the energetic rhythm analyst to be particularly reflexive about his or her positionality. Preferably, as this book, he or she should run in Anderson's analytical auto-ethnography shoes, as well as engaging with and researching other running bodies – younger and older, faster and slower – to create a diverse, communal and ultimately far more interesting ethnography of the rich and polyrhythmic world that marathons have become.

## Notes

1  This section is a revised version of parts of a Danish book chapter (Larsen, 2018b).
2  Wacquant (2005) reacted negatively when his boxing study was referred to in a review as auto-ethnographic (Fine, 2004). Wacquant mocked the method for its postmodern 'anything goes attitude', its narcissism, its valorisation of the aesthetic and personal, and its lack of any desire or ability to understand how structures shape and enable social action. He even describes his study as 'anti-auto-ethnography' because his book deals as much with other boxers as with himself.

# 4

# INNOVATING NEW ASPIRATIONS

## The birth of ordinary marathon practices and extraordinary marathons

### Introduction

This chapter is informed by practice theory's attention to 'meanings' and how practices change when they become associated with new meanings and practitioners (chapter 2). In this context, it explores the changing meanings, ideas and aspirations associated with marathon running over time as an established rhythmic practice and spatial event. I focus on key historical moments and those movements that gave new meanings to running and races. Such moments and movements innovated new and relatively inclusive practices and rhythms of running for ordinary able-bodied people, along with extraordinary street marathons for such ordinary runners.

First, I begin with a historical account of the serious, exclusive and sport-focused nature of running throughout much of the twentieth century, when marathons were small-scale exclusive events for the select few who competed against each other and against the clock. I discuss how sport rhythms of running value time, achievement, and improvement. Second, I consider how the jogging movement from the 1960s onwards de-sportified running. This movement invented casual and slow rhythms of running by cutting ties with the world of sport, embracing instead discourses of health and active lifestyles. Third, while the jogging movement championed unexacting and brief running, I explain how parts of this movement redefined and popularised marathons for ordinary men and women. Marathons became extraordinary, atmospheric and visually striking mass street events in which thousands of bodies with very different abilities and aspirations participated. I reflect on how marathon finish times slowed down and new aspirations related to experiencing exciting places became associated with marathons. Against this background, the final sections analyse my interviews and observations to discuss the multiple aspirations and meanings associated with marathons today.

DOI: 10.4324/9781003125068-4

## History of running and early marathons

### *Achievement running and the significance of time*

Throughout much of the twentieth century, running was a serious, competitive niche sport that appealed to physically competent devotees, mostly young men. They joined clubs, trained daily and participated in races where everybody ran to win (Bale, 2004; Bryant, 2006; Scheerder et al., 2015; Smith, 1998). Bale termed such running, which was concerned with 'learning running techniques, maintaining personal records, seeking personal best performances and taking part in competitions' (Bale, 2004, p. 18), 'achievement running'. Running, competition and sport were – to use a practice theory term – closely 'bundled'. 'Racing' against the clock on a standardised and recognised distance along a measured route defined achievement running as a rhythmic practice and spatial practice. 'Achievement running' was, and still is, a sport where practitioners train meticulously to mould a body that is perfectly conditioned to move rapidly across a set distance – such as 5 km or 10 km – on a race day in as little time as possible, and faster than the opponents (Carter, 2018; Smith, 2002). Thus, racing, or 'achievement running', is a *temporal* practice (Bale, 2004) where success is measured in clock time – and faster is always better, as everything else is secondary to a person's finish time, entailing constant efforts to reduce the amount of time needed to run a specific distance (Bale, 2004, p. 19). Smith clarifies:

> The temporal dimension is a conspicuous feature of the talk and activity of runners at every level of ability and involvement. Close students of running and runners themselves take a keen interest in the 'lap times', 'personal bests' and 'records'. ... Time, that omnipresent characteristic of social life, has special significance in the running world. Runners learn to attend to time as finely tuned markers of running achievement, as careers with stages and turning points, and as cyclical calendars.
>
> *(2002, p. 343)*

The point is that clock time is crucial to racing, and the idea of racing without timing an event is unthinkable, even absurd. Race running is a serious matter where time is never forgotten, unlike children's games or more playful or mediative forms of sport where people experience flow and there is a sense that time is 'flying by'. Time and distance are always present and recorded in serious 'achievement running', as suggested by Bale:

> Achievement running is a world of numbers, ranks, hierarchy, records, and a sense of certainty. ... It is a serious business. The record provides certainty and security – 'safety in numbers'. The statistic, the rank, and record, identifies the runner as a number – a 10-second man, a 15-minute woman, decontextualizing the performance and dehumanizing the runners. Athletes become 'statistical persons'. The measured time, to a tenth or hundredth of a second, appears definitive and unambiguous.
>
> *(2004, p. 25)*

Bale (2004) identified important links between running and modernity and the use of stopwatches on tracks and in factories. These timed, outcome-oriented and statistical principles clearly resemble capitalist ideologies, not least in the rationalisation and standardisation that typified modern work where floor managers with stopwatches turned work into a drill of abstract repetitions to secure fast and effective rhythms of work (Cresswell, 2006; Lefebvre, 2004). However, this focus on running time as dehumanising, as claimed by Bale, is questionable. Many people obviously take pleasure from achievement running against time, as I will demonstrate in this present book.

What is also unique about running is that winning (for example, in football or tennis) or coming in first (for example, in cycling) is not everything. While winning *matters*, the winning time is often more important. Those who do not win may be jubilant and feel like winners if they have beaten *their* all-time 'personal record' (PR – also called 'personal best' (PB)) for that particular distance. Improving their own time drives them forward and makes it possible for 'also-rans' to feel like winners.

Marathons as serious, small-scale events for elite runners have been around for a long time and have always been part of a 'racing culture'. The first city marathon was the Boston Marathon, which has taken place every year since 1897, the year after the first successful Olympic Marathon in Athens in 1896. For a long time, marathons drew relatively few athletes and were often dominated by well-conditioned labourers and working-class men. On the other hand, shorter track events and field athletics were largely upper-middle-class activities (Tulle, 2007, p. 334). Marathons, as Bryant describes,

> were high-class races, with fiercely fast fields. But only a few dozen runners would ever show up, maybe a hundred or so at most for a championship event. They were grim affairs, full of hardened, anorexic-looking men, proud of their athletic club vests, their reputations as runners and their exclusive membership of a brotherhood of suffering. … Traditionally the marathon was always seen as a man-killer of an event. It existed at the outer rim of what was considered possible even for the toughest and hardest-trained of athletes.
>
> *(2005, pp. 4, 11)*

Marathon courses were often closed after four hours, and late finishers' results sometimes went unrecorded. Marathons were considered an extreme and even inhuman exertion for eccentricity – even amongst 'achievement runners'. It was a resolutely male form of sport, largely excluding women. Men widely believed that endurance running was detrimental to the health and appearance of the female body. An American woman, Bobbi Gibb, tried to enter the 1966 Boston Marathon but was turned down with the following condescending words from the president of the Boston Athletic Association: 'Women are not physiologically able to run marathon distances and we can't take the medical liability' (Ross, 2018, unpaginated). Despite being denied a start number, she successfully 'gate-crashed' the race by concealing her female features and ran an impressive time. A year later, a woman named Katrine Switzer was less fortunate. Using her last name to sign up, she cheated her way into the race and was given an official start number. The Boston race director was infamously captured by a photographer when, his face twisted with anger, he aggressively tried to pull her out when he realised that the semi-disguised runner was in fact a woman. However, she managed to finish the race. From around 1970 onwards, marathons began to welcome women. However, the first Olympics Marathon for women was held as late as 1984 (Chase, 2015; Schultz, 2019).

## The invention of leisurely jogging

For much of the twentieth century, running was considered a sport for the super-fit. Running for fun and fitness was not encouraged, being looked down upon as deviant, bohemian and subject to ridicule. Walking was considered more appropriate, as described by Bale:

> Adults seen running through streets or over open country tended to be serious runners taking part in organized events such as road or cross-county races. Walking was considered much more appropriate as a form of keeping fit, something that was also believed by many serious athletes.
>
> *(Bale, 2004, p. 16)*

This also reflects that in the post-Second World War decades, 'it was rare for American men or women over the age of 30 – outside of work – to partake in any physical activity more strenuous than yard work, bowling, golf, or light calisthenics' (Latham, 2015, p. 104). Recreational running in suburban neighbourhoods and parks was uncommon. Runners were seen as odd, even suspicious people. A 1968 New York Times article described how runners were chased by the police as suspicious, or were ticketed for the 'illegal use of the highway by a pedestrian' (Higdon, cited in Groth & Krahn, 2017, p. 6). The commonly held views of runners changed slowly from the late 1960s with the emergence of the jogging movement in the US, and later in Europe. However, in the early days, joggers were still stigmatised, insulted and called names (Scheerder et al., 2015). Little by little, running gradually became seen as appropriate for both women and middle-aged and older adults. While there were as few as 100,000 joggers in the United States in 1968, the figure had risen to 27 million eleven years later (Gotaas, 2009, p. 265; Plymire, 2004).

Crucially, the jogging movement 'invented a new practice of running that was suitable for increasingly sedentary and overweight men and women habituated to motorized travel, desk jobs and energy-rich diets' (Larsen, 2019a, p. 47). We may say that jogging and automobility are modern twins. The jogging movement was a reaction to the fact that Americans were trapped in an unhealthy ecology of practices and mobilities, leisure and eating practices that made them inactive and victim to various new lifestyle chronic diseases (Agger, 2011; Latham, 2015). Modern comforts made people ill. The new prescribed medicine was exercise:

Fifty years ago 'exercise' as a concept did not exist. Physical activity meant walking or cycling, and work was remunerated activity not passivity ... and motorised transportation and energy-rich diets have condemned us either to the tyrant of exercise or to the indignity of obesity.

*(Roberts, 2010, p. 118)*

Running became associated with urbanised well-being and health in a sedentary, overweight and accelerated car-dominated society where bodies were highly mobile but seldom moved on foot, as clarified by Latham:

'Jogging' was designed to counter the systematic diminution of necessary corporeal effort occurring throughout the urban environment – whether that be through the substitution of the automobile for walking, lifts and escalators for stairs, or television for more physically demanding pastimes.

*(2015, p. 104)*

Before the jogging movement, exercise was not generally prescribed by doctors and recognised among medical professionals and the general population. Vigorous, high-intensity training was considered potentially dangerous for middle-aged people in particular. Rather than training, middle-aged people were made to feel that they should accept the fact that their bodies were in a state of inevitable decrepitude (Latham, 2015, p. 111). Exercise was considered vanity at best and dangerous at worst.

However, the jogging movement portrayed this necessary exercise as pleasurable and meaningful rather than cruel. 'Joggers' were a great deal larger than the leaner racing man. They jogged for exercise purposes and to lose weight, not to set personal records. They invented a form of running that was instrumental in helping them to lose weight and prevent disease yet was also fun and pleasurable. Their rhythms were not dictated by their watch, as explained below:

One important consequence of the jogging craze was that millions of people began running without ever giving a thought to competition. Jogging at a pleasant, steady pace, LSD – long slow distance, as it was called – brought a new dimension to running. The point was the exercise itself, not setting the fastest pace or keeping an eye on the clock. The main aims were improved health, well-being and fun rather than personal records. ... The masses only began running once training routines had become more enjoyable.

*(Gotaas, 2009, p. 259)*

The jogging movement cut the ties with the racing movement of leaner men and 'achievement running'. Instead, this movement bundled their way of exercising with emerging health discourses and personal well-being as a gentle and pleasurable exercise.

The jogging movement, increasingly endorsed by doctors, advocated for moderate 'jogging' as doable for inactive and obese people. It was seen as a healthy and necessary individual palliative response to the physical degeneration and rise of hypokinetic diseases in sedentary and high-calorie western societies. Running was then conceived as an effective way to burn calories and to restore the heart and the body's overall musculature system. Moreover, the jogging movement was associated with spirituality. A combination of mediation and running was understood to be good for mental health, lifting people's moods and easing their problems. An unhurried and meandering jog of some distance was deemed effective in achieving a mental boost. Moreover, it was believed that would-be practitioners needed careful support, guidance and instructions. 'How-to-jog' articles and books were popular, teaching adults that running was good and 'do-able' for them (Gotaas, 2009; Latham, 2015). Over time, jogging also became scripted as a route to a slim and attractive body (Abbas, 2004; Berking & Neckel, 1993, p. 67; Smith, 1998).

## Slow rhythms and urban running

Whereas 'achievement running' puts emphasis on speed and overcoming a distance as quickly as possible, jogging came to value slow and gentle rhythms of movement in itself. It was designed for people for whom corporeal mobility was otherwise reduced to brief bursts of walking. A defining principle for all advice and programmes regarding jogging was a gradual and very slow build-up of speed and distance. In the early stages of a jogging programme, walking was an integral part of a training plan, and the running speed was not much faster than a brisk walk. We may say that jogging was a progression of walking. One Swedish jogging instructor articulated:

> All proper jogging starts with careful walks. You simply walk at a leisurely tempo. … Walk, try it out for a few hundred metres, perhaps a kilometre. Pick up your pace slightly and take a few quick steps. You are jogging!
>
> *(Cited in Qviström, 2017, p. 353)*

As people became fitter and lighter, they could run longer and faster without compromising the ethos of running at a gentle conversational pace. By adhering to training programmes, people understood that they would develop the required habits, capabilities and aspirations to become joggers without injuring themselves (Latham, 2015; chapter 5). The meanings and competences of running were 'desportified' and running became do-able for less fit and portly middle-aged bodies that otherwise lived sedentary car-centric lives.

The jogging movement also invented new urban geographies for running. It moved out of tracks and forests and taught people to run in cities, on tarmac and in their immediate neighbourhoods as well as local parks. This resulted in a low entrance barrier and a distinct urban sensibility. Jogging appealed to urban dwellers, who began to run close to their homes – on the pavements of their front paths. The jogging boom 'pushed the physically active body back into the public environment' (Latham, 2015, p. 118). Bowerman and Harris wrote in *Jogging*:

Jogging country is everywhere … . Jog right out the door, jog in a schoolyard, on a city street, at the beach, on a country road or a vacant lot. Jog down a bicycle path, on a school track, around a golf course, through a park, in a backyard, in a gymnasium, in a supermarket parking lot – anywhere.

*(Cited in Latham, 2015, p. 66)*

However, this public display also made running somewhat transgressive and 'out of place', especially for women:

Running allowed for people to exercise in public, sweating, their bodies being exposed – something that was prior to that time limited to confined areas such as school gyms and tennis courts, or working contexts such as farms and factories. In short, running signaled something new and rebellious, in a time that screamed out change and rallied against public order.

*(Breedveld et al., 2015, p. 243)*

This also illustrates how the jogging movement did not push for specific urban infrastructures designed especially for them. Runners had to adapt to existing urban infrastructures where their outfit and rhythms were somewhat 'out of place'. Nor did they push for special sport equipment or expensive memberships at clubs or associations. An exception here is Sweden, where jogging became associated with designed trails in woods (Qviström, 2017). However, in most other parts of Europe and Asia, where jogging boomed in the 1970s, joggers found themselves running on pavement and park trials designed for and dominated by walkers.

Running attracted many practitioners because unfit people could participate, and the required equipment, such as running shoes and pavements/paths to run on, was easily available. Unlike most sports, jogging was characterised as inherently 'democratic' because it could be practised almost everywhere, at all hours and by anyone, requiring only a relatively cheap pair of running shoes (Qviström, 2017, p. 353). Jogging was scripted as a locally emplaced and individualised practice, as many people were indeed 'running alone'. This practice was part of a wider trend of individualised sports at the expense of civic associations. Jogging made sense to 'time-squeezed' professionals because it was easy to organise and delivered high aerobic benefits in a short time. This made jogging attractive to women, who took it up in greater numbers (Breedveld et al., 2015, p. 247).

Jogging was cheap and time-efficient, as people did not waste time travelling to specific sports venues where they might be dependent upon other people's presence and commitment to engage in this activity. Indeed, in *Bowling Alone*, Putnam (2000) denounced the rise of solitary bowling at the expense of organised bowling, seeing it as a metaphor for a decline of social capital in America. Due to extensive commuting and television watching, people were less involved in collective sports and civic associations. While an individualised practice, jogging also created communities where experienced practitioners encouraged novices and people ran together. Parts of the jogging movement also became associated with running events that generated social capital as people were 'running together' in multiple ways (Larsen & Bærenholdt, 2019). Some joggers became relatively serious runners, and road races slowly began to attract joggers, building upon jogging's basic architecture, which eventually came to dominate such races.

## The marathon boom and the emergence of the extraordinary marathon

The 1970s marked the first boom in marathons across the US, Asia and Europe. Ironically, this boom would not have occurred without the jogging boom, because jogging was supposed to be about short, easy distances and fitness running, not gruelling distances such as marathons that took a toll on the body. It was also paradoxical because marathons used to be the very opposite of jogging: fiercely competitive, exclusive, elitist, brutal and at times detrimental to one's health. However, some joggers became devoted practitioners and began running long distances as part of their training routines. They were attracted to the many races that popped up and catered to them just as much as to elite runners, as explained by Plymire:

> The millions of people who began running in the 1960s and 1970s often ran far more than … recommended, however. Scores of road races of varying distances sprang up in cities and towns across the United States catering to the swelling population of runners, and though not all runners were marathon runners, the 26.2-mile race occupied a special place in running culture.
>
> *(2004, p. 197)*

Jogging was soon sportised. Many people went from being casual joggers to serious runners following achievement running's ethos of racing, time, speed and personal records (Carter, 2018, p. 16).

However, I argue that many joggers became marathon runners because marathons were becoming exciting and extraordinary. Marathon officials learned from the jogging movement that streets were suitable and exciting venues for running, and from this time onwards, marathons became big city events. The New York Marathon illustrates the transformation of the marathon scene. For the first six years (1970–75), this was a very low-key, inconspicuous event whose course consisted of repeated loops around Central Park. The runners were not separated from bicyclists, pedestrians and horse riders:

> On 13 September 1970 126 runners took part in the first New York City Marathon. The 55 runners who had completed four circuits in Central Park without attracting the attention of the press or the television and they were clapped home by family, friends and enthusiasts. Few of the other people who happened to be in the park that day – skaters, dog walkers and courting couples – knew anything about the marathon apart from the fact it was a strange Olympic event and one that attracted cranks.
>
> *(Gotaas, 2009, p. 262)*

Marathon enthusiasm took off in 1976 when the course consisted of closed-off boulevards with no traffic throughout all five boroughs of New York City. Instead of cars, it was packed with spectators, implying an escape of running from parks and pavements. The New York Marathon became known as one of the first marathons to reclaim the streets as a legitimate space for running. For this day only, parts of the city became a 'Running Polis' and not a 'Car Polis'. The marathon demonstrated that streets could be used for people, not just for cars. Running on streets provided highly emotive sensations and different understandings of movement:

> They all knew the roads but now they were trying them without wheels and engines and discovering that everything felt completely different when travelling on foot. It was all up to you, up to your own strength and performance and nothing to do with the accelerator pedal.
>
> *(Gotaas, 2009, p. 259)*

Musicians and cheering spectators made marathons atmospheric, fun to participate in and much less serious than old school marathons (Bale, 2004, p. 71). Spectators realised that people like them, of similar ages, bodies and potential, participated. This had a contagious effect in that many more people found themselves participating as runners in the years to follow.

Importantly, marathons began to attract much slower runners, as the maximum time to complete the event was extended from four hours to six hours. In a couple of years, more than one third of the 12,000 runners finished after four hours, and the number of slow runners increased year by year. Officials and crowds treated everyone as winners and worthy of attention. The presence of such runners meant that 'the marathon had become less of a competition to achieve a good placing or good time and more of a ritual to be gone though, a symbol of vigour and will' (Gotaas, 2009, p. 265). However, at the same time, the New York Marathon became highly competitive, attracting the best marathon runners with huge prize moneys. The New York Marathon 'simultaneously emerged as a mass-participation sport and as a professional sport' (Suozzo, 2006, p. 24). The event was now highly heterogeneous and polyrhythmic. As Cooper elucidated:

> For those less inner-directed, the New York City Marathon provided a festival atmosphere and symbols, such as finishers' medals and race T-shirts, which assured all who actually completed the course, no matter how slowly, that they were part of an elite group. The New York City Marathon found ways to accommodate and sanction a wide variety of reasons for entering a 26.2-mile footrace.
>
> *(1998, p. 387)*

Soon, the number of participants in this race increased dramatically, attracting runners from many different places – it became an obligatory event for many runners. As Gotaas elaborated: 'The New York City Marathon was the joggers' Olympia and they made pilgrimages from afar simply to take part in its tough rituals' (2009, p. 267).

In addition, a significant number of city marathons were staged across Europe, and a trend started in the late 1970s and the 1980s of new marathons, such as the Chicago Marathon (1977) and the London Marathon (1981), while more people participated in older marathons, such as the Berlin Marathon (1974) (Scheerder et al., 2015). From that time onwards, it was the norm for marathon practices to multiply, associated with different aspirations and meanings for diverse groups of runners. A Swedish jogging journal in 1979 explained that 'jogging is a sport for all … but many are probably looking for a goal to achieve. This is one of the reasons why … [we] initiated the Stockholm Marathon' (Hässelby, cited in Qviström, 2017, p. 353). This was the birth of what Suozzo terms the *modern* marathon,

> that enlists the energies of entire cities and celebrates not only athletic accomplishment but also the vitality and dynamism of the cities that sponsor it. … the marathon becomes not so much a contest, but rather a mass celebration in which thousands of extremely diverse individuals engage in a vast urban procession.
>
> *(2006, pp. 7−9)*

Such events also celebrated tourist travel and the new excitement that came with travelling to big cities as places of touring and sightseeing. While marathons started as relatively local events, they soon became national and later international events that generated much tourist travel. Marathons were exciting partly because they took place in exciting locations such as New York, Boston, London, Berlin and Tokyo. However, equally fast marathons, such as the Frankfurt Marathon, attracted a smaller crowd because they were less appealing to the tourist gaze (Larsen, 2019a; Latham & McCormack, 2012).

The meaning of marathons changed as running marathons became personal goals tied up with a reflexive project of self-transformation (Reischer, 2001) and self-identity that more broadly came to define modern societies (Giddens, 1991). Finishing a marathon was something extraordinary, a personal milestone (Carter, 2018, p. 5). It conveyed specific desirable attributes such as endurance and perseverance, and marathon runners were perceived to embody such positive attributes more broadly (Carter, 2018). Being a marathon runner supposedly looked good on one's curriculum vitae: 'Marathon races are particularly well suited to attest in a way visible to everyone to personality features that can only infrequently be demonstrated in the calmer course of everyday life: bravery, battle-readiness, composure' (Berking & Neckel, 1993, p. 75). Marathon running became, in Bourdieu's (1984) terms, a way of acquiring and displaying 'cultural capital'. Marathons took the form of 'disciplined leisure' that appealed to the middle classes, as will be discussed next.

## Class, age and gender

Leisure and sport are ordered around class distinctions (Tomlinson, 2004). As discussed previously, marathon running was originally a working-class sport (Havens,

2015, p. 12). However, with the jogging boom, marathon running became associated with the middle classes, an activity for people with sedentary professions, desk jobs and good incomes. The Yale-educated law student, Frank Shorter, who won a gold medal in the 1972 Munich Olympic Marathon for the US, was a role model for enticing such professionals to marathon running (Cooper, 1992, p. 249). This class upscaling was also initiated by the New York Marathon after an entrepreneur, Fred Lebow, took control of the event with the intention of increasing revenue. The key for Lebow was to attract affluent runners – both men and women – with great spending power, to increase the starting fee and ameliorate the sponsor deals (Cooper, 1998, p. 141).

Since then, marathon running has enticed middle-class people, or the 'petty bourgeoisie' (Bourdieu, 1984). The practice was appropriated by well-educated, rational men and women. They appreciated that gratification was delayed, and that hard work, self-discipline and rational, schematic training rather than exceptional talent, made a marathon runner. As Suozzo (2006, pp. 10–11) wrote, 'The race embodies middle-class virtues that they cultivate: discipline, long-range planning and deferred gratification.' This appealed to a rational mind. In 1993, Berking and Neckel penned the following:

> today the marathon has become the national sport of rational people, the passion of teachers, the obsession of technicians and white-collar workers, engineers, doctors, and intellectuals … it is probably no coincidence that the social structure of marathon runners is almost identical to that of the urban middle class. The marathon runner requires personal virtues which are unequally distributed in class society because they are not equally useful to everyone. Among them: trust in one's own abilities, belief in the future and reason, and a drive for ruthless self-improvement.
>
> *(1993, p. 69)*

To this day, marathon running attracts relatively affluent middle-class people who are mobile, which also explains why municipalities, sponsors and tourism organisations support urban marathons. Accordingly, *Runner's World* is reputedly one of the most expensive and most coveted magazine in the world in which to advertise (Vorm, 2017, p. 272). Moreover, it explains why, especially in the UK, marathons are part of a huge (health) charity economy where participants are obligated to raise significant donations to secure a bib through a charity organisation. The 2017 edition of the London Marathon 'raised £59.4m, setting a new world record for fundraising in a single day' (C. Jones, 2017).

Marathons are now unique sport events that attract runners of diverse ages, not just young and highly able-bodied runners. There is in fact a 'greying' of marathon practitioners (Breedveld et al., 2015). Studies of millions of marathon data records show that the average male finisher is around forty years old, while the average female finisher is 36 years old. The 40–49 age group is the largest group for men, and the 50–59 age group outnumbers the 20–29 age group (RunnerClick), which testifies to the significance of so-called veteran marathon runners (Tulle, 2007).

As touched on, women were long excluded from long-distance running and marathons. From 1928 until 1960, they were prohibited from running distances longer than 400 m at the Olympics. It was widely believed by medical authorities, sports organisations and prevailing social mores that arduous training would interfere with women's reproductive ability and health. Pulsing beneath these health anxieties were social and aesthetic discourses that stipulated that running was not a proper female activity. Despite this prohibition and such stereotyping, women began to 'gate-crash' marathons from 1960s, as discussed above. In *Breaking into the Marathon: Women's Distance Running as Political Activism*, Schultz (2019) discusses how such pioneer female marathon runners practised political activism by demonstrating the female body's physical capability to run marathons, empowering and inspiring other women to do distance running events (2019, pp. 1–2).

Over the next few decades, many women took up marathon running, and the gender gap between male and female practitioners shrank. However, a male bias remained. According to Runrepeat (Andersen, 2021), only 32 per cent of all recent marathon runners were women. One structural explanation provided was that women do more domestic work than men and struggle to find the time required for such a time-consuming activity (Serravallo, 2000; see chapter 5). The most egalitarian countries in terms of male–female parity in marathon running are the US, Canada and Iceland (43%, 37% and 36% women, respectively), while men heavily dominate races in Spain, Switzerland and India (13%, 12% and 9% women, respectively) (Andersen, 2021).

In summary, the meanings and rhythms ascribed to marathon running have changed over time. From an emphasis on time and competition, a broader focus on personal achievement and experiences had taken its place as marathons became inclusive and spectacular street events. The practice of marathon running now attracts many different-abled bodies with different aspirations and ambitions. Accordingly, in the final section, I analyse the interviews I conducted with respect to how the interviewees ascribe meanings and aspirations to the practices of marathon running.

## Contemporary meanings

### Novices

My fieldwork reveal that marathons contain multiple meanings and that practitioners sometimes run for different reasons. This is related, in part, to their specific running biographies. Those who were running a marathon for the first time were generally intrigued by the extraordinary nature of marathons. As one marathon 'novice' commented at the Berlin Marathon:

> To try something extraordinary. A 10 km race is something everyone can do. Running a marathon requires training, perseverance. It is fascinating for me to test myself and see if I can stand the distance and run 42 km.
>
> *(Jurgen, personal communication, my translation)*

For first-time runners, the marathon is a liminal experience and the most physical trial that they will likely undertake in their otherwise sedentary life. The key is to test themselves against this mythical distance. While they vaguely aspire to a certain finish time, their main goal is to become a marathon finisher. Moreover, they are excited about being part of the whole event, running in a sea of others and experiencing exciting cities.

## Time and achievement running

For repeat runners, this meaning is partly overshadowed by other aspirations of 'achievement running'. Few are now content with 'just finishing'. One such aspiration is running faster: 'I expect a PR ... It has become more organized with the trainer, diet, preparation, how I should run and hydrate during the race. It means a lot when you have tried it many times before' (Helle, personal communication, my translation). Most of my interviewees wondered how fast they could run *this* time. When I asked them their expectations for the upcoming race, many reported aiming for a new personal record (PR/PB). Alternatively, if their preparation had been patchy, they hoped for a decent time that would not be too embarrassing. This testifies to Hewitt's observation that the first marathon is 'the only time you will run a marathon wondering simply whether you can finish it. For all the rest, you will be wondering whether you can run faster than you've run before' (2012, p. 14).

Thus, the time-obsessed nature of elite running has somewhat permeated non-elite runners. Beating their 'personal records' motivates them to run another marathon. Jannick elaborates upon the meaning and significance of beating a 'personal record':

> PR is the best time you have ever run. It is a very good thing to aim for so that you have something to aspire for in training. One can make the argument that if you have run a marathon you have run all of them because they are all 42,195 km no matter where in the world you run them. So there has to be something that drives you. And for many that is training to have a fair shot at your PR. Constantly improving oneself.
>
> *(Personal communication, my translation)*

This focus on becoming faster and improving resonated with both younger and older runners. Very few said that time did not matter. Some appreciate marathon running because it allows them to be competitive and track their progress from one training session or race to another. They love the fact that running produces indisputable numbers through multiple timing devices (chapter 5). One interviewee, Carsten, a former football player and now a young professional with a business degree, misses having 'fun with the ball', but loves the fact that running is easy to 'measure' and calculate, which football is not: 'In football, it's a bit elusive ... with running, it is very easy to measure. It's just a time, and maybe a little weight and distance. There is a lot you can start playing with. It's easier to make it quantifiable.' Like Carsten, Lone says she enjoys marathons because 'I have a science education, a lot of focus on structure and logic. That of following a plan and seeing that it works, it's cool. The goal you are navigating towards. ... I can detect progress ... and development. I can always compare myself to myself' (both personal communications, my translation). Carsten and Lone love running because it is quantifiable. Their educations have taught them to be competitive, to appreciate numbers and to think about success in such terms. Carsten elaborates by saying that 'running a marathon is something very "business-schoolish" – it looks good on the CV' and works well in a job interview as it 'says something about your personality – that you are steadfast and persistent' (personal communication, my translation). This reflects, as discussed above, that marathon running is associated with the rational and quantifying mind and middle-class virtues, and with the continuing acquisition of 'cultural capital' (Bourdieu, 1984).

Other interviewees – especially those with an engineering, business or social science degree – also praise running for being amenable to tracking and producing numbers with GPS watches, heart rate monitors, running apps and race bibs, ensuring that personal progress can be measured, compared and shown to others (chapter 5). Indeed, I argue that they partly run to produce numbers and would probably not participate if no numbers were produced – they run with watches as much as with their bodies. Numbers, we may say, are the currency of 'sport capital', which is easily transferred to 'cultural capital'. More broadly, such ambitious runners are keen to develop their skills and develop careers in this sport (Stebbins, 1992). For them, leisure time is not merely about relaxing, having no ambitions and being passive.

### Defeating age

The interviews also gave insight into why runners in their mid-thirties and forties are attracted to marathon running and achievement running. Many of my interviewees are also serious runners and still chasing personal bests despite, or perhaps because of, their advanced age. As Scott, a man in his forties, declared: 'I run marathons to compete with myself and improve myself. To prove that I can still optimise myself, despite getting older' (personal communication, my translation). This is in contrast to sports such as football, where one cannot improve after a certain age. Here, one is easily one of those slow 'old boys players' who are a pale shadow of their former ability and rhythmic vigour. This ability to defeat age was also stressed by one female interviewee:

> I really wanted to run sub 3:30 ... In the spring I ran 3:33 ... I have given birth to two children and I want to prove to myself that I can ... that one is

not limited by one's physique [in the 30s] ... It's cool to meet other women in their 30s and 40s who run long and fast.

*(Vera, personal communication, my translation)*

This illustrates that 'older' runners are attracted to marathons because they can excel in them and produce impressive times. Equally important, it supposedly halts the perceived biological rhythms of ageing; they feel and look younger than they are. Although sporting abilities normally decline rapidly with age because speed and aerobic capacity decreases with age, this is less true of endurance sports (Lara et al., 2014, p. 2014). While elite marathons are won by runners in their late twenties and mid-thirties and younger athletes outcompete older runners at shorter distances, the average marathon runner in his forties is slightly faster than the average twenty-something man; the overall fastest age group for men is 40−49. However, the age group between 50−59 is slower than all the younger groups, so we may say that marathon men age in their fifties (RunnerClick). Despite some physiological disadvantages, older runners keep up with their younger counterparts because they are more experienced − it is often claimed that marathon runners first peak after seven years of running − and train more often than their younger counterparts. 'A key differential appears to be the hours the two groups are willing to put in. According to *Strava* [a mobile application and website which connects millions of runners and cyclists, see chapter 5], older runners average 28 miles (45 km) a week about three months before race-day, compared with 24 miles for those in their 20s' (Balch, 2019, unpaginated).

The ability to run fast, set personal records and train on an equal footing with much younger runners makes marathons attractive to people in their late thirties and forties. My middle-aged interviewees felt young and energetic, not middle-aged, overweight and decaying. The discourse of bodily decline with increasing age is prevalent (Tulle, 2007), but this decline can be somewhat circumvented with marathon running, where one can excel at a higher age because this practice requires experience and endurance rather than speed and agility. However, such runners are often ridiculed by non-runners. They find such runners' ambitions vain and their training regimen excessive and a sign of mid-life crises. They are also accused of running away from problems and domestic responsibility. If they get injured, people tell them that it is a sure sign that they are training too much for their age and getting too old for such exertion.

I also interviewed another middle-aged man who had been running marathons 'on and off' for two decades. At the age of 50, Oskar felt that his body had peaked and that the chance of a new personal record was long gone. However, in the summer, he ran a new record and finally became a proud sub-three-hour runner. At the time of the interview, he was 54 years old and half-heartedly hoping for another personal record, but he was also aware that the next upcoming marathon would probably be his last chance, feeling that age was slowly catching up with him. He envisaged his marathons in the future as being about having rich experiences and not so much about records and running fast. However, this would not be a major transition for him as he had run many 'experience marathons' before and, while different, they were equally exciting for him. This illustrates a second theme in the interviews, that marathons are very exciting to participate in and provide extraordinary experiences, especially when competing in various great locations.

### Extraordinary experiences

Most interviewees also associated marathons with other meanings and sensuous experiences besides racing. First, as discussed in chapter 8, marathons are linked to the sensuous excitement of being part of a big crowd and being cheered on:

> I'm not in the shape I was a year or two ago, so I just want to enjoy the race this time, taking in all the sights, running through the Brandenburg Gate and enjoying all that. ... I'm hoping to keep my time under four hours for my personal pride, so I don't embarrass myself. I just hope to enjoy the scenery and take it in and experience doing it in a foreign country. The sightseeing element and taking in the crowd and the energy. I ran the Boston a couple of years ago, and I have heard that here it is very good with people coming out, cheering you on. So, I'm excited about taking that in.
>
> *(Matthew, personal communication)*

Second, I argue that marathon meanings are also related to the excitement of tourist travel and sightseeing, as practices of marathon running and tourist travel are often 'bundled'. Runners are willing to travel to marathons that take place in exciting cities, and many interviewees had rich so-called 'event travel careers' (Getz & Andersson, 2010; Getz & McConnell, 2011; Shipway & Jones, 2007). They had participated in several marathons in their home countries and abroad and were accustomed to 'accumulating places' through running events and extending them into weekend breaks, or sometimes even longer. This also reflects that marathons often attract those with a mobile lifestyle and substantial income. Such 'expectations' to run in faraway places and attend obligatory (Shipway & Jones, 2007; Urry, 2007) 'must do' marathons means that this otherwise cheap and localised sport easily becomes relatively expensive and exclusive.

Some interviewees described marathon running as an excuse for travelling and seeing great cities. This is possible because my interviewees sometimes travel with their (often non-running) partner or family members, who want much more than just experiencing the marathon and supporting their partner. The American man cited above commented laconically that 'we are here for the marathon and to do some sightseeing as well', while his partner followed up by uttering that marathons 'are a good excuse to travel' (Rita, personal communication). Two 'distant' friends in their thirties from the US and South Korea, Donald and Claire, use marathons to meet up intermittently in different places. They told me:

> We are not super serious. We do it hopefully for fun. But it is a challenge every time we do it, a challenge to finish. So, it is quite an accomplishment to

get to the finish line… We both look for marathons out there that are special in some way. She did the Two Oceans Marathon in Africa. It is special because it is a great place to be able to go. Just the ability to go to interesting places in the world.

*(Personal communication)*

This ties into the notion of 'networking through tourism' where distant friends and family members use holidays and weekends to come together in specific places (Larsen et al., 2007). On the same day I interviewed Donald and Claire, I interviewed three mature American women who usually travel together to marathons. While they also run US marathons, they have a ten-year goal to complete a marathon on each continent. They explain why:

JANE: Because we are hitting those bigger numbers, fifties and sixties, it seemed like a good challenge to do within ten years. This year we are doing Europe, probably our next one is going to be New Zealand. ...

ESTHER: The motivation is to do something that's different, so you incorporate the travel. It is the reason to train. Keeps you to your training because you know that you are paying out a lot to travel ... and when you go you want to do it well. If it is at home, and the weather is not good, you might say no and may not do it. If you have paid a lot of a money, you go and do it. It is the reason, why we come together to London, and now coming here to Berlin. And we are going to New York City together.

JO: And you learn something about each country that you go to, and that's what has been so interesting ... I don't know if I would ever have come to Berlin for a vacation. It has been a great city to explore.

*(Personal communication)*

I conducted other 'group interviews' where distant friends explained that they came together at specific marathons and kept 'in touch' by following each other on Strava (chapter 5). This also illustrates how signing up for 'big marathons' and booking flights and hotels together with others motivates daily training routines. As people become 'friends' by running together, they become more committed runners. It is not only slower runners who 'bundle' marathon running and tourist travel. Some say, half-jokingly, that marathon running is an excuse for travelling and seeing great cities. The seductive combination of travel, 'must-do' events and famous cities is nowhere so crystal clear as with World Marathon Majors.

## World Marathon Majors

World Marathon Majors now comprise some of the largest and most iconic marathons, and they are placed in equally famous cities on three different continents: New York, Boston, Chicago, London, Berlin and Tokyo. These marathons are partly famous because they are located in famous cities. A large part of the lure of World Marathon Majors is that ordinary people, so-called 'everyday champions', can become victorious 'six-star finishers' by finishing all six marathons, which, especially for non-Americans, presupposes that one can afford to live a high-carbon life with several long-haul flights and many overnight stays in expensive cities. Given that these marathons are notoriously oversubscribed, they are difficult to plan for, and travel with a running travel agency that guarantees a starting bib is extremely expensive. In 2019 there were more than 6,000 'six-star finishers' from 88 countries, most of whom were high earners in their late forties (Larsen, 2021).

While travelling to specific 'places' certainly matters to marathons, particular cities can also be partly overshadowed by specific 'events', as I experienced with the Berlin Marathon and especially the Tokyo Marathon. This was particularly the case with the North American and Asian runners whom I interviewed at the Berlin Marathon and the European and North American runners at the Tokyo Marathon. When I asked them why they ran the Tokyo Marathon, the interviewees declared, quite frankly, that they were lured there because this event was part of the World Marathon Majors, not because they had always dreamt about visiting and seeing Tokyo; they said that they would almost certainly not have run the Tokyo Marathon (at least this year) if they were not on a quest to become a 'six-star finisher'. As the two European, Ben and Hanna rationalised:

> I want to complete all the six major marathons. I have done London and New York, so this is the next one, and I got the other three ones later in the year. I got entry in all of them.
>
> *(Ben, personal communication)*

> It's my 13th marathon, including Berlin − five times. Then, we decided to run New York and then we decided to do the six major marathons, and Tokyo was the next where we could get the starting number. ... In the autumn, we are in Chicago.
>
> *(Hanna, personal communication)*

While the event was the 'reason to go', they were nonetheless excited about being there; similarly, some turn this running weekend into a longer holiday in Japan. The interviewees stressed that it was wonderful that this event 'gives them the opportunity to experience this exotic place, and that the six-star finisher project is alluring because it allows them or gives an excuse for (re)visiting must-see cities, and to combine their love for running with tourist travel' (Larsen, 2021, p. 132).

At the Expo I do hours of observations in the World Major Marathon booth and note how it

> swarms with especially western runners waiting for their turn to be photographed as a proud soon-to-be six-star finisher or to take pictures of the glass-framed cabinets with the individual medals for each of six marathons and the whopping six-star medal. ... The prospect of collecting yet another prestigious medal and acquiring, or getting one step closer to, that conspicuous holy grail

of international marathon running clearly entices many to come to Japan for this particular event.

*(Larsen, 2021, p. 131)*

I argue that this whopping medal is a form of 'conspicuous consumption' (Veblen, 2005) whereby middle-aged and upper-middle-class people of mainly western origin live high-carbon 'mobile lives' (Elliot & Urry, 2010), flashing a shining cocktail of wealth, cosmopolitanism and athletic accomplishment. In part, people participate in marathons because it gives them a reason to visit exciting places together with family members or running friends.

## Habitual training, friendships and social capital

So far I have stressed the sheer excitement of running marathons, especially in a new place. This overlooks the 'everydayness' and habitual nature of marathon running, that is, the more or less daily training in one's immediate environment. Most runners will only run one or two marathons (perhaps one abroad) per year. The interviews indicate that such everyday training largely shapes marathon meanings and identities. This is the pleasure and drill of marathon running. Shortly after dropping out of a marathon where he had aimed for a personal best, I asked Scoot if the poor result ruined it all:

A marathon is more than the race itself. It is also the whole prelude. Half-year training sessions in Utterslev Mose with friends, either in heatwave and bare upper-body, or fighting headwinds and … mud. All the good times, hard times, all the prelude, all the planning … all the partying afterwards.

*(Personal communication, my translation)*

While running is an individualised and flexible sport (Atkinson, 2015; Robinson et al., 2014) and my interviewees often run on their own, many also run with others and join loose and individualised running communities, such as NBRO, when they became more committed. An NBRO runner stated: 'Socialising and travelling is what makes running fun. It also drives the motivation to come here and meet others who like to run and talk about running' (personal communication, my translation). Further, interviewees explained how their extensive training schedule gives a certain structure to their leisure life in that they have learned to appreciate and shape other practices. Those who are committed to marathon running enjoy the everyday drills of training, often because they are running with others, forming relationships. While running associations such as NBRO in principle are 'liquid communities' where obligations and ties are non-committal and fluid (Pedersen et al., 2018), my research shows that NBRO runners form common social worlds (Robinson et al., 2014), friendships, meet obligations to others and develop a strong collective identity that enable them to do things together. They develop the kind of 'trust, norms and networks' that Putnam argues enable voluntary organisations – including sports associations – to produce social capital and facilitate 'coordinated actions' (Putnam, 1993, p. 167; Elmose-Østerlund & van der Roest, 2017).

## Marathon biographies and defection

However, for others, running fails to settle as a structure or becomes too much of a structure – an unhealthy burden. A key aspect of practice theory is to account for the recruitment and defection of practitioners of a given practice (chapter 2). It seems that marathon running is typified by much 'substitution'. For some runners, running marathons is an enduring lifestyle, but for many others it is just a once-in-a-lifetime experience, and they return to casual jogging after achieving this ambition. Reischer wrote that 'most people who run a marathon will do so only once' (2001, p. 19). Similarly, Higdon claimed that 'a large percentage of people entering the most popular marathons are running their first marathon – and it may turn into their only marathon. Thirty-six percent of those who run the Chicago each year are first timers, and that percentage is typical of most major marathons' (2011, p. 4).[1] Thus, marathons need to entice many new practitioners each year. An increase in marathon running has occurred even though many people abandon running marathons after a brief flirtation, often because the training is too demanding or time consuming, or they suffer a serious injury (chapter 6).

Marathon runners may have different careers throughout their lives, and they may give up on marathon running for shorter or longer spells, if ever returning. We need to acknowledge that practitioners may move from one category to another. My research indicates that we should not assume that runners necessarily become more committed or competent over the years, although many evidently do. Rather, runners' biographies are dynamic, contingent and in flux. For instance, they may change in accordance with their other obligations, such as work and family life. In some cases, serious runners become casual runners when they become pregnant or when they become parents for the first or second time. For instance, this was the case for Oskar who stopped running marathons for six years after becoming a father for the first time. He said: 'I just could not justify the many training hours that I did to my family, also taking into consideration that I had a demanding professional career' (personal communication, my translation). He then began running marathons 'on and off' for a couple of years with different friends, but without being too serious and without training too much. However, a few years later, he intensified his training and became very committed when agreeing with his then running partner that they should do 'The Majors' together (at the time of the interview, he had just become a six-star finisher). When peaking as a runner at the age of fifty, he had a personal coach and ran with equally committed friends. At this point, he considered himself very 'serious' about running.

I have witnessed and talked with many runners who have defected from serious running for shorter and longer spells, if not completely. Three years after completing his first two sub-three-hour marathons, I interviewed Karl about why he stopped running. He explained that he was jubilant when he crossed the finish line with a new, impressive PB. High on success, he only thought about stepping up his training and running even faster in the next marathon. However, the joy did not last long, and he soon had second thoughts: After taking a long run one day, he started to experience knee pain, forcing him not to run for several months. In fact, he never returned to the NBRO or running, even when he became injury-free. He realised that chasing personal bests was a somewhat shallow and never-ending pursuit that would only steal more time from his family. Karl told me that

> Time became important because it was what could be improved. I also think that was why I stopped. If I had to improve, I just had to run even more. Right after the marathon, I was not happy. Immediately I said I should run 2.48, but I did not feel like it. Then you just do it. … Then I got a knee injury. Got injury-free and had a hard time coming back. Started playing some football again.
>
> *(Personal communication, my translation)*

He realised that the only way to improve his personal record was to spend more time on training, 'squeezing' (Southerton, 2003) even more running time into his family life. In hindsight, he believed that his family suffered a little from his, what he now considers, excessive running. Thus, the extensive nature of marathon running, coupled with the premium of improving one's time, means that some people eventually relinquish it. Marathon running is for many a short-lived practice that does not make sense, or cannot be integrated into their wider arrangement of everyday practices, in the long run.

While this person stopped running of his own accord, injuries may force others out of running against their will for shorter or longer spells. They might fall out of the habit of running or come to the heart-breaking conclusion that their body cannot cope with extensive marathon training. This can be devasting because they enjoy running, are fit and identify themselves as runners. Further, they lose regular contact with their running friends. Injuries play a part in the marathon drama of rhythms as they strike unexpectedly and provide a fatal blow to one's brilliant form in the short run and one's running identity and friendships in the long run. Running injuries lead to damaged identities (Allen-Collinson, 2003; Allen-Collinson & Hockey, 2007), often leading to mild forms of depression.

## Conclusion

This chapter has traced some key moments in the historical and contemporary metamorphosis of marathon running and recreational running. I have shown how marathons have transformed from small, competitive events for young male elite runners to inclusive mass street events and relatively ordinary practices. Marathons now comprise diverse bodies, men and women, young and old, fast and slow. The rest of this book discusses how this distinct medley of people provide the routinised, dramatic and spectacular polyrhythmic qualities typifying contemporary city marathons and the required time-consuming everyday marathon training.

However, competition and time – achievement running – remain crucial. My interviewees compete against themselves and their last personal record. Given the emphasis on personal goals and not of those of others, people's overall standing has little impact on how they experience victory when they cross the finish line (Berking & Neckel, 1993, p. 69). This is the beauty of this unique event. I have suggested that less ambitious and sometimes older runners associate marathons with less competitive meanings, such as experiences, friendships and travel (Masters & Ogles, 1995; Ogles & Masters, 2003; Rupprecht & Matkin, 2012). I have argued that marathon running is a 'way of travelling'. Marathons attract well-off middle-class runners because this practice provides mobile lifestyles and extraordinary experiences, which I term 'experience running'. While marathon training is a localised and routinised practice, marathons, I maintain, are nothing without exciting cities. It is the design of such extraordinary places that I will discuss next.

## Note

1 It is difficult to say whether this is entirely correct as I have not come across any specific data on this point.

# 5

# MATERIALITIES OF MARATHON RUNNING

## Designing practices and places

## Introduction

Kerr (2014) has argued that sport scholars have tended to overlook the power of the nonhuman in staging sport. In chapter 2 I discussed how 'mobilities design', 'practice theory' and non-representational theory all highlight the role of material affordances of things and environments in enabling corporeal mobile practices. These approaches understand cities as human and non-human assemblages to explore the extraordinary and mundane material affordances of objects and environments and the manipulation and redesign of such affordances in *in situ* practices. They discuss how 'infrastructures, technologies, materialities, and spaces that are integral to the embodied movements of human subjects' (Merriman, 2014, p. 177) and how certain 'social situations' (Jensen et al., 2016) and practices are informed by but also actualise specific affordances. This chapter examines specific *material* affordances of marathon running and events. I argue that marathon running is influenced by a variety of materialities that are seldom discussed together. These marathon materialities include non-human infrastructure (such as roads and road signs), road materials (asphalt and gravel), specialised consumer objects (GPS watches and shoes) and weather conditions (such as storm and heat). Such materialities enable, disable, facilitate and transmit embodied rhythms and places of running. Since non-humans never exist in a social vacuum, I explore how, for instance, race orga-nisers – in collaboration with sponsors, authorities, municipalities and runners – use and manipulate particular non-humans according to their 'design will'.

First, drawing on my notion of 'course-places' (chapter 2), I analyse how race-courses are designed, 'staged from above' (Jensen, 2013), and describe how orga-nisers and volunteers avail themselves of roads, metal fences and other items to secure generic, fast, timed and protected running *courses* on the one hand and, on the other, atmospheric and sight-packed *places*. I argue that attractive marathons excel in both parameters. Second, I discuss in detail how organisers plan and erect

DOI: 10.4324/9781003125068-5

marathons as rhythmic places on a practical level. This section draws on the relatively few studies that have explored the design and management competences and protocols involved in operating such materials and organising marathons (García-Vallejo et al., 2020; Hall et al., 2019). I then note how such material ordering can be disrupted by terror attacks and poor weather. Third, I examine the changing role of various timing technologies in organising marathons and running as a temporal rhythmic practice. Fourth, I turn to the affordances of shoes and clothing in facilitating specific bodies and corporeal rhythms of running. Drawing on practice theory, it is argued that the affordances of such mundane objects enable and sometimes change particular embodied forms and rhythms of running. While practices are usually relatively stable (chapter 2), they can change with technological developments and new material objects. I also show that their sign-values (Lash & Urry, 1993; Michael, 2000) communicate desirable meanings about marathon running.

## Designing marathons

### Redesigning streets

The last chapter discussed how the birth of the 'marathon boom' blossomed in 1976 when Lebow persuaded New York City politicians and municipality officers to move the New York Marathon out of Central Park and into the streets of the five boroughs, and to that end – and this was the tricky part – banned vehicles and pedestrians from using or crossing them (Cooper, 1992). From that day onwards, urban marathons have been *street* events and disrupted and immobilised other mobilities (less prestigious marathons may still use paths). They became in a sense urban street experiments that reconfigured the street as an 'urban common' that produces 'relatively smooth "corridors"' (Sheller & Urry, 2006, p. 213) for runners, in contradistinction to the traffic that is usually privileged on these routes.

However, elsewhere, this seizure was not always as smooth as in New York. While the Copenhagen Marathon was a street marathon in the 1980s, participants were in places forced to run on paths and in 'the gutter' of the street, crammed in between parked and driving vehicles. Moreover, because it was crucial not to disturb traffic, the route was not very scenic or central. This reflects, as the former race director recalls, that the authorities were not ready to conduct such experiment:

> It was really hard to gain understanding from police and other authorities for the first many years. For example, we had to be responsible for roadblocks, and that meant that the runners had to run in and out between cars, as much of the route was simply not blocked off.[1]

One of my interviewees, Oskar, who ran both Copenhagen and New York in the mid-1990s explained that they were completely different courses and experiences:

In Copenhagen the traffic was not blocked off, so we ran in and out between the cars. The route was dead boring, really dead boring. When you were not running on the paths in parks … you had to take care about cars. Not at all like today. And then you come over to New York in 95 and all the route is barred. … You turn around the corner and goosebumps rise when you look up the First Avenue and you just have those six-eight lanes and there is not one car. Everything is just blocked off. … Imagine the contrast to Copenhagen.

*(Personal communication, my translation)*

However, over the last two decades, municipalities in Copenhagen and many other places have become much more positive towards marathons, which now form part of an extensive process of 'eventification' through which cities compete to produce spectacular experiences that promote place branding and boost tourist consumption (Smith, 2016). Moreover, as running have become associated with healthy lifestyles, urban liveability, and sustainability, and the hegemonic roles of cars have been called into question, the necessary political support has become much more forthcoming.

Crucially, urban marathons reverse the order of things on the street. Whereas everyday running takes place in pedestrian paths and pavements, and is interjected by walkers, cyclists, red lights, and dangerous cars (see next chapter), urban marathon takes place on streets where traffic lights are off or bypassed and cars, cyclists, and passing pedestrians are temporally banned. Marathon organisers have obtained a temporary permission and power to reorganise streets from the local municipality and police, so that this annual occasion belongs exclusively to the ticketed runners (Smith, 2016, p. 97). This also explain why marathons tend to take place on Sunday mornings, when many of the usual weekly rhythms of the city are suspended or less hectic, with an absence of school children, commuters, and many shoppers, whereas such closing-off on any other day of the week would cause havoc and arouse opposition. Nonetheless, many non-participants are annoyed with such public events that disrupt their mobilities and 'right to the city' (Smith, 2016, p. 46). They believe that the racecourse, with its policing, erection of crowd barriers, and the exclusion of vehicular passage on these and adjacent roads (Boyle & Haggerty, 2009), make their usual mobile rhythms impossible. Indeed, it is 'hard to remove around city spaces when these events are being staged. Road crossings are restricted to designated points/times, large crowds prevent free movement, and transit to and from the roadside is often highly constrained by crowd control measures' (Smith, 2016, p. 73).

## Rhythmic templates

### 'Courses'

I now discuss how marathons are designed as what I call 'courses'. Marathons are organised and ranked according to the international regulations and design manuals of the AIMS/IAAF (International Association of Athletic Federation), which standardise marathons as codified *athletic* places (www.iaaf.org/competitions/iaaf-label-road-races).

Marathons strive to be labelled one of the 'leading road races around the world' by being awarded a gold, silver or bronze medal by IAAF.[2] The Berlin Marathon, Valencia Marathon, Tokyo Marathon and Frankfurt Marathon have gold labels, while the Copenhagen Marathon has bronze status. To receive such labels, they need to excel in media services, health and safety and attract an 'international elite field', and in addition they must deliver world-class finishing times and high prize moneys. The racecourse must be closed to vehicular traffic and pedestrians and include nutrition and water stations every three or five kilometres. Moreover, it has to be measured and electronically timed according to Association of International Marathons and Distance Races (AIMS) standards and include electronic timing. Organisers are obliged to provide individual start numbers, timing chips and split times every five kilometres, and display split times, finish times and rankings (also according to age and gender) on public result lists. Thus, 'gold label' indicates to all runners that the racecourse is fast and ideal for a personal best attempt and that the whole race is well organised (Edensor & Larsen, 2018). This is priceless branding for any marathon, especially for marathons – such as the Frankfurt Marathon – that take place in a city where normally few tourists roam.

In order to deliver 'world-class finishing times', marathons need to design a racecourse that affords high speed and linear movement. More broadly, as Bale writes, a race

> has a beginning and an end. Its logic is characterized by the spatial metaphor, 'linear'. Physical work – the race included – requires the physical organization of space. A manufacturing process – making a car or making a race – starts here (now) and ends there (then). … The starting and finishing lines are clearly marked, but in racing the destination itself has no inherent significance; it can indeed be identical with the starting point: 'What is important is speed – speed in directed space'.
>
> *(2004, p. 19)*

Speed is indeed pivotal in the organisation of marathons. Race managers try to select streets that are wide and whose tarmac is smooth and without (too many) cobblestones. They search for long stretches with pervasive flatness and without speed-reducing sharp turns. Asphalt is the fastest city surface and is easy to maintain a steady rhythm on (Bloom, 2015). Smooth and linear asphalt is ideal for energy-efficient running. Like running tracks in stadiums, urban marathons transform typically traffic-bound streets into an extended racecourse (with regular nutrition and medical stations), along which running is the master rhythm.

Marathons appropriate up to 42,195 kilometres of city streets, as major marathons never do repeat 'loops' and only include small parts where the same streets are run twice. The complex, labyrinth-like city 'is transformed in the marathon into the orderliness of a path formed of bodies which no longer has any wrong tracks' (Berking & Neckel, 1993, p. 71). A marathon is what Franck and Stevens (2007) term a 'tight place', being highly structured and typified by order and control, as well as turning a public space into a 'commodity' (Smith, 2016). The clearly designated racecourse affords linear movement, and it is simply impossible to get lost, or *resist* the route.

Thus, a disciplinary isorhythmia is produced that fosters linear progression from start to finish, reflecting that 'sport places, in their ideal type, are placeless: they afford speed, measurement and not least comparability *between* races. Speed overrules aesthetic considerations. They are places of inattention' (Bale, 1996, p. 165). 'Placelessness' is valued as something positive because it affords speed and seamless mobility. Yet, crucially, my argument is that this is only one part of the design: marathons are designed not only as 'courses' but also as exciting and stimulating 'places'.

## 'Places'

Runners not only request fast courses; they also desire to experience places with unique local features and rhythms of support, as well as a distinct atmosphere produced by locals. Municipalities and tourism organisations wish to showcase the city's major sights and attractive features to runners, spectators and TV viewers (as they generally do with major sport events, Smith, 2016). During mega events, 'urban civic space is a canvas willingly given over to the territorialising tendencies of brandscaping where parks, squares and buildings are opened up to commodification processes ... offering up the host city's cultural, civic and architectural assets for commercial exploitation' (McGillivray & Frew, 2015, pp. 2650–2651). Accordingly, organisers facilitate an affective atmospheric event by transforming streets into a vibrant outdoor stadium, encouraging bands to play along the route and distributing 'clapping devices' and free maps that spectators can fold up and deploy as clappers (chapter 8). Moreover, marathons are more than standardised sport spaces – they promote place-specific qualities, making them attractive to tourists. For instance, the Berlin Marathon organisers once wrote:

> The BMW BERLIN-MARATHON offers one of the most attractive courses at the 42.195k distance. Not only is the course in Germany's capital flat and ideal for setting personal bests, but it is also extremely attractive for tourists. A sightseeing tour could not have more spots in its program. The loop course is great for spectators following the race. Live music – ranging in style from classical to jazz to samba – lines the course.
>
> *(Cited in Larsen, 2019a, p. 50)*

This marathon starts and ends in Tiergarten and includes a symbolic run through the Brandenburg Gate as runners enter the final run-up stretch in Tiergarten. In between, they pass some the city's most spectacular sights, such as the Reichstag, Kurfürstendamm Boulevard, Neue Nationalgalerie, the Berliner Philharmonie, Potsdamerplatz, the two cathedrals on Gendarmenmarkt Square, Unter den Linden boulevard and the socialist architecture of Karl Marx Strasse. They also run through multicultural and hip neighbourhoods such as Kreutzberg and the green and affluent south-western neighbourhoods[3] (Larsen, 2019a, p. 50).

Another example is the Kyoto Marathon. The course design effusively utilises the city's world-famous sights and is promoted as perfect for sightseeing and getting to know Kyoto. The organisers write:

Running the course while enjoying the attractions that only Kyoto can offer!
…

Located along the course are the seven UNESCO World Cultural Heritage sites … Runners follow a course along the Katsura River with a view of Togetsukyo Bridge in Arashiyama, and then pass through the picturesque Sagano area and Hirosawa-no-ike Pond. The course then leads to Kinukake-no-michi Road, which has been famous for its scenic beauty for over 1,000 years, passes through the Kyoto Botanical Gardens, extends along the Kamo River, a symbol of Kyoto, and then takes the runners on a trip through history in the verdant Kyoto Gyoen National Garden (Kyoto Imperial Place). Yet another major thrill of the Kyoto Marathon is the view of the five mountains that are the focus of the Gozan no Okuribi festival.

*(Cited in Larsen, 2021, p. 128)*

Indeed, this marathon emphasises sightseeing (place) over speed (course). The many temples are located in a very hilly terrain and this course does not afford fast finish times (Larsen, 2021).

Other marathons are known for their spectacular and highly *place*-specific start and finish areas. The Valencia Marathon commences and ends at the city's highly spectacular post-modern landmark, the stunning 'Príncipe Felipe' science museum, which is part of the larger City of Arts and Sciences, one of the most significant tourist attractions in Valencia. City of Arts and Sciences is a huge cultural and architectural complex situated in a massive sunken green park in a former riverbed. After a calamitous flood in 1957, the Turia River was drained and rerouted and its old riverbed subsequently turned into a park with this huge cultural complex. This emplacement makes the race photogenic, distinctive and approvingly atmospheric. The same is true of the flamboyant, ear-splitting disco-infused final inside a massive sport arena at the Frankfurt Marathon.

## *Weathering of course-places*

In chapter 2 it was argued that the weather – as a material force – impacts running rhythms, and organisers must take account of this in their planning. Yet the weather is an uncontrollable factor that give courses a place-like feel. Runners have an open relation to the world, and the weather conditions are specific to marathon course-places (and training grounds, see chapter 6) with volumes of air, heat and rain that surround and touch the body (Larsen & Jensen, 2021). There is a seasonal pattern to urban marathons. Most marathons take place in spring and autumn to ensure ideal running weather or at least avoid adverse weather conditions such as high and low temperatures (and snow), which impede fast and comfortable running and increase the likelihood of illness. However, on the day of the race, the weather must help the runners along or at least not meddle too much in their runs. While the event takes place on same day of the year, the actual weather can differ dramatically from one year to the next, meaning that managers and runners are always fretful about the weather that will be thrown at

**FIGURE 5.1** The finish line at the Valencia Marathon
Photo credit: The Valencia Marathon.

them *this* particular year (chapter 7). This is the contingent variable, as studies show that the weather impacts overall finish times and dropout rates. Statistically speaking, the optimal weather is an air temperature between 8–10°C, an overcast sky, no or a slight wind, and light drizzle or no rain at all. Heat seems to be the key factor, with studies showing a connection between temperatures above 8–10°C and slower finish times. High heat and humidity also make dehydration and heat strokes common (Spellman, 1996; Vihma, 2010; Vugts, 1997). This relatively low temperature also explains why most marathons start early in the morning, although most runners (especially slower runners) will often run the latter part of the race in warmer temperatures (Larsen & Jensen, 2021). The temperature should be so low because bodies quickly 'heat up' and produce excess heat and, by running in proximate groups, they also warm each other up (Allen-Collinson et al., 2018; Cheuvront & Haymes, 2001). While runners build up weather competences and adjust their clothing and training to the weather, runners often fail to control it as it is a volatile and agile phenomenon, so the 'weathering of the running body' is a matter of distributed agency between the running body and the immediate environment (Larsen & Jensen, 2021, p. 77).

To sum up, municipalities, race managers and multiple others co-impose a rigid order over time and space to ensure the efficient and smooth progress of the marathon as an attractive course-place and to ensure disciplinary isorhythmia. This illustrates that inscribing new rhythms on streets and places more broadly requires vigilant management, design procedures, technological augmentation, numerous mundane objects and many 'volunteering hands'. Moreover, different marathons are strikingly similar *and* different, and I have suggested understanding them as what I have termed course-places. They are similar as *courses*, being designed for smooth speed, auto-pilot movement and tunnel vision. But they are more than 'motorways'. They are simultaneously designed as exciting sites for gazing and as local places. While international design regulations and procedures standardise them, the local neighbourhoods, weather, topography and scenic qualities make each of them unique as *places*, and these differences will be sensed by the runners and impact their possible pace, rhythms and experiences. The next section discusses in more detail how organisers go about designing and organising racecourses as rhythmic spaces on a practical level.

## Planning and erecting courses

As Roche (2003, p. 99) insists, mega-events like marathons are temporary occasions that have 'long-lived pre- and post-event social dimensions', and organisers, administrators, police and volunteers tend to be well prepared for the medley of roles that they have to enact before and during events. Annual marathon events demand months of intensive planning and management to redesign streets as a running space attractive to sponsors, spectators, and runners, and to ensure that the many rhythms of the day proceed smoothly (Coppieters, 2012; García-Vallejo et al., 2020). These strategies reveal how managers and the authorities 'utilize and manipulate time, dates, time-tables' (Lefebvre, 2004, p. 68), prescribing rhythmic and temporal order, norms and atmospheres. As Edensor and Sumartojo argue more broadly, 'designers set "the conditions in which the atmosphere appears", creating "tuned" spaces with tones, hues and shapes, and it is no stretch to identify the multiple ways in which spaces of all kinds are managed so as to produce a particular feel, mood or ambience' (2015, p. 253).

Marathons 'come to life' through being designed and staged by race organisers in collaboration with municipalities, professional event companies, sponsors, media, police, tourism organisations, medical teams and volunteers, requiring the coordination of various procedures that synchronise their actions. While key managers are in charge of these authoritative practices, this staging requires the synchronisation of and coordination between volunteers and diverse professionals, illuminating how staging is strewn amongst many co-producers (Edensor & Larsen, 2018, p. 743). Indeed, studies show that volunteers, social networks and social capital are crucial for organising tourism (sport) events (Larsen & Bærenholdt, 2019; Richards et al., 2013; Richards & Wilson, 2005).

In the preceding months and up to immediately before the race, following regulations and design manuals, managers and their staff and volunteers are laying down the rhythmic templates that enforce strictures upon participants and seek to produce a disciplinary isorhythmia and vibrant atmosphere. They are busy negotiating commercial sponsorships, running marketing and press campaigns, and designing a racecourse that the local authorities and police will approve. They are trying to 'design out' a variety of risks, as managers are well aware that street marathons 'are susceptible to various risks, both natural and man-made' such as 'inclement weather; bomb threat; crowd control; medical issues; active shooter; logistical failure; and emergency response time' (Hall et al., 2019, p. 11). This has implications for the medical teams, for example:

> In preparing for medical coverage of a mass participation event such as a marathon, race directors and their medical staff members need to account for the unexpected. Extremes in weather as well as the potential for outside threats need to be given consideration before race day in order to adequately prepare.
>
> *(Chiampas & Jaworski, 2009, p. 131)*

My informal running-with-interview with the former race coordinator of Copenhagen Marathon provided insight into some of the laborious work, political negotiations and many agents involved in getting the racecourse – the heart of the race – designed on paper, approved by the municipalities and the police, and then staged on the race weekend. Each year they submit to the municipalities a huge visual presentation of the racecourse and – most importantly – a detailed description of how it will affect the traffic, what streets will be blocked, and where they will place specific road fences, signs and anti-terror bollards. They will normally only make incremental changes to the course, sometimes forced by feedback from runners, ongoing construction work or instructions of the authorities. Once the plan is approved, the marathon organisers, not the police, are in charge of executing this traffic plan on the race day.

A week or two before the race itself, written notes will be placed on front doors and street information stands to inform affected locals that certain streets will be closed for parking (cars will ultimately be removed prior to the race) and driving, suggesting alternate routes. The actual start-and-finish area is erected a few days before the race day and there is no guarantee that things will go according to the plan, especially when external partners and volunteers are involved, the event takes place in the unpredictable weather-world and complex urban centres (Hall et al., 2019, p. 11).

At the race weekend the start area is bustling with final activities to guarantee that the race rhythms proceed effortlessly. Professionals and volunteers erect the start-and-finish area with show rooms, info stands, lockers and toilets, while specialised sport event companies set up timing devices and busy hands prepare large amounts of fruit and energy-rich drinks that runners will fuel and hydrate their bodies with. This is a nervy time; there is very little time to erect the racecourse with fences and bollards because they are first allowed to close off the streets on the race day itself. The former racecourse coordinator tells me that like many other marathon organisers they rent the metal crowd barriers that prevent vehicular and pedestrian passage (Boyle & Haggerty, 2009) from a German company. They are dropped off on the pavement along the racecourse so that they can be easily erected Sunday morning:

> We are first allowed to start fencing of the street from 6 o'clock in the morning but we are first allowed to block the street completely two hours

before the race starts: sometimes we have not fully finished the last part of the course when the race commences.

*(Personal communication, my translation)*

Simultaneously, numerous other hardworking hands are diligently setting up nutrition stations, timing devices, DJ booths, medical units and photography stations and cheering zones along the 'stretched out' route.

During the race itself and along the course, thousands of volunteers hand out drinks and foodstuffs or nurse injured runners (Pedeo, 2007; Ewert, 2007) and, not least, ensure – in tandem with the metal fences – that 'others' do not interfere with and restrict runners. This is more intense in some races than others, with Japanese marathons being the extreme, having one long thick string of volunteers throughout the race. A race like Copenhagen Marathon is more relaxed, and yet 'we have at least two volunteers at each crossing' (former racecourse coordinator, personal communication).

In the aftermath of the Boston Marathon bombings, when three people were killed and a further 260 injured, there is a growing recognition between race organisers and the authorities that marathons given their open access and distributed nature are difficult to safeguard in their entirety. They are thus susceptible to terror attacks, so police officers, CCTV cameras, bollards and drones are increasingly employed, especially in high-profile and therefore high-risk marathons. According to Schrotenboer, 'perhaps no sporting event in the world is harder to safeguard from terrorism than a giant footrace in a big city' (cited in Hall et al., 2019, p. 12). For example, 'the 2017 Boston Marathon organisers dispatched 5,000 law enforcement officers along the marathon

**FIGURE 5.2** 'Fencing off' Karl Marx Strasse, Berlin Marathon

route … and the Chicago Marathon utilizes more than 22,000 cameras across the city on race day' (Hall et al., 2019, p. 14). These forces generate what Adey (2014) in his work on airports terms 'security atmospheres', and we may say that marathons are increasingly fortified and bubble-like.

Such 'security atmospheres' can also be seen in the spatio-temporal organisation and ordering of runners in the start area. As mass events with up to 40,000 runners, a logistic challenge is avoiding an arrhythmic start caused by congestion at the front and interspersing of fast and slow runners. Accordingly, the start line is divided into fenced-off and controlled corrals where runners are 'sorted' into specific start groups based on their intended finish time and previous times (disclosed and documented as part of the registration process). The appointed corral is clearly communicated on the start number and is carefully 'checked' by volunteers when the runner enters the corral; runners will be refused movement into another corral. The fastest runners start first, while the slowest commence up to half an hour later, which ensures a relatively smooth and frictionless start, where each second counts for many runners. Indeed, the start will slide into rhythmic chaos if runners do not accede to this rhythmic ordering.

This ordering is only acceptable because of recent technological innovations. 'Waiting' while others are running and the official time is 'clicking away' would be deeply frustrating if 'gun time' still mattered. In this case, time-obsessed runners (chapter 4) would not accept being placed at the back, and there would be more pushing and aggression. It is only acceptable because new *individualised* timing technologies have made 'gun time' irrelevant, as now discussed.

## Timing and numberisation of corporal rhythms

### Chip-time and net-time

Time-keeping used to be dictated by the gun-time and manually recorded (although runners used their own digital wrist watches to record their actual time). As marathons grew in attendance, runners often found themselves blocked at the start and even at the finish line. As Allen writes:

> For years, race organizers depended on numbered race bibs with pull-off tags to record marathon times and preserve the correct order of finish. The runner would cross the finish line, her race number and finish time would be written down and a pull-off tag at the bottom of her race bib (which included important informa-tion like name and age) would be ripped off and put on a spindle in the order of finish … . As marathons became a bit larger, finishers were hustled into finishing chutes until volunteers could tear off the tags from the athlete's shirt-front.

Finishing chutes easily became crowed with frustrated runners who had to wait seconds, even minutes, before their time could be recorded, which it goes without saying was incredibly frustrating for time-obsessed runners when the time was clicking away (Mitchell, 2001). Individual chip-time is a relatively recent innovation; it was first introduced in 1996 in the London Marathon (Bryant, 2006, p. 171; Austen, 2001). The ordering through corrals and 'delayed starts' explain why absolute gun-time (gross-time) now plays an inferior role to the individual net-time, recorded by a computer chip, often attached to the shoe of the runner.

Today, with *individualised* timing technologies and the focus on 'net-time', the wait to start is not a problem. Except for the very front runners, runners have slower gross-times than net-times (up to half an hour for the last runners), as net-time starts the moment the 'chip-runner' first crosses the starting mat and not when the race time officially starts (that is, gun-time). Crucially, this discrepancy does not matter as runners (except the very elite runners) only care about and measure personal records in net-time. Net-time is

> the duration between the moment your body crosses the first magnetized mat at the start until the time you pass the last one at the finish. A small plastic disc containing an RFID chip is tied to your laces and read by the magnetized mats placed throughout the race. The net time figure produced with chip timing is critical to mass participation events, and marks a certain seriousness. Chip timing allows something like a marathon to be a mass participation event and have its eventness organized around nearly 35,000 individual races. It allows runners to start way back in the pack, with dozens of corrals of thousands in front of them, and still run their race, for their time.
>
> *(McLoughlin, 2010, p. 77)*

Modern mass marathons and rhythms of running would had been very different without chip timing, as accurate timing would have been impossible for the vast majority of the runners. This tiny electronic chip is programmed with the runner's specific identification and is attached to shoelaces or the start number (the latter is common in Denmark; Sailors, 2019). The chip is a tracking device 'that marks out the course of the body, in time and space' (McLoughlin, 2010, p. 77) that is read continuously when runners cross the start line and finish line and every five kilometres along the route by timing mats. Accordingly, the runner becomes a 'data-assemblage' (Lupton, 2015) and rhythms of pacing and running are endlessly tracked and recorded in a process of 'data-production' that ensures correct individual timing throughout the course. More recently, it allows 'live tracking' of specific runners so that 'live supporters' know when to expect a runner at a specific place (or kilometre sign), while absent acquaintances can cheer from a distance.

## Running watches and self-tracking

Runners are not only being tracked and their data disclosed; they are self-tracking their movement with increasingly sophisticated GPS watches and displaying the data on associated apps and social media sites for runners (and other sport practitioners) such as Garmin Connect (if running with a Garman watch) and Strava (West, 2015).

However, such time recording is nothing new as such. Reflecting modern societies' preoccupation with recording of time, watches have long been standard equipment amongst urban dwellers and 'coordinated' modern mobile life (Larsen et al., 2008), while stop watches were used in factories to make work mobilities effective and rational (Cresswell, 2006). Similarly, stopwatches have always been used extensively by coaches to time runners (Bale, 2004), and runners have been equipped with digital watches since the 1980s. However, a significant moment was in 2003 when Garmin launched their first GPS running watch. Since then, satellite tracking has improved greatly and watches now include mapping features, heart rate monitoring, running dynamics, and much more. As part of a wider digitisation of many social practices (Carlén & Maivorsdotter, 2017; Esmonde, 2019; Lupton, 2015; Lupton et al., 2018), self-tracking and data production are now an integrated part of the running body (Salazar, 2020). This also illustrates that serious running is not cheap, as watches cost between €200 and €800 and runners frequently buy new ones (see also the next section about shoes).

I largely concur with non-representational and emplacement approaches to self-tracking. They show how tracking devices condition *ongoing* mobile practices as cyclists and runners move through the world and produce 'data in the environment (with the body), rather than as producing data about the body' (Pink & Fors, 2017, p. 379; Esmonde, 2019; Lupton et al., 2018; Sumartojo et al., 2016). As demonstrated later (chapters 6 and 7), embodied rhythms of running are almost always mediated and evaluated through lively and agentic – rather than dead – 'numbers' (Lupton, 2016, p. 709) measuring ongoing speed, distance, and heartbeat. This is because time is invisible to the senses and can only be observed through indicating technologies, such as the watch (Urry, 2000, p. 105).

My research shows that training and competing with GPS watches has become the norm. Most of my interviewees use such watches, and virtually no one heads out for a run without tracking it in terms of location and perhaps heartbeat, but most importantly, distance, speed on certain stretches and overall pace. Some also wear a chest strap to monitor their heart rate more correctly. They run *with* GPS watches and analyse their movements and progress while on the move in specific environments through such quantitative measurement technologies as much as through their lively, feeling bodies. They believe that such watches and practices of 'live analysing' afford them rhythmic control during outings and a precise measurement of how far and fast they run during particular stretches and on average. Competent runners are skilled at both listening to their body and reading their watch, viewing such information as complementary rather than conflicting. Moreover, runners make sense of this data in relation to the environment and weather-world that they are emplaced in. So, 'while self-tracking technologies might appear on the surface to belong to a quantified world of measurement … they participate considerably in how people "feel" or sense in their everyday environments' (Pink & Fors, 2017, p. 376). Runners are enmeshed within variegated places and networked with the technologies they run with, and these technologies '"get under the skin" to shape their bodies and experiences' (Esmonde, 2019, p. 806). However, some runners are aware and worried that these 'bodily quantification practices can lead to an emphasis on data over feeling and numbers over haptic sensations' (Esmonde, 2019, p. 807).

## Representing running data

What is not discussed much by non-representational approaches is that tracking technologies not only mediate ongoing practices but also produce *representational* data about these runs. I thus suggest that we need to account for both the repre-sentational and non-presentational aspects of such tracking practices, as these tech-nologies produce valuable shared numbers about embodied running, as we saw above with the public result lists. At the end of a run, a watch immediately makes a brief 'race report' about distance, mileage time, heart rate and overall pace. More-over, many runners by default 'connect' their watch with, for instance, a private Garmin Connect account and public Strava account, producing more data about speed and heartbeat on different stretches. Data are also produced on the traversed environment, as routes are visualised on maps and measured in relation to kilo-metre splits, gradients and the weather and the run is compared to how other

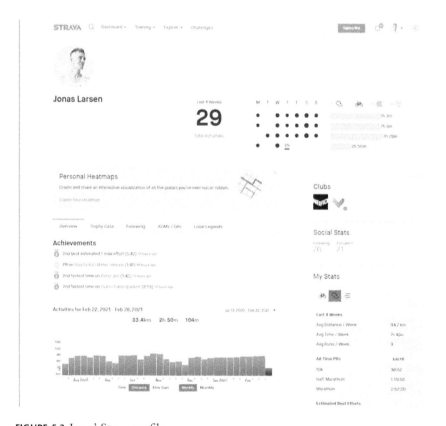

**FIGURE 5.3** Jonas' Strava profile

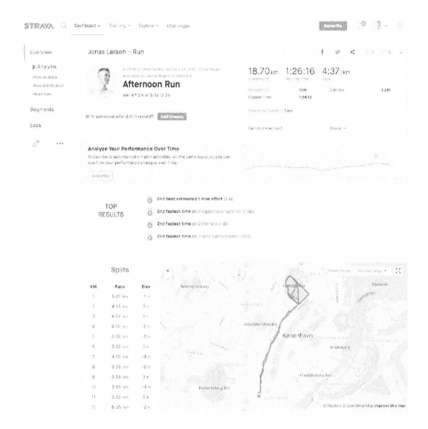

**FIGURE 5.4** Interval training in Fælledparken

runners have run (part of) them (called 'segments'). This represented data is then public. At Strava, all training activities and weekly mileages of each participant are fully visible, allowing runners to easily keep track of how others are training in terms of distance (on a weekly basis), speed and location (see Figure 5.3). I argue that this 'strava-isation' means that runners in part run to produce and display impressive numbers, and the languages of rhythms and corporeal sensations are objective numbers as much as subjective expressive sentiments.

This also illustrates how digital self-tracking requires skills and competences to analyse one's own data and those of others (Carlén & Maivorsdotter, 2017; Pink et al., 2018). Moreover, running data are *produced* by a particular 'watch-runner' who makes production choices when turning it 'off' and 'on' – or forgetting – at red/green lights, taking breaks, and 'jogging' (note how I forgot to pause my watch when taking a break after the third round of intervals (12 km); see Figure 5.4). Two co-running 'trackers' may thus produce different data on the same run. Moreover, whether a particular average pace or 'running time' on a certain route uploaded to Strava is impressive in part comes down to how and where the runner ran the session (chapter 5), and how he or she 'paused' the watch. Data collection is thus 'always interdependent with and contingent on human, bodily, sensory, emotional, environmental and other material circumstances that [are] not necessarily predictable or reliable' (Pink et al., 2018, p. 5). This is different from races, where it is the official time that counts and 'pausing' one's watch – for instance if stopping for lacing one's shoes – is considered cheating if uploaded as an official marathon time (Esmonde, 2019, p. 210). Moreover, as discussed in chapter 6, the displayed data matter because they *produce* significant 'training grounds'.

Finally, representational data matter in relation to sociality and positioning. Connected runners, being 'data assemblages', might be running very much alone, but their data reveal their engagement in (virtual) running communities where runs are often noticed and acknowledged. Self-tracking is also about communication (Lomborg & Frandsen, 2016; Spotswood et al., 2020) and creating tangible training logs (Barratt, 2017, p. 330). As Barratt notes in relation to cycling:

> These devices, and their scripts, augment the ride structuring and shaping connections which can be engaged with both on and off the bike. ... A bike ride is no longer something that just happened, a memory, a calorie deficit to be annulled, it endures, it becomes tangible – it is a record in a training log, a time on a leaderboard, a route to be shared amongst friends and strangers.
>
> *(Barratt, 2017, p. 328)*

Strava is largely digitising and making public the old habit of keeping written private training logs (Lupton et al., 2018, p. 256), and studies shows that individualised runners appreciate the support and camaraderie of fellow runners and friends living elsewhere (Carlén & Maivorsdotter, 2017, p. 27; Spotswood et al., 2020). This reflects Strava's mission statement that 'Strava makes fitness a social experience, providing motivation and camaraderie even if you're exercising alone' (www.strava.com/about).

Competition is another side to Strava (Barratt, 2017; Lupton et al., 2018, p. 658). A more sinister reading is that Strava enforces neo-liberal exposure, angst and competition, with 'friends' comparing themselves against each other and in that process belittling themselves and others – there is always someone doing better, or more, or running faster. For instance, the 'side by side competition' function measures one 'friend' against another in terms of weekly mileages and all-time personal records (PR). Runners may become addicted to watches, data production and comparison, with running making little or indeed no sense without such a combined social media component (Sailors, 2019). The Danish sociologist Petersen (2016) has coined the notion of the 'achievement society', and it is clear that Strava and marathon data more broadly are designed to demonstrate tangible and impressive achievements that boost what we might call 'sport capital', a form of 'cultural capital'. The societal problem with the 'achievement society', according to Petersen, is that constant hunt for new achievements easily causes depression.

Next, I discuss the role of clothing and especially shoes in mediating corporeal practices and rhythms of running, while also arguing that such objects tie running and the consumer society closely together.

## Shoes, clothes and the consumer society

> The registration area is located at the very end of the EXPO, so people have to walk through the commercial part where rhythms of browsing and shopping dominate. European marathon expos are almost always identical in design although they are always flavoured by the local context. There are representatives from European marathons and elsewhere, companies selling specialised running shoes and clothes, or running watches, while others sell all sorts of 'scientific' sport nutrition, be it gels, before/during/after energy bars, tablets for sport drinks, and much more. All such products are branded as 'necessary' and crucial for running smoothly, for not 'hitting the marathon wall', or going into cramps, or dehydrating: they tap forcefully into runners' aspirations about success and fears about failure; how can one resist buying and using some of it?
>
> *(Field notes, Frankfurt Marathon 2016)*

Places and events are closely aligned with the rhythms of shopping (Kärrholm, 2009). This includes sporting mega-events such as marathons where rhythms of registration overlap with shopping and commercial displays of new running specific shoes; sweat-absorbing t-shirs and shorts; running socks; compression socks; running t-shirts; singlets; race souvenirs; energy bars and gels; powder to make energy drinks; gels belts; band aids; Vaseline; and leaflets for adventurous marathons elsewhere. Many wear trainers and track suits. On race day, people will run in an almost new pair of their favourite light racing shoes, not in washed-out shorts, singlets and t-shirts. Worn-out training shoes are not suitable for this occasion.

**FIGURE 5.5** 'Visit Japan. Run Japan', Frankfurt Marathon

Arms are decorated with expensive running watches and pockets are packed with nutrition products. Practitioners are race-ready, well trained (chapter 6), and fully equipped to run a marathon. While running is a matter of responsive openness and osmosis between the body and the world, this 'exchange' is mediated by more or less specialised clothing that allows bodies to breathe and be cushioned (Larsen & Jensen, 2021).

This testifies to the fact that marathon running and serious leisure running in particular have become commercialised and the running industry is a lucrative business spearheaded by giant brands such as Garmin, Adidas and Nike (Askwith, 2015; Metzler, 2019; Sailors, 2009). Becoming and being a marathon runner is also about buying specific products, dressing 'correctly' and buying into the 'commercial hype'. Indeed, marathon runners – of similar ability – dress remarkably similarly. Running shoes in particular are fetishised semiotic objects and a ritualised part of this practice, something that runners talk much about. Many swear loyalty to a specific brand, often as part of a group affiliation. For instance, NBRO runners only print the club logo on a Nike garment and pledge overwhelming support to Nike shoes (NBRO is loosely part of the Nike-related brand community; Kornum et al., 2017). The required materials of running – as with many other practices – have expanded and become increasingly specialised *consumer* goods.

This reflects, on the one hand, the precepts of practice theory that practices create consumer wants. Thus, 'it is the fact of engagement in the practice, rather than any personal decision about a course of conduct, that explains the nature and process of consumption' (Warde, 2005, p. 138), which means that 'patterns of consumption – of expenditures, possessions, portfolios of cultural activities can therefore be explained and accounted for partly by volume of practices and commitment to practices' (Warde, 2005, p. 144). Moreover, practice scholars are primarily concerned with the material affordances of consumer objects and how they afford certain human actions, such as running, rather than with their symbolic words. Practice theorists would therefore argue that running gear is essential insofar it creates a better and more comfortable running experience. For instance, above we saw how watches allow the timing of running. Shoes are, in this view, crucial to runners as they mediate interactions between the runner's feet/leg and the traversed ground and, in the process, are something that 'fundamentally reshapes the body's capacity to run' (Picciotto, 2016, p. 332) on specific surfaces. This need for comfort and absorption reflects the fact that such 'groundwork' (Ingold, 2004) potentially has hazardous repercussions: when running, 'from step to step, muscles and skin shake vigorously, and the force of each step's impact is distributed across the runner's whole body' (Picciotto, 2016, p. 333; Brown, 2017). Running shoes are 'an extension of a runner's skin' and runners are 'in touch' with specific surfaces through their footwear as much as their feet. Indeed, as discussed by Ingold (2004) and Michael (2000), shoes are affordances that mediate the affordances between humans and the environment. Particular shoes make certain surfaces more walkable and runnable in terms of comfort, speed, or stability. Alternatively, they can become 'parasites' if they start to gnaw, feel heavy and clumsy, wear down, take in water, cause blisters or give too little support (Michael, 2000; chapter 8).

I will now exemplify how different shoes afford different embodied sensations and rhythms of running by discussing the 'evolution' of running shoes, starting with the significance of the jogging movement (chapter 4) in creating new consumer demands. More broadly, this section responds to Ingold's (2004, p. 331) call to attend to how 'knowledge of the environment is altered by techniques of footwork and by the many and varied devices we attach to our feet'. Prior to the 'jogging boom', running shoes were ultrathin and afforded minimal protection:

> The most popular running shoes of the 1960s … had almost no cushioning at all, just a flat robber outsole; a barely-there insole layer between the runner's foot and the ground; and a wafer-thin, lightweight upper made from leather, canvas, or nylon.
>
> *(Metzler, 2019, p. 30)*

Such shoes were designed for fast running – literally 'flying over the asphalt'. They were also designed for a specific practitioner: the super light, biomechanically sound and highly skilled, efficient runner with perfect posture, foot stride and forefoot landings as well as access to running tracks (Metzler, 2019; Sailors, 2009).

However, this changed dramatically with the arrival of the urban sidewalk jogger, the corpulent heel-striking novice who valued comfort over speed or demanded plenteous cushioning between foot and ground. Pounding pavements makes running a high-impact sport – on the legs and the lower body – with a high injury rate, especially so for not-so-slim people (Allen-Collinson, 2003; Bloom, 2015). Running shoe companies experimented with different materials (such as plastics, rubbers, leathers and synthetic fabrics) to develop comfortable shoes that were suitable for and gave enough cushion protection to afford pleasant running on the callous asphalt world of sidewalks and not just on the more forgiving surfaces in forests, fields and running tracks (Metzler, 2019; Mills, 2003; Sailors, 2002). At the same time, 'joggers' also craved cool-looking shoes, and running shoes suddenly transformed in street fashion objects and *normal* everyday shoes; they were comfortable to walk in and flaunted an active lifestyle and fashion sensibility (Hockey et al., 2015; as Michael (2000) shows with walking boots). Brands such as Nike co-created the jogging movement by innovating the footwear for this particular form of casual – yet chic – form of running. This reflects more broadly that product innovation needs 'to develop the activity, not just the product' (Shove & Pantzar, 2005, p. 52). As Metzler writes:

> running was changing, with a premium placed on comfort, stability, and looks. New runners didn't necessarily want to run as fast or as often, so lightweight, minimally designed shoes were lost on them. What they wanted was to feel comfortable and avoid soreness and injuries. And they wanted to wear their running shoes while doing things other than just running. So how a running

shoe looked became paramount and a reason for brands to push the envelope of design in new directions.

*(2019, p. 57)*

The sale of running shoes skyrocketed (Metzler, 2019, pp. 47, 63) as running shoes acquired new meanings; they felt and looked appealing, and they worked well for many other active practices. Running shoes thereby de-sportified and became everyday items, often being renamed trainers. This reflects that companies realised that they could *sell* more shoes by reaching new practitioners. This was done through marketing hype, sharp design and striking colours, exemplified by the fancy Nike Air model. We should not forget, as Metzler writes, that 'running shoes are a commodity, and every running shoe company is in the business of designing and manufacturing shoes for the sake of selling as many as possible. … updates, tweaks and innovations are mostly about one thing: selling more shoes' (2019, pp. 96, 151). Their first priority was not improving performance or reducing injuries; indeed, there is little research-based evidence that running shoes in themselves can prevent injuries (Metzler, 2019, pp. 91–93). As all runners know, one cannot stay loyal to one specific shoe as the brands constantly 'update' existing models with new features or introduce whole models supposedly superior to last year's model, which reflects a wider design process of 'planned obsolescence'.

Sometimes such innovations are 'paradigmatic'. This was so when the maximum cushion movement gave way to the minimalist running movement that claimed – popularised by the best-selling book *Born to Run* (McDougall, 2010) – that excessive cushioning was 'unnatural' and even harmful since it encouraged heavy heel striking rather than the natural forefoot gait, which was supposedly gentler on the body and more effective. This had the effect that almost all brands began to produce 'minimal' shoes with less cushioning (Metzler, 2019). Such shoes provided a feeling of apparent 'shoelessness' and an intimate, direct touch with the ground. Picciotto describes how 'maximalist shoes push runners' feet up to the clouds and minimalist shoes pull them down to the ground' (2016, p. 336). However, contrary to Picciotto's observation, I argue that minimalist shoes in practice force people upwards; the hard feel impels one to run lighter, to be on one's forefeet and 'to fly on asphalt', as each landing sends callous vibrations through one's legs if landing heavily with a heel gait.

However, now the trend has changed once again as cushioned shoes are back in fashion. However, they are much lighter and faster than the first generation of highly cushioned shoes. I now turn to the 'hype' around the Nike Vaporfly 4% shoe to illustrate how shoes might actually make one run faster.

### The Nike Vaporfly 4% shoe and the sub two-hour quest

Nike's Vaporfly 4% racing shoe is intimately associated with possibly the greatest marketing event in marathon history, let alone running history: the Breaking2 project. The arduous goal was to design an event that would afford an opportunity to break the magical two-hour barrier. When Nike announced the project in November 2016, the marathon record stood at 2:02:57 and had been dropping very slowly over the

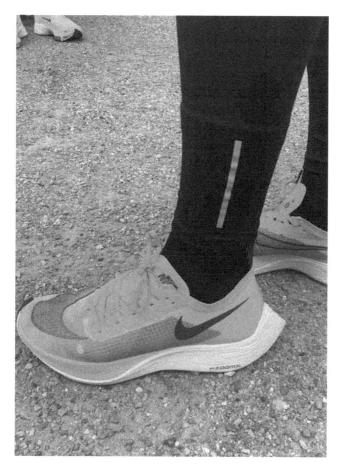

**FIGURE 5.6** The Nike Vaporfly 4% (ZoomX Vaporfly Next%)

previous years. The last two record breakers wore Adidas, and Nike was desperate to be associated with the record by designing the most recent fastest marathon shoes. The Breaking2 project was designed to achieve the fastest marathon time and showcase a marathon racing shoe specifically designed for this event (Rhodes, 2017). The event itself was not to be a conventional city marathon with public mass participation and the risk of poor weather, as such an event was not considered fast or predictable enough.

Instead, Nike 'technologically engineered' their own race. Nike's experts opted for a private race with an organised team of three carefully selected world runners (Lelisa Desisa Benti, Eliud Kipchoge and Zersenay Tadese) and a dense rotation of professional pacesetters (who trained together for the race under the supervision of Nike) in charge of keeping an exact pace and forming a wedge-shaped wind protective shield. They choose the super-fast (completely flat, no curves, smooth asphalt, oxygen-dense) automobile racetrack in Italy (the historic Autodromo Nazionale di Monza) on a day with – statistically speaking – perfect running weather. Yet 'instead of scheduling the event for a particular day, the Nike team determined a three-day window in which conditions were calculated to be most favorable' (Sailors, 2019, p. 3). The last crucial cog in this 'speed machine' was Nike's new Vaporfly 4% shoe. This shoe became known for its extra-cushioned thick midsole foam and especially the carbon-fibre plate in the sole. Nike claimed – as suggested by the name – that the shoe alone would improve running efficiency by 4 per cent by reducing fatigue, minimizing energy loss and 'creating a momentum boosting downhill running sensation in every stride' (Metzler, 2019, p. 170). The carbon-fibre plate stores and releases energy with each stride to propel runners forward, acting as bouncy catapult. This sensation is boosted by the bouncy or springier midsole foam, which increases comfort and speed (Burns & Tam, 2020; Lindsey, 2019).

Although the Breaking2 project eventually narrowly failed (Kipchoge's finish time was 2:00:25, still the fastest unofficial marathon record[4]), from that time onwards, the distinctive Vaporfly 4% (in various ongoing 'updates') became known as the fastest marathon shoe and was highly sought after despite the extremely heavy price tag (combined with low durability, as the shoe wears out after a few hundred kilometres). A year later (2018) in those shoes, Kipchoge ran a new official world record at the Berlin Marathon of 2:01:39. Vaporfly's prominence increased further in 2019 when Eliud Kipchoge broke the two-hour barrier in a new attempt (now called the Ineos 1:59 Challenge) – this time in an equally engineered park environment in Vienna with long straightaways and recently paved road. While Nike was no longer the sponsor, Kipchoge and his 49 pacers wore the new pink Vaporfly (now called Vaporfly NEXT%): 'Anyone who saw Eliud Kipchoge of Kenya break the two-hour marathon barrier in October very likely saw something else, too: the thick-soled Nike running shoes on his feet, and, in a blaze of pink, on the feet of the pacers surrounding him' (Keh, 2019).

There is little doubt that these shoes have enabled faster marathon times for the elite and serious leisure runners, who also began to run in these bright coloured shoes in great numbers (Burns & Tam, 2020; Kelly, 2019; Quealy & Kats, 2019). In the final months of 2019, 41 per cent of all the sub-three-hour marathon finishers wore these shoes (Quealy & Kats, 2019). Indeed, Quealy and Kats claim – based on a big data analysis – that those wearing these shoes are '2 to 3 percent faster than runners in the next-fastest popular shoe'. Another study suggests a 3.4 per cent increase in running speed (Burns & Tam, 2020, p. 1), which equals a minimum of a one-minute to 90-second improvement for elite runners and even more for slower runners (Ingle, 2020a, b).

Some observers thus accused these shoes of giving unfair advantages (especially when they were not widely available) and for being tantamount to 'mechanical doping'. Exercise physiologist Ross Tucker wrote: 'Any device inserted into the shoe, and which purports to add to energy return … should be banned' (cited in Lindsey, 2019). While Vaporfly gives runners an advantage, IAAF decided that they do not violate current rules for running shoes (Ingle, 2020a, b, 2021).

## Conclusion

This chapter has discussed significant 'materials' of marathon environs and practices. I began with the urban context, discussing the spatial transformation of existing streets-capes into attractive course-places. I then discussed the medley of spatial-temporal designs that constitute marathon courses as rhythmic course-places. They afford smooth, fast and atmospheric rhythms on the day for the many participants. Marathons are carefully designed to reverse the order of things, being temporarily 'transgressive' (Cidell, 2014), substituting for the usual rhythms of the city and providing a smooth, unhindered flow of running on a clearly designated racecourse. This affords fast running. I have also argued that city marathons are special: they are carefully staged to include and celebrate iconic, spectacular sites and exciting neighbourhoods and to provide a festive street party atmosphere to 'egg people on'. This occupation of streets bestows on the marathon a sense of specialness.

Smith suggests that running events such as marathons commodify running *and* urban spaces. Runners 'now pay a lot of money to complete a course that they could run for nothing whenever they wanted. … the streets are commodified as a venue and involvement of sponsors means that they are also commercialized …' (Smith, 2016, p. 141). This commercial impetus is evident, for example, in the ways in which advertisements are situated at particular junctures along the route. This chapter has shown that marathons are commercial products that to some extent commercialise streets and urban places, while marathon running is a consumer practice tied up with specific consumer objects. However, Smith fails to understand the nature of running and how running in the middle of streets-turned-racecourses afford very different experiences and sensations to running on the same street when busy and subject to red lights; these are two very different running environments and experiences, as discussed in the forthcoming chapters.

This chapter has foregrounded the power of organisers in designing racecourses and attuning its atmospheric qualities. Yet, as discussed in the following chapters,

> designers depend upon their acceptance of the feel of an atmosphere but can never be sure whether a crowd or group will charge the atmosphere with unwanted or unexpected tones or play the roles envisaged. Similarly, particular conditions – a blackout, sudden rainstorm or newsflash that may utterly transform an atmosphere – cannot be anticipated.
>
> *(Edensor & Sumartojo, 2015, p. 252)*

Various non-human and human forces might disrupt this material ordering of the race, turning it into a drama of rhythms.

The chapter also examined significant (wearable) technologies associated with running, arguing that such technologies crucially mediate competences of running and affordances of places. Chip timing and GPS watches afford the mechanical and precise timing and tracking of how bodies are moving through space in terms of speed, distance, heartbeat and routes. GPS technologies simultaneously track bodily data and spatial data, and we may say that bodily data are always 'emplaced'. Such designs and data are now integral to embodied running and sensuous forms of accessing movement and bodies. Indeed, runners note and make sense of these data 'on the move', using them as a second opinion on how their bodies are doing and if there is a need to slow down or accelerate. Rhythms are partly sensed through visceral, kinaesthetic sensations and partly through data.

Finally, I discussed how specific shoes afford specific running experiences and corporeal sensations of variegated 'grounds', and established that shoes have the potential to speed runners up and create faster finish times. However, I also noted how such designs and technologies not only mediate and improve but also constitute and communicate 'meanings' about being a proper runner and belonging to running communities. Objects have sign-value as much as use-value. Serious running is commercialised as running events, made expensive and complicated, by the global vortex of consumer capitalism and all their 'experts'. As Askwith laments: 'runners are born free, and everywhere they run in chains. Or, if you prefer, in chain stores' (2015, p. 17).

## Notes

1  https://copenhagenmarathon.dk/fra-pionerloeb-til-folkefest-40-aars-maratonhistor ie-kulminerer-paa-soendag/
2  http://dt9guucc6nuua.cloudfront.net/competitioninfo/c2127e60-9aa 4-40d9-bd90-43fd7db3d607.pdf
3  www.bmw-berlin-marathon.com/en/race-day/course.html
4  The time was not officially recognised as a world record because it was not run under normal conditions.

# 6

# PREPARATORY RHYTHMS

## Everyday running and training grounds

### Introduction

Marathon running involves dramatic events, time-consuming localised everyday practices and training places. 'In terms of time and effort expended,' as G. Smith writes, 'training constitutes the larger part of running activity; typically, races are the "ends" to which training is the "means"' (2002, p. 348). This chapter examines the *socially* produced (Cresswell, 2006) nature of *everyday* marathon training, focusing on the mundane, habitual and largely unspectacular everyday practices and spatialities of marathon running in connection with academic discussions of both 'the everyday' and the training of the body. While the runner is 'a rhythmic figure par excellence' (Edensor et al., 2018, p. 112), relatively little is known about how specific running rhythms are socially produced and learned. In this context, I explore marathon training as a mundane rhythmic everyday practice in which cities become 'training grounds'.

Expanding on chapters 2 and 3, I first argue that both everyday life and training are performed in the ambivalent space between scripts, repetitions and improvisational practices. While always scripted by experts and discourses, everyday practices such as training are not predetermined and practices are learned in action, often from experienced practitioners. Moreover, while the everyday and training imply dressage, unreflexive routines, repetitions and local places, they are not merely grey, uneventful and instrumental, but also meaningful and pleasurable.

The second section, focusing on five marathon training books (Allen et al., 2012; Cook, 2015; Higdon, 2011; Hilditch, 2014; Nerurkar, 2012) for ordinary runners, discusses the rhythmic principles of marathon training as *scripted* by experts as a highly codified rhythmic practice requiring specialised sessions and variegated rhythms that both sit with and depart from Lefebvre's notion of dressage.

Drawing on my fieldwork, I then explore how and how much such knowledge structures practices of daily training. I discuss how such daily training is enacted and felt

DOI: 10.4324/9781003125068-6

and then how the interviewees develop training routines and social relations, and incorporate them into their daily practices. Finally, I discuss how the weather conditions training and geographical significance of training, showing that while runners are often 'out of place', their habits and tracking practices produce significant 'training grounds'. I draw these discussions together in three vignettes about emplaced training sessions and significant training grounds.

## The everyday and training

However, 'the everyday' is made up of contradictions. It is the realm of the quotidian, unreflexive, and ordinary, but pleasures, creativity and subversion are always within reach. The everyday consists of ordinary, unquestioned practices, the collective scheduling of when to eat, move, work and play, daily grinds and scripted routines. Such unreflexive habits are inscribed on the body, constituting a shared common sense (Edensor, 2012; Larsen, 2008) of temporal rhythms dominated by the drills of work, commuting and passive, recuperating leisure (Lefebvre, 2004). However, there is more to everyday life than this, for everyday practices can allow creativity, subversion and resistance (de Certeau, 1998), altering everyday scripts. Scholars have highlighted the often sensuously rich, pleasurable and meaningful aspects of everyday routines and local places. For instance, Edensor (2003) argues that repetitive commuting should not be understood as uneventful and motorways as 'non-places'. Leisure scholars show that there is more to leisure than 'recuperation'. Leisure can be 'serious' (Stebbins, 1992), as when hobbyists develop skills and career biographies and join associations, through which practitioners come to appreciate their local environments in new ways while developing event travel biographies. However, 'serious leisure' is first and foremost a localised daily practice in which competences are honed through scripted training.

As discussed in chapter 2, mastering a practice entails learning requirements on competence, materials and meanings. As Wacquant (2004) argues in his boxing study, such skills are learned in practice and in interaction with other boxers and one's coach. Ingold (2010) and practice scholars argue that novices learn by accompanying experienced hands or legs who pass on practical know-how (Pink, 2009). However, mobile practices are simultaneously governed by representations and scripts about correct procedures (Cresswell, 2006). As noted, training resembles to some extent what Lefebvre termed dressage, training bodies to absorb rhythm through protracted repetition so that it becomes habitual, 'second nature'. Lefebvre briefly suggested that military marching, with its repetitive, mechanical and other-directed collective rhythms, serious gestures and assertive march music, typifies dressage, arguing that dressage underwrites all practices. Dressage produces docile bodies with marching competences, guaranteeing an 'automatism of repetitions'. Repetitions are the key (Lefebvre, 2004, pp. 48–49) and also the link between dressage and training. Drills are repeated to produce eurhythmia: 'Intervention through rhythm … in *sporting* and military training … has a goal, an objective: to strengthen or re-establish eurhythmia' (Lefebvre, 2004, p. 78, my italics). This echoes the 'docile bodies' produced by disciplinary practices identified by Michel Foucault (Elden, 2004; Lyon, 2018) and studies inspired by Foucault of sport science that demonstrate how coaches, through prescribed repetitions, produce docile and 'mechanical' sports bodies (Markula & Pringle, 2006). From the perspective of boxing training, Wacquant also notes the significance of repetitions: 'the most striking character of [boxing] is its repetitive … quality: its different phases are infinitely repeated day after day, week after week with only barely perceptible variations' (2004, p. 60). Similarly, I adduce the repetitive, coerced and abstract nature of much marathon training, but demonstrate that marathon running is organised through *different* rhythms and involves self-reflexive monitoring. In contrast to Lefebvre and in line with Wacquant (2005, pp. 68–69), I stress that marathon training is an enabling practice, that runners are active and reflexive, and that prescribed, measured rhythms and repetitive training can be evocative, pleasurable and social. I also emphasis that running rhythms include play, reflexivity and autonomy.

## Scripted training

### Learning process

Becker (1953) showed that people need to learn (from others) to appreciate 'being high' when smoking marijuana. Marathon running is also a learning process (Lev, 2019), and realising its bodily sensations is a biological and social process learned in words and actions. Practitioners need to 'learn to reframe muscular "burn", stiffness, breathlessness, a pounding heart and exhaustion as both immediate pleasures … and as signs of achievement and well-being' (Crossley, 2006, p. 40).

Most able-bodied adults have marathon potential. Humans are built to move rapidly on foot and transport their bodies at moderate speed over significant distances. Lieberman (an anthropologist) and Bramble (a biologist) argue that the popularity of marathon running makes perfect sense in an evolutionary sense, as it 'is a testament to our species' capability for endurance running' and 'although humans no longer need to run, the capacity and proclivity to run marathons is the modern manifestation of a uniquely human trait that help make humans what they are' (2007, pp. 288, 290). While genetics influences peoples' talent, *becoming* a marathon runner requires submitting oneself to systematised training contrary to the idea that some are 'predisposed' to run, while others are not. Bodies are not fixed, and training, not talent, largely determines marathon performance. As Bryant writes, 'The reassuring truth is that a marathon runner can go further on hard work and less natural ability than any other sports event. You don't need much talent, but you do need consistency' (2006, p. 196). Or as Seaton puts it: 'the marathon is an honest distance, and you reap on race day what you sow in training' (cited in Nerurkar, 2012, p.17). As discussed below, marathon training – like all serious leisure practices – requires 'coaching' and 'significant personal effort based on specially acquired knowledge, training, or skill' (Stebbins, 2007, p. 202; Green & Jones, 2005; Lev & Zach, 2020, p. 8; Shipway et al., 2013).

## Coaching

Marathon running is not for restless souls who demand instant results. Training programmes stipulate months of sustained training to build up the required physiological capacity and 'embodied mind'. Most books about marathon coaching often start with a caution aimed at joggers and 'novices' who suddenly desire to run a marathon. Most recommend running for a year before starting basic marathon training. Readers are warned that injuries proliferate because of premature excitement. While accustomed to long-term planning, ambitious professionals often train too hard before their bodies are sufficiently conditioned. A slow build-up of the body is vital and 'training for a marathon is something that should never be rushed' (Cook, 2015, p. 4). One coach teaches, 'the secret is to be patient and enjoy seeing your fitness improve gradually over time' (Nerurkar, 2012, p. 3).

The five aforementioned and analysed marathon training books are written for novices and accomplished runners, the authors are predominately former elite runners informed by training principles for *elite* runners and sport *science* principles about the physiology of the running body (Sperlich, 2016; Zinner, 2016). These books highlight

> the body as a mechanistic hierarchical system where episodes of running or training are concerned with the continual improvement in the efficient function and form of the running body. The focus is on improving the cardiovascular system, body strength, biomechanics and fuelling of the body. The focus of the body on objectification and quantification suggests that while the sporting body can in principle be for leisure or play it is increasingly rationalised into a self-regulated work like form.
>
> *(Ettorre, 2016, p. 66)*

Coaches' adherence to detailed training plans and scientific and systematic principles resembles Taylorism, transforming workers from ineffective and habitual into effective, speedy and machine-like bodies through rational science, mechanisation and mechanical clock timing (Cresswell, 2006; Shilling, 2012). Critical sport scholars argue that this turns leisure running into work, putting a premium on repetitive drills and executing prescribed abstract exercises (Mills & Denison, 2013, 2015, Denison & Mills, 2014), and inculcates a power relation in which coaches know right from wrong training and expect docile runners to follow their drilling without thinking for themselves. This resonates with Bale's suggestion that coaches convert runners into pets (2004, pp. 89–91) and Lefebvre's claims that 'dressage is based on repetition' (2004, p. 39), whereby 'humans break themselves in [*se dressent*] like animals' (2004, p. 48).

The analysed marathon training books outline the established principles behind marathon training, physiology and training principles and sessions, and we may understand them as substitutes for coaches. Overall, they convey that unstructured marathon training is risky and ineffective, whereas they as experts know how to design effective plans that ensure peak performance on race day. Crucially, they all provide marathon training programmes tailored to novice, intermediate and experienced runners (some offer individualised training programmes for a fee). They assume that runners lack knowledge about effective training and that, apprised by exercise and medical science and past achievements, they can help runners avoid injuries and improve their personal bests. Moreover, they script marathon training as a rational and scientific endeavour for rhythmic training. Readers are, for instance, lectured that *variegated* rhythms and paces of running are essential, contrary to the common habit of darting along at the same pace or running too fast in an addiction to a 'high average speed' (which tracking technologies encourage). Higdon informs novices that they must become sensitive to *different* rhythms:

> If I had to cite one mistake made by inexperienced marathoners when they seek to improve their performance, it is that they run too many of their miles at the same pace and over the same distance. There is little variety, and that limits their improvement. ... To improve, you need to add intensity to your program. ... In order to train at a high level of intensity on certain days, most of us need to train at a low level of intensity on other days. That's where slow running comes in.
>
> *(2011, p. 67)*

Readers are also warned against the common mistake of suddenly increasing one's weekly mileage by more than 10 per cent (Higdon, 2011, p. 77; Nerurkar, 2012, p. 33). The body needs time to adapt gradually to new stresses and physiological changes in its energy and musculoskeletal systems. To use Lefebvre's terminology, the prescribed linear rhythms of training must be aligned with the runner's cyclical biological rhythms.

## Prescribed rhythms

Overall, all the marathon training programmes in the five books are organised around daily, weekly and yearly rhythms as well as variegated temporal and spatial rhythms. In terms of yearly rhythms, they recommend a maximum of two marathons as intensive training, as the event itself leaves the body extremely weary and sore: it needs a month's rest (with only light running). Most schedules include three to four months of progressively intensive training. So-called 'periodisation' is integrated into training programmes that progress slowly through weekly phases as speed, duration and distance gradually increase (often with a slight drop every third or fourth week to allow rest before the next period of intensification). For instance, Higdon's (2011, appendix) 'novices' start at 24 kilometres and peak at 64 kilometres spread over four days, while his 'advanced' programmes peak at around 90 km per week and involve six days of running. Programmes normally last between 12 and 18 weeks.[1]

Playing with the notion of a taskscape, we might understand such programmes as rhythmic taskscapes (Howe & Morris, 2009, p. 314; Ingold, 2002, p. 195) that delineate daily spatio-temporal running tasks organised around specific rhythms at different speeds and intensities. These rhythmic taskscapes involve such tasks as speed intervals, high-tempo runs, marathon pace runs, the marathon-defining long runs and moderate recovery runs.

Such repetitive tasks have specific rational purposes and presuppose the exact and ongoing timing of distance, pace, splits (and sometimes heart rate) and subsequent 'filing' in a training log. The weekly programme is periodised. 'Hard days' (involving intervals and tempo) must be followed by 'easy days' (recovery run or rest) to allow requisite rest. 'Hard, easy. Hard, easy. … Rest! That may be the single most important word you will read in this book' (Higdon, 2011, p. 29). The key is to increase the mileage (quantity) without sacrificing speed and intensity (quality) (Higdon, 2011, p. 79).

These 'sessions' are combined in different ways for novices and experienced runners. Overall, beginner programmes focus on aerobic training that is relatively light on untrained bodies and predisposing runners' circular, respiratory and musculoskeletal systems to running. Slightly more advanced programmes, such as Higdon's 'immediate program 1',[2] prescribe five days of running and one day of gym cross training. Each session in this programme is measured in distance, but only indirectly in speed. For instance, 'midweek training' should be done 'at a comparatively easy pace', with a relatively low pulse and at a conversional pace. Therefore, the disciplining dressage here involves slowing down runners' habitual pace. The intensity picks up on Saturdays, where the focus is on the anticipated marathon pace ('pace' on the training charts). A sub-four-hour aspiring runner must master a 5:39 km pace and should use this session to make this pace 'second nature' (feel natural) and learn how it feels kinaesthetically as their bodies respond to it with fresh and tired legs. The final session is the weekend *long run* where endurance and 'digging in' (Hockey & Allen-Collinson, 2015) are trained. One should run slow and not be out of breath, with the recommended pace being '30 to 90 or more seconds per mile slower than their marathon pace'[3] (the speed may only be increased at the end). These long runs start at 13 km and end with two runs of 32 km. Here, the musculoskeletal system and 'mind' must learn to attune to pounding streets for hours, appreciating or ignoring the burning sensations of fatigue and soreness in muscles and bones and keeping motivated for hours. Long runs should not exceed 33 km because greater distances are too draining.

Higdon's 'advanced training programmes'[4] designed for seasoned runners add extra intensity through speed sessions such as taxing hill repeats, speedy intervals and high-tempo runs; this form of anaerobic training is crucial for improving speed. Hill repeats involve running up a slope at almost full speed and catching one's breath on the decline. The rhythm is then repeated, starting with three repetitions in week 1 and ending with seven repetitions in week 13. Intervals involve running close to one's maximum on distances between 200 m and 2 km. Immediately after recovering one's breath, the drill is repeated. Lastly, the tempo run is described as progressive, meaning that most start with a gentle pace for 10–15 minutes before slowly building to reach one's 10 km race pace, which must be sustained for a set time before the pace drops again at the end.

This illustrates that runners are clearly instructed when and how to run (and rest) in terms of speed, distance, and repetition. The tasks are painstakingly scheduled and ready to be 'ticked off'. Thus, they instantiate a regular series of exercises that demand *divergent* rhythms. This is interesting in the context of dressage where, typically, we might think of endlessly repetitive actions that do not vary, like much military drill. Overall, varied rhythms of running are said to be needed to build up physiological and musculoskeletal strength so that a body gradually becomes conditioned to sustaining a consistent eurythmic pace over long distances as well as maintaining a stoic consciousness to 'dig in' (Hockey & Allen-Collison, 2016, p. 229) when faced with somatic sensations of pain, fatigue and geographic and climatic stressors.

However, these coaches do not expect runners' bodies to be fully docile, like soldiers. Programmes presuppose individual adaptation since runners – based upon past results or tests – need to work out a realistic pace for each 'task', and many consults online 'race predictors' that determine training splits based upon one's previous or anticipated race results at different distances. A runner with a recent run of 10 km in 45 minutes will be told to do long runs in 05:44, marathon pace sessions in 04:55, tempo runs in 04:36, and intervals in 04:14, and to expect a 03:27:12 marathon time if well prepared.[5] This illustrates how individual adoptions of generic programmes typically rest on abstract time and predictions, on future aspirations, and not only on 'what feels right' in the moment.

Runners are also instructed to detect when their bodies revolt against the drill, when a tough session must be replaced by an easy one or some rest. Hilditch empowers runners by stating that 'endurance training is not an exact science … . Only you know your body and how it is responding to training – the best advice is to listen to it' (2014, p. 11). Nerurkar writes, 'use the training schedules sensibly and be prepared to modify them according to your lifestyle' (2012, p. 21). This acknowledges a milder form of dressage compared to, for instance, the soldier's. In the absence of a coach, runners are expected to mediate the programme through their own reflexivity. However, in the same breath, this transfers blame to the runner if they are injured while following a programme. Conditioning the body becomes a self-reflexive, individualised project.

This focus on rational training and temporal rhythms also explains certain lacunae in these books. First, they do not promote sensuous sensations or aesthetic pleasures of running in different places and landscapes. This is in contrast to the literature on casual running (Edensor et al., 2018) and 'fell running' (Askwith, 2015), where sensations of running are linked to immersion in and contact with variegated surfaces, gradients and beautiful environments (Lorimer, 2012; Nettleton, 2015). While not oblivious to landscape aesthetics, marathon coaches primarily focus on places as concrete 'land' and only secondarily as aesthetic 'landscape' (Howe & Morris, 2009; MacNaughton & Urry, 2001). Parks and forests are recommended because their soft surfaces reduce the chance of injury as much as for their landscape qualities. Their concern is how specific 'surfaces and slopes' (Lorimer, 2012) affect rhythms of running and impact on the body. Nerurkar writes: 'Ideally you should do some of your running off-road, perhaps in a nearby park or along some dirt trails: your legs suffer less pounding on softer surfaces and your surroundings will make you feel more at ease' (2012, p. 20). They also teach runners to scout for spatial affordances, such as gradient topographies for 'hill sprints' and flat and undisturbed ones for fast sessions. Overall, they recommend avoiding tarmac in favour of softer surfaces (such as gravel) for slower sessions – except speed sessions – as tarmac is fast but hard on the legs. Readers also learn that different tasks and surfaces necessitate specific shoes to be effective or protective: 'I wear heavy, protective shoes on those easy days when I run slow. When I run fast, I prefer a light shoe, and I often wear racing flats for my speed workouts and a semilight pair for long runs' (Higdon, 2011, p. 135).

Second, these books do not explain how training becomes routinized and how it sits with other everyday practices, which is also true of the sport science literature (Sutton, 2016). This is striking, given that many are reluctant runners (Hitchings & Latham, 2017a) who give up on running because they fail to appreciate its pleasures or synchronise it with their wider everyday practices as discussed below.

## Enacting training rhythms

Having discussed how marathon training is scripted by experts, the next section draws on my interviews and observations within the NBRO to discuss the everyday practices of marathon training where things seldom go according to plan. I begin by discussing how my interviewees use programmes. Reflecting the diversity of marathon runners, my interviewees cover everything from 30 to 120 km, run three to six days, and spend 5–12 hours running each week. Not surprisingly, generally speaking, the fastest runners do the most kilometres. While some follow such programmes slavishly, others bend them to their own ends, while others resist being coached. I then focus on how this extensive training is performed in everyday practice.

### Following programmes

The interviews revealed that much of their training prior to a marathon was structured through programmes or indirectly through their underlying principles. Some follow a generic programme, such as those discussed above, with simple 'running tasks' adjusted to their competences and aspirations. Some personalise these programmes using race-time predictors. As Jurgen said:

> This time I used løbeprogrammet.dk. I entered my 5 km time and then it made a running programme based on it, which I then followed slavishly. I am very disciplined; if it says that I have to run 10 km, then I never run 9.9, but I sometimes run 11 km. … The running programme definitely gives me some structure, but it also gives me an understanding of how my training should be structured that I did not have before – involving both short and long trips, intervals.
>
> *(Personal communication, my translation)*

Following a programme is both structuring and motivating. The day before the marathon, several interviewees said that following a programme meant that they feel ready for the task ahead: 'Having a programme' 'means that you "check off"' your daily training and that you can stand here today with a good conscience. You just have to train, even if it's rain. Ok, if it's raining really hard, I'll wait until tomorrow' (Bente, personal communication, my translation). The latter illustrates that tasks are intermittently rescheduled when adverse circumstances arise, but not dramatically so.

## Following coaches

Others hire a coach to devise a programme tailored to their specific fitness level, often based on physiological tests, race ambitions and wider everyday life. They have regular dialogues with their coaches about their 'running data' and well-being, and their programmes are continuously adjusted. Helle, in her forties, said:

> I have chosen to have a personal trainer this time ... who I email with and who makes my new programme - based on time. So, it is adapted to my everyday life and fitness. The fact that I have been able to put it in a system has meant that I have had more time in my everyday life. It has been optimised: I train maybe less, but better.
>
> *(Personal communication, my translation)*

Runners consult coaches to make their somewhat ineffective training – in terms of time and results – more effective, as Ravn illustrates:

> In the fall, I ran a lot more structured because I got a trainer ... I was missing something. ... The programme is based on training peaks, then dialogue and follow-up with the coach... . That's the positivist, scientific approach. ... Not just 'feel' or 'just do it' but testing of my body to start with and then ongoing feed-back... .
>
> *(Personal communication, my translation)*

Kenneth also stresses his regard for a science-based approach and the discipline offered by a coach, who

> has a lot of experience and studied sport science at university. ... The cool thing is, I do not have to think about whether this is the right thing to do. I just go out and execute according to the program. Then, I report back and then we adjust from there.
>
> *(Personal communication, my translation)*

Interviewees find programmes and expert coaches highly trustworthy, motivating their daily training, and believe that they improve their race-day performance and reduce the risk of injury. They appreciate the expert's commands on how to run, as they only follow the order and perform the prescribed drills. However, they often end up running on their own, as their daily tasks are very specific and nonnegotiable. As with Taylorism, we see here a division between the runners' physical work and the coach's mental work. Such runners, feeling a lack of knowledge, almost blindly follow their coach's advice. This ties into the idea that 'dressage fills the place of the unforeseen' (Lefebvre, 2004, p. 49) and liberates the acting body from thinking (Lyon, 2018, p. 27).

## Self-made programmes

Others construct their own ad hoc programmes and track them via Excel sheets or on Garmin and Strava. Some are apathetic towards being 'other-directed' and resent the idea of following someone's programme or being told how to run, resisting such dressage. While more loosely organised and ad hoc, they generally have clear targets for weekly mileage and must-do sessions, and they can be equally ambitious. However, tasks are never fully pre-determined, and they often negotiate pace and distance with fellow runners and adjust their intensity to how their body feels on that particular day. *Not* running with an individualised fixed programme with a determined task gives them freedom to be spontaneous and social, unlike what we might call the 'programmed runner'.

They are often 'experienced', understand the basic principles of marathon training, and join clubs where recurrent training sessions are largely conducive to marathon training. For instance, the recurrent weekly NBRO schedule involves tempo runs on Mondays, intervals on Wednesdays and long runs on Saturday, with 'slower runs' on Tuesdays, Thursdays and Fridays. However, NBRO does not have a coach or follow a programme. While framed by certain habitual routes and routines, finer details about pace, duration, speed and routes are negotiated on the spot among those present. As NBRO has always opposed traditional running clubs where training is scripted by coaches and there is less space for everyday improvisation and playfulness, relatively few NBRO runners follow individual programmes that decouple them from the collective rhythms of NBRO.

## Clock rhythms: watches and data

Despite these differences, almost all my interviewees and NBRO members routinely use running watches when training to detect and record their *ongoing* movements. They do so in part because programmes and coaches work through the logic of meticulous timing and recording, but also because numbers are easy to understand and talk about. Tempo and bodily rhythms are assessed through 'numbers' as much as felt sensations. While skilled runners can roughly access their speed based on their breathing and kinaesthetic sense (Allen-Collinson, 2008), they nonetheless routinely consult their watches to 'objectively' monitor if they are slower or faster than their prescribed or planned pace. If their breathing is ragged, many will also check their heart rate figures as a second source of verification. When running in groups, runners use these data to evaluate and negotiate their shared pace. Once a session is completed, runners habitually affirm the average pace and distance by talking about how hard or easy it felt. Such lively, embodied non-representational data also has a representational after-life on Garmin and Strava as race accounts, expressed in maps, graphs, figures,

**FIGURE 6.1** The NBRO week
Photo credit: Henrik Thorn

numerous numbers and possible user-generated stories, comments and 'kudos'. Here, such data become a vital part of each runner's weekly and yearly mileage and overall adds to their cumulative running biography (chapter 5). Those who love and work with numbers often rejoice in the analysis of such data and view it as integral to the pleasures of running:

> When running a long run … I have fun and pain, fatigue, for the 1½–2 hours, but I enjoy analysing heart rate data and everything else for many hours after. I log a race story … I would not get so much pleasure out of it without this data. The joy of a run is extended.
>
> *(Scoot, personal communication, my translation)*

However, while most runners habitually analyse their recent data, they do so in minutes rather than hours. Nonetheless, my argument is that people partly run to make and communicate impressive 'numbers' – just as tourists go on holidays to produce photographs. There would probably be much less marathon running without such number-producing technologies and platforms, just as tourism would have been very different without the invention of photography (Urry & Larsen, 2011).

## Routinising and socialising running

> To run 80–90 kms and to do an hour or two in the gym means that my weekly training totals some 10 hours spread out over six days. It is a logistical challenge to

find the time as a professor with a partner and two sons. I fiddle around with my work hours, sometimes coming in late (because I had run in the morning) or leaving early because I need to run. Sometimes I run to the station and I get off the train early and run the last 9 km. Or I run during my lunch break or whenever it suits me when working from home. I now consider running as important as my work. I have never worked so little. Sometimes, my body is so knackered that other activities seem like hard work. I take for granted that I have to run every day and that domestic responsibilities and social arrangements need to be accommodated by these routines.

*(Field notes)*

I now discuss how the actual enactment of abstract programmes and marathon training depends on the development of routines and social arrangements. Programmes tell people to run (almost) daily, but seldom how to make it a habitual practice. Chapter 2 discusses the rhythmic nature of social life and how particular practices display distinctive rhythms and 'micro organizations of routine'. Highmore writes that 'we establish our own daily routines to give our lives rhythm and predictability' (2004, p. 307). Sport practices depend on the synchronisation of supporting practices and rhythms (Edensor et al., 2018). Blue argues that synchronisation essentially is about 'developing and maintaining eurhythmia' between different practices and making training a dominant 'temporal anchor' that outcompetes other practices:

I noticed a significant change in other daily practices as well. Socialising with friends outside of the gym, going out and having a drink were all off the cards, partly for abstinence reasons (hangovers and getting punched in the head don't really mix!), but partly because resting, recovering and even getting in another training session seemed to take priority. Working and studying, became practices that were 'slotted in' around the expanding temporal demands of training.

*(2017, p. 348)*

Hockey has described his daily running routines with his partner Allen-Collinson, paying particular attention to their late afternoon routine, wherein they unreflexively and habitually transform from scholars into serious runners. This was also the case with Scoot, a father who trains up to six times a week:

I do not regard it as work, but as a habit. I do not have to spend any effort at all to think about when I come home from work: … get some food, take off my clothes and put on my running clothes; I get going, no matter how awfully tired I am.

*(Personal communication, my translation)*

Hockey and this interviewee give the impression that this transition is fairly easy once routines are established. However, I suggest that it is easy for Hockey and Allen-Collinson because they (seem to) live and run together without children. They do not need to negotiate running time with a non-running partner or care for children. The above interviewee only has a childless routine during the week his children stay with their mother (they are divorced). Few people can leave their families daily for an afternoon run. Hockey does not discuss how many younger runners need to synchronise their training routines with family rhythms, how it 'requires, massive support, encouragement, permission, acceptance, cooperation, and understanding … from the spouse of the runner' (Lev & Zach, 2020, p. 513). This may partly explain why fewer women run marathons (chapter 4), for, generally speaking, they do more domestic and emotional work than men. Hockey misses the complexity, emotional stress and guilt that haunt many marathon runners with young families (Cook et al., 2016; Goodsell & Harris, 2011; Goodsell et al., 2013; Shipway & Holloway, 2016). As I noted, guilt-ridden once again:

> Just a quick jog before I need to pick up my son. His kindergarten is just opposite our flat. However, they leave for a bigger place at 8.30 and return at 15.30, but they remain open until 5 pm. Today – where I work from home – I head out five minutes before the bus is due and parents are already waiting. I'm guilt-ridden once again for choosing running and not Wilson. I try to comfort myself that he loves the 'pick-up kindergarten'. My bad conscience is aggravated when running into my running partner who is about to pick up his child. He runs significantly less now that he has become a father of two. To make things worse, the bus passes by. I fear that Wilson or a staff member will notice me and weigh up the situation: 'He prefers running to spending time with his son'. I decide to shorten the route and run faster, and jump some red lights. I arrive at the kindergarten at 16.10. There are only a handful of children left.
>
> *(Field notes)*

My interviews and fieldwork suggest that runners are aware that their running habits mean that they often 'miss out' on family time, their children spend more time in childcare, and their partners do more domestic work (at least at certain hours). They often compensate by cutting down on other activities. They are conscious that 'others' find their training routines obsessive and must deal with uncanny questions: how do you find the time to all this training and what is your family saying? 'Finding time' for the next run can cause constant conflicts and stress.

Overall, runners tend to negotiate certain set training routines with their partners on specific days where they can train with friends or clubs, but they also need to be flexible and pragmatic and run at hours least inconvenient to others, exploiting how running is a time-effective sport that often can be performed in a nearby environment (but see later). Sometimes they head out very early to be back when the family wakes up or the morning table is set or into the dark night when the children have been put to bed. As the father Kenneth said:

> I compromise a lot … I get up sometimes at 5 a.m. to be in my shoes at 5.30 a.m. I often wear running clothes when I drop off my son at school and have time to run 10–15 km. I'm really good at thinking of it as transportation in relation to my work. … Sometimes I run straight home, sometimes I make a

detour … it has become completely normal for me to remember to pack running clothes, not eating too late.

*(Personal communication, my translation)*

Several interviewees explained that their training habits upset old routines, such as reading, watching television and socialising. Marathon routines are combined and aligned with certain practices, while also ruling out engagement with practices unsuited to or too time-consuming for intense marathon training. Carsten, a young adult who trains up to 120 km weekly, said with slight melancholy:

Not much time for friends … you are extremely tired after 21 km in marathon pace and you have no energy to watch the Champions League with the boys. You fall asleep at half past nine … . Some say that running energises them, but that's not the case at such an intense level.

*(Personal communication, my translation)*

This extensive training takes much of his time and energy, leaving him too exhausted to do much else or see others. Training and resting become 'anchor points', common in the second part of a training programme.

However, as Kenneth indicated above, one way to avoid compromises and give up other practices is to use running as a form of transport (Cook et al., 2016; Edensor et al., 2018). Several run to work on occasion, when visiting family members, and while undertaking 'excursions' where the rest of the family bike or drive. Transforming passive commuting routines into active ones – walking, running, and cycling – is effective from an everyday life perspective (Larsen, 2018a).

It is evident that running suits those with flexible working hours, such as professionals in managerial positions (main marathon segment, chapter 4) or with ample home-working opportunities. While many professionals work long hours, they often have flexibility and autonomy to coordinate their *own* work and sometimes that of others; they incorporate running into their 'work hours' as extended lunch breaks or breaks between meetings, or stretch their work hours into the night and over weekends. They arrive and leave late or early based upon when they need to run. As one such interviewee said frankly:

I spend a lot of time at work, … working odd hours. It must be the exception to say no to a training session. But then I'm also working at 9 p.m. again. Sometimes I tell my employees [late in the afternoon] to have a draft ready in two hours. No one should say that to me, because 'I am out running' there.

*(Personal communication, my translation)*

Moreover, the seated, indeed sedentary nature of their work is ideal for restitution. Those with substantial temporal autonomy in their work arrangements can find pockets of time for running, whether from the doorstep of one's home or from work. Developing such routines is a privilege for the few.

## Training with others

Many say that 'running with others' or being part of a running community transforms running into something social and communicative, providing a valued social boost to an otherwise individualised sport (chapter 4; see also Shipway et al., 2013; Barnfield, 2018). Social relations motivate people to form and stick to their training routines, and novices learn new skills and the running lingo from seasoned runners. As Jannick, a NBRO runner said:

> It means a lot that you have someone to run with. It may be possible without one, but then you really have to kick yourself in the ass. It's easier to get out the door when it's windy and cold and you're tired when someone is waiting for you. You are responsible to someone. In NBRO, running is very much a team sport.
>
> *(Personal communication, my translation)*

Running with others also reduces feelings of discomfort and unsafety when running in potentially dodgy or dark places (Allen-Collinson, 2008; Gimlin, 2010). A key to becoming a dedicated marathon practitioner is to run with others and form affective and supportive bonds. To cite Vera,

> I would not have run so fast if it wasn't for all the cool women ... who showed that it was possible. ... And I would not have thrown myself into [a marathon] without that community and knowing other women who said, 'you can easily do that, you must try'.
>
> *(Personal communication, my translation)*

People desire to learn from and share their passion with runners with more know-how and 'faster legs'. For instance, learning in NBRO is very experience-based, with runners imitating each other and sharing good and bad experiences. One member said: 'Those that you train with spur you forward. If I had trained on my own, I would never have run sub-three-hours. I would lack the inclination to train that much' (Ravn, personal communication, my translation). However, coaches warn that training with 'others' is potentially dangerous: 'But beware: a companion danger is that you may train too hard, resulting in staleness ... or injury' (Higdon, 2011, p. 116). One must keep an eye on the watch when training with others; a common observation amongst NBRO runners is that they end up running faster than the agreed pace as well as their own habitual pace.

However, NBRO members also run together because they appreciate the companionship and form friendships, and these 'liquid tribes' (Maffesoli, 1995) partly satisfy the need to socialise and 'hang out' with friends at other times. Their social life and running life are tightly 'bundled', in part because they spend so much time together and in part because running – like few other sports – is perfect for talking, and runners 'kill time' by talking together (or listen to podcasts or music when running alone).

To sum up, developing extensive marathon training routines comes with a price, and one's family members may 'suffer' from it. Marathon runners constantly justify their excessive training routines to themselves and others, and if they fail, they may stop. In chapter 4, Karl was quoted as having absconded from running because he had had enough of slavishly following a time-consuming programme that left him an 'absent father':

> Followed a program … . Average of 80 km per week. … It was time consuming. Spent a lot of time planning the trips, how I should execute all those kilometres in relation to work and my family life. … In the end, it was probably a big planning burden … it was stressful to fit in and remember to bring the running clothes to these different places, to achieve those kilometres.
>
> *(Personal communication, my translation)*

Today, he does not miss the daily training grind. I ask him if others were negatively affected by it at the time. He pauses and then states,

> A little. Got a nanny to look after my son when I was running. It seemed damn weird. This is where it became clear that the time I spent running, I could have been at home and together with my son.
>
> *(Personal communication, my translation)*

Having discussed how marathon running is routinised and socially organised within a wider network of practices and social relations, I now consider how such routinized marathon practices are emplaced within seasonal weather worlds and localised places.

## Seasonality and weathering training

The last chapter discussed how seasonal marathons are scheduled to ensure good weather. However, training takes place in all types of weather and seasons (unlike, for instance, winter sports such as skiing) (Atkinson & Drust, 2005) and practitioners are uniquely thrown into the visceral realities of seasonal weather worlds. Seasonal weather shapes local training grounds, as well as moods and motivations (Ingold, 2010, p. 131). Humans perceive weather as part of their 'dwelling in world' through ongoing sensory weather work and interpretation (Allen-Collinson et al., 2019; Barry et al., 2021). As Vannini et al. noted, 'To weather is an active, reflexive, practical disposition to endure, sense, struggle, manipulate, mature, change, and grow in processes that, over time, implicate the place-making of one's dwelling' (2012, p. 362). Weather work is thus a competence acquired through specific practice.

Seasoned runners are not discouraged by poor weather (as casual runners are; Atkinson & Drust, 2005), but adapt to and 'dress for it'. They normally run in all types of weather and are skilled at weather work, assessing how snow and rain affect surfaces and high and low temperatures affect one's thermoception (Allen-Collinson, 2018; Allen-Collinson et al., 2019; Hockey & Allen-Collinson, 2017, 2019):

For runners too, we are intertwined with, and immersed in this weather-world, and often highly 'attuned' to atmospheres, including air quality … . Hence, part of the socialisation into both the cultural and physiological practices of this athletic endeavour consists of experiencing the ways in which varying temperatures and climatic conditions impact upon the running body, and understanding one's own strengths and weaknesses in relation to these impacts. Given the physically demanding nature of the sport, in hot weather a rise in body temperature occurs relatively quickly, and thermoception is a sense to which runners need to attend, and become well attuned.

(Hockey & Allen-Collinson, 2017, p. 52)

Seasoned marathon runners know how their bodies respond to different weather conditions, and routes are contingent on weather conditions and seasonal changes. Those who routinely run the same routes will notice how seasonal changes alter surfaces, visibilities, temperatures, flows of people, vegetation and non-human life. The feel and sound differ across distinctive times of the year (Edensor et al., 2018).

If not running in 'adverse' weather, one's body will never become marathon-ready. Those well-prepared for a spring marathon have endured testing and troublesome cold runs with ice-cold fingers on muddy autumn trails, low visibility on pitch-dark routes, and snowy and icy streets and paths that make running – especially intervals and tempo runs – unpleasant, difficult and dangerous. There are also temporal rhythms to the attunement to the weather-world. During dark winter months, runners often run late in the morning and early afternoons to avoid pitch-dark routes and eventually learn to run with small strides when it is icy and to 'see through darkness' (Cook & Edensor, 2017). Accordingly, sweltering summer days bother those preparing for an autumn marathon. Speedwork or a 'long run' in the midst of a midday heat wave is a recipe for disaster; the only alternative is a gentle run. They need to dress very lightly in sweat-absorbing fabrics and run early in the morning or late in the evening, adjusting their intensity to the hot temperatures. All this reflects the fact that 'good running weather' is contingent on the specific 'taskscape' that awaits the runner on that particular day (Larsen & Jensen, 2021).

## Local training grounds

Similar to the weather, I now analyse how specific places also condition moods and motivations, and runners become skilled at determining how different environments afford specific running experiences and 'designing' routes for specific running tasks. While the jogging movement pleaded that running can take place everywhere, places matter to running (Cook et al., 2016; Edensor et al., 2018; Qviström, 2017). This is especially true for serious marathon training.

Runners first become competent in assessing material affordances as part of their habitual training, often building up 'extensive and detailed knowledge of their training route' (Hockey and Allen-Collinson, 2006, pp. 195). While running is an embodied practice, it does not exist in a vacuum; it is always an interaction between the body (mediated by objects) and the environment on the ground and in the air (chapter 2). As Esmonde writes,

> The locales in which jogging takes place are inseparable from the act itself. It is the feeling of looking up at a hill before ascending; the precarious sensation of uneven terrain on a running trail; the repetition of running around a track. Whether on a treadmill in the gym, on a remote trail, through the local neighbourhood, or while exploring a new place, the entanglement of bodies and their environments is inescapably apparent in the act of running.
>
> *(2019, p. 804)*

Studies show that runners experience places in multi-sensuous ways, in part because the weather always condition how places feel that particular days. Some have highlighted the crucial role of seeing and hearing the proximate environment (Allen-Collinson, 2008; Allen-Collinson & Hockey, 2011). This includes accessing the well-being of fellow runners and, not least, diligently and actively scanning pavements, streets and crossings for information about potential imminent human and non-human obstacles and dangerous situations (cyclists, walkers, cars, dogs, icy streets, uneven pavements, puddles, drunk or suspicious people, and many more). Based on this visual and aural information, runners – sometimes in an instant – change pace or direction, or come to a complete stop, negotiate encounters with others, and prevent accidents and injuries (Cook et al., 2016; Hockey & Collinson, 2006).

Research has also found that the somatic sensations of ground surfaces constitute an important dimension of running and that the weather always conditions how surfaces feel that particular day (Brown, 2017; Edensor et al., 2018; Howe & Morris, 2009; Lorimer, 2012). Such accounts are inspired by Ingold (2004), who highlighted 'grounded perception' and the significance of sensing places haptically with the feet, mediated by footwear (see chapter 5). Moreover, Ingold (2004, p. 331) argues that perception is a function of movement (flying, driving, biking or walking) within different landscapes. In fact, running produces not one but different landscapes according to *how* people run; for instance, long runs and tempo runs yield very different landscapes (Cook et al., 2016). As routes with particular material and topographical affordances as well as mobility rhythms are chosen for specific training sessions, 'with these practical concerns in mind, runners become highly attuned and attentive to the nature of terrain and its possibilities for enhancing their performance' (Hockey & Allen-Collinson, 2006, p. 77). Places are sometimes valued for gravel paths that are 'soft on the legs', steep gradients for hill sprints, flat streets with smooth tarmac, no stop lights and few pedestrians for intervals, or attractive scenery for long runs. They are also treasured if they have good lightning, few traffic lights, little traffic and easy crossings to maximise visibility and flow, and also if they have public water stations, toilets and kiosks to cater to bodily needs.

Such sensuous local knowledge and competencies are particularly important for urban runners. In cities, runners belong to pavements and paths, but they are seldom ideal, dominated by and designed for others; runners' largely rational rhythms are 'out of sync' with the slower, staccato-like, stop-and-go, irregular rhythms of walkers (Cook et al., 2016; Edensor, 2010), window shoppers, tourists, outdoor café guests, groups of chattering teenagers, hand–in–hand couples, and families with dogs on a long leash, much as cyclists are the inferiors on car–dominated streets and need to improvise rhythms (Jones, 2012; Spinney, 2010, p. 114). Running thus intermingles and (de)synchronises with various other rhythms. Busy pavements do seldom afford a eurythmic run but demand a constant adjustment of one's pace to avoid near collisions and impacts with commercial signs, parked bikes, e–scooters, and those walking in pairs and groups or engaging in the numerous 'stationary activities' that now occupy many pavements. Pavements are designed for walkability (Forsyth, 2015) but not for hurried running (Ettema, 2015). Runners belong on pavements but seldom feel completely at home or ease there.

Runners, therefore, often break the law by intermittently running on the bike path or on the street (very common in NBRO). Moreover, physical, sweaty and huffing and puffing runners are 'out of place', dirty and contaminating, 'in a western culture obsessed with distancing from embodied reality' (P. Jones, 2017, p. 309). In particular, during COVID-19, runners' breath was conceived as potentially contaminating (Jensen, 2021). Many runners prefer instead urban parks or other green areas with gravel paths, but here they are 'out of sync' with the dominant rhythms of leisurely walking, easily 'devolving into arrhythmia' and 'undesirable disruptive rhythms' (Edensor et al., 2018, p. 105). This was the reason that running (but not walking) was temporarily banned in my local park during the COVID-19 lock-down.

The above has problematised the misconceived assumption that 'one of the advantages of running … is the ubiquity of its availability' as it can be 'done … anywhere and at any time' (Cidell, 2014, p. 577). Effective or pleasurable running cannot occur everywhere in cities. In some cities, it is almost impossible to find a place and time for running, as I experienced in Tokyo:

> I finish the last interview of the day and I ache for a gentle 6 km run back to my flat. I'm used to running more or less everywhere in Copenhagen… I was about to learn that this is not the case in Tokyo (and many other cities), where crammed pavements dominated by rhythms of walking make it virtually impossible and indeed 'transgressive' to run. I soon give up and jump on the tube. Later in the evening, when googling 'running in Tokyo', I learn that running is an early-morning activity and that it takes place in parks, along canals and, not least, around a 5 km loop around the Imperial Palace, not on pavements … . The day after the marathon I run the Imperial Palace loop. While it affords a nice unhindered running flow and the panorama is riveting, I commiserate with the local runners who must be really bored with endlessly circling around in this restricted loop to the sound of speeding cars.
>
> *(Larsen, 2021, p. 134)*

In many major cities, it can be difficult and dangerous to run on the pavement, forcing runners to run very early in the morning or in the late evening when visibility is low and fewer protecting eyes are out – or to stick to a few running-friendly environments again and again.

Even in Copenhagen it can at times be a little difficult to find safe and convenient running places, especially during peak hours and when it gets dark. Practitioners need practical knowledge about what places at particular hours are appropriate for specific running tasks. Drawing on my own and NBRO training routines in Copenhagen, I now give three accounts of how specific running sessions are social, 'emplaced' within and producing particular seasonal training grounds. They analytically highlight some of the unique ways that runners simultaneously sense somatic sensations and rhythms within their moving bodies and the streets, paths and seasonal weather worlds they habitually move through, track, and visualise. Through such habitual practices, I argue that they lay the seeds and breeding grounds for routes to become significant collective training grounds that attract many runners and become well-trodden, beaten tracks. Embodied running and digital tracking produce training grounds, some volatile, others long-lasting.

## Mondays

A habit I have adopted recently is to combine hill repeats and fartlek every Monday afternoon in a beautiful and undulating local park called Søndermarken. 'Fartlek' is a looser type of speedwork than intervals originating in the Swedish woods that involves speeding up and down at will in harmony with the landscape (for instance, racing between five lampposts, ten trees, or from one bench to another; Bale, 2004; Mills & Denison, 2015). The park is only 1.5 km from my flat, and the zig-zag run on the busy, narrow pavement is only effective as a gentle warm-up before the hard work begins.

I have been running in this park for several years. The 2.5 km circuit is a treat for one's legs, eyes and mind, with its soft gravel, landscape beauty and tranquillity. However, I had fallen out of the habit of running here, as the swelling nature of the circuit troubled my injury-plagued knees. Now that my knees are fine, I recently returned to it to integrate hill sprints and fartlek into my training habits, thereby changing the landscape. Now, it is 'land', a 'taskscape', not a landscape where my mind was wandering.

I have specifically chosen the steepest and flattest parts of this circuit. I sprint at a maximum speed 300 m to the top, focusing exclusively on running smoothly, pushing forward and reaching the top. My vision is reduced to avoiding collisions with others. My head is empty. At the top, I almost collapse, bend forward, desperately gasping for air. I catch my breath and jog slowly, a few hundred metres into the only flat part of the park – a spacious grass lawn surrounded by a 300-metre circular path. When turning the first corner, I accelerate to almost full speed and keep that pace for the next 300 m. It feels like my lungs are being ripped out. However, the speed is thrilling. I descend at a leisurely pace along a meandering route. Now at this time, the visual splendour always gets me, but not for long. Ahead is the hill. The drill is repeated six times. The taxing hills and speed will leave my legs sore tomorrow.

**FIGURE 6.2** The Søndermarken hill

## Wednesday intervals

It is Wednesday evening at 17.30, so NBRO meets for its weekly interval training at the tracks at Østerbro Stadium. People wear light clothes and racing shoes. This rationalised form of speed work is best performed on a 400-metre athletic track that Bale (2004) described as a 'machine for running' – and denounced for being sterile and anaesthetic. We disagree. Nothing beats the fast, generic, measured environment of tracks for practising intervals where time, speed and flow are everything. There is always an electric atmosphere when we perform intervals in this beautiful stadium. This is a key session, with people relying on each other to complete the callous intervals; successful execution requires not only a fitting material environment but also a social one. The thought of doing solitary intervals is disconcerting, collective intervals exhilarating and empowering.

The training always commences with a high-profile member outlining the 'track rules' and then asking the 30–60 runners to propose specific training sessions that others can join:

> Yes, Frank. 'I'm doing 6 × 1 km in 3.35ish with active jogging for a minute in between. Feel free to join in.' Yes, Peter, what are you doing? '12 × 400 m, full out in 3.15.' … Any slower sessions? 'Yes, I'm doing 5 × 1000 in 4.00 pace' … . Let's get started and remember the track rules.
>
> *(Field notes)*

Regulars know the lingo and who to run with, but bewildered 'rookies' busily scan the crowd for runners of similar ability in the few minutes before groups are off. The front person is in charge of keeping the announced pace *throughout* the session and is often told off for going too fast, too slow or arrhythmically. At stake here is a 'relational sociality' where runners 'are continually responsive to the movements of others' (Ingold, 2011, p. 43). Watches are consulted incessantly and checked against our bodies and the breathing of co-runners. We appreciate the smooth, protective and super-fast synthetic surface and the unobstructed movement, where running for once is the master rhythm. No one is troubled about this dressage: that they are constrained within a circle, *must* run in a straight narrow line on the inner track and anti-clockwise (according to the 'track rules'). People count 'rounds', track pace and aim to run effectively, relishing that running with others makes them stronger and a part of a collective organism. At the completion of each repetition, there is high-fiving applause, exchanges about pace and flow, and sup-port shouted to groups whizzing by. After a minute or so, when our pulses have abated, the groups repeat the same (or slightly different) session on the inner track 5–10 times. At the end, we jog home and catch up on all the talk our arduous session precluded.

The COVID-19 lock-down forced us to establish new interval routines. The sta-dium was closed and we were not allowed to meet under the auspices of the NBRO. Smaller informal groups of friends met to devise a track-like environment. A nearby park (Fælledparken) was an obvious candidate, super flat and fairly free on a Wed-nesday evening. I was vocally in favour of the gravel 'parkrun' 5 km circuit, but my running peers desired faster ground under their feet, so we began looping *around* the park on streets and bike lanes, hardly ever sticking to the narrow pavement. NBRO members invented, named, measured and tracked various 'loops' *around* the park and painted small kilometre marks on the asphalt. This mundane, insignificant roadscape became a training ground where week in and week out members did countless intervals and tempo runs. With time, we felt at home here despite its few obvious attractive features. My argument is that this odd place-less route became a significant training ground for us – a place of records, memories, friendships and races.

## Saturday long run

Saturday long runs at 10 a.m. have been a set custom in NBRO for the last decade. The classic route is the 21 km 'Mosen' ('the bog'), which involves running back

**FIGURE 6.3** 'The loop'

and forth to Utterslev Mose from Nørrebro and doing a full round around the bog. NBRO originally desired a long run out of the asphalt world into green spaces with nice gravel paths. The 9 km circular route around the bog fit this purpose.

NBRO's approach to running 'Mosen' is habitual despite a constant turnover of members and includes time-honoured rhythms of jogging, resting, speeding, photographing and socialising. This knowledge is passed on in action (similar to Wacquant's study of boxing). Seldom do we talk about this route and why we run it, we just do it, as we did last week and the week before that. This route works because we know it and how to run it so well. Despite this highly choreographed and repetitive nature, though, each run has unique moments. Mosen is always in process, always becoming something else, especially in relation to changing seasons and weather conditions, scenery and non-human life. Moreover, the social composition of people running together is never the same. Finally, how hard people run it depends on whether a marathon is on the near horizon.

Running with others is particularly appreciated on long weekend runs. Many dread solitary long runs with nothing but the scenery, or perhaps podcasts and music as distractions. Before 'heading off', at the usual meeting point there is a prompt organisation into loosely organised pace groups. Then comes the warm-up transport on the tarmac to Mosen, where the pace is conversational. As we enter Mosen, one immediately notices the softer tactile sensations of gravel underfoot and the absence of cars. The first collective stop is the first water post, where people wait for others, sip water, urinate and take the obligatory team photo to upload to Facebook and Instagram.

Next on the programme is marathon- or half-marathon-specific speedwork until the next water post 4.5 km ahead. We group into smaller pace groups, and as the speed picks up, ragged breathing eventually replaces bantering and we become comparatively oblivious to the visual sensations around us. Groups often end up running slightly faster than agreed, egging each other forward in friendly competition. People then normally head home at a moderate pace, paying little attention to their watches. We now enjoy the scenery and chat non-stop – about running, football, politics and our families – to disassociate from the relative monotony of running long distances at a moderate pace, which, however, is ideal for talking. Long runs afford a unique space for talking with 'others', and participation in Mosen long runs makes little sense without contributing to the conversational landscape. Moreover, 'casual chatting' distracts our minds from the burning in our heavy legs near the end and prevent our returning to the faster rhythms. Now bonds are formed as rhythms slow down.

## Conclusion

This chapter has established the rhythmic nature of marathon training. It began by teasing out how these rhythms are scripted as 'mechanical' and regulated by programmes and coaches. Based on long-established rational principles of industrial time and sport science, programmes and coaches authoritatively outline (almost) daily training drills (structured in weekly plans) with variegated rhythms – of pace, distance and intensity – of running.

I have shown how many runners follow training programmes or structure their individual training more or less in accordance with established principles of 'achievement running'. While this might be seen as a form of dressage that programmes prescribed tasks with rationalised, linear rhythms, practitioners do not seem to feel particularly alienated or estranged. Here the linear rhythm and instrumentalism become part of the attraction itself. However, as noted, many runners do not follow them unreflexively or to the letter; they bend them to their own aspirations and other everyday practices. Accordingly, I discussed how extensive marathon training must be synchronised with other everyday practices, but also how they sometimes clash with and prevent other routines and obligations. The latter is a cause of conflict within families and one reason that people stop running marathons.

Lastly, I have analysed how 'training geographies' differ from race-day geographies. Race geographies are designed and valued for steady pacing, fast tarmac, 'perfect weather', unhindered flows and thick atmospheres (see chapters 5, 7 and 8). The places of training are more complex, variegated and contingent, as they must afford a variety of tasks and rhythms. Except for stadium tracks, they are not designed for runners, so runners need to rework their affordances. The geographies of training involve different topographies and surfaces, green spaces and roads, slow and fast running, short and long distances, solitary runs and long conversational runs, early and late runs, and boiling hot and freezing cold runs. I have stressed that while eurhythmic training is difficult in cities, runners are skilled at reimagining and redesigning streets and paths as significant and meaningful training grounds. Nonetheless, it is the relatively impoverished conditions for everyday running that make the experience of running marathons so extraordinary, as discussed in the next chapters.

## Notes

1   www.halhigdon.com/training/marathon-training/
2   www.halhigdon.com/training-programs/marathon-training/intermediate-1-marathon/
3   www.halhigdon.com/training-programs/marathon-training/intermediate-1-marathon/
4   www.halhigdon.com/training-programs/marathon-training/advanced-1-marathon/
5   http://loebesiden.dk/beregninger/

# 7

# DRAMATIC RACE RHYTHMS

## Introduction

Movement of any kind is 'the spatialization of time and temporalization of space' (Cresswell, 2006, p. 4) while Urry (2000, p. 105) argues that 'mobilities are all about temporality' and are organised through clock time. Nowhere is the significance of time greater than in achievement running, where marathons are about designing *fast* courses and running a fixed distance in as *little* time as possible to set new *time* records (chapter 4). This chapter describes how specific *pacing* rhythms are required to achieve this temporal goal in marathon running. Pace emphasises the somewhat under-explored temporal dimensions of mobility. More broadly as Salazar and Amit reflect, pace highlights connections between moving bodies, spaces and timing (chapter 4):

> how we move is always also a matter of tempo, duration, intensity and timing. … Yet scholarly efforts to work through the temporal dimensions of mobility have often tended to take a back seat to the denotation and mapping of spatial trajectories.
>
> *(2020, p. 2)*

Accordingly, I discuss how race rhythms revolve around labouring an even pace (conditioned through repetitive drilling, as argued in the previous chapter), adopting a tunnel vision that reads spaces for relevant information and treats routes as courses. This chapter focuses on racing ('achievement running') as a temporal sport practice organised around rhythms of pacing and routes as *courses* (in contrast, the next chapter focuses on marathons as atmospheric *places* and on 'experience running', chapters 4-5).

It does so by attending to the dramas, pains and pleasures of attempting to beat one's personal best. Despite the extensive organisation and training conditioning courses and runners, I argue that marathons are dramatical, as hopeful runners often

DOI: 10.4324/9781003125068-7

run into problems (arrhythmia), typically during different stages of the race, ending up bitterly disappointed. As marathon lore holds that a marathon begins at 30 km, the work that awaits is partly beyond preparation. Moreover, the 'stoicism of consciousness' developed through training 'is never total or complete', for 'vulnerability is always liable to emerge, as one inevitably has "bad days" in … racing' (Hockey & Allen-Collinson, 2016, p. 229). There is no assurance that marathon training will pay off. 'Long runs' seldom exceed 30–32 km, are run on a moderate pace and include numerous stops, while marathon race-pace sessions are typically short, with breaks in between (chapter 6). In a marathon it is time to run 42.195 km in one continuous stretch and at a highly consistent pace away from one's usual safe training grounds and habitual training routines, perhaps abroad. Lastly, the weather is a major unknown factor (chapter 5; Hockey & Allen-Collinson, 2007, pp. 126–127) and bad or unanticipated weather can affect one's moods, cause stress and lead to arrhythmic rhythms. Moreover, the individual stakes are extremely high. Much pain will be involved, and one's face or character is on the line. Can one handle the pain? Live up to the dreams, expectations, and predictions? 'Race fever' is building.

This chapter is descriptive, suggestive and analytical. It aims at an evocative, fleshy, and lively rhythmanalysis of marathon running as embodied rhythmic practice and marathon routes as mobile rhythmic *courses*. This chapter in particular enlivens rhythmanalysis and the rhythm analyst by connecting them with non-representational theory, carnal sociology and (auto)ethnography's focus on 'lived bodies in actions', flesh and blood, and lively, expressive forms of writing about and from the sensuous body (see chapter 3 for a detailed account of this method).

The chapter is divided into five evocative and lively vignettes, each discussing and providing a 'live commentary' from particular stretches.[1] They stress the shifting metabolic, thermoregulatory and physiological demands on runners and how they affect, disturb and reshuffle the paces and rhythms of running. I attend to runners' embodied rhythms and 'mechanical' clock rhythms at various stages, taking physical, physiological and 'tracked' sensations of running seriously. However, I start with a more conventional discussion of how experts script marathon pacing and then analyse the pacing strategies of my interviewees. Runners are taught not only how to train (chapter 6) but also how to race.

## Pacing

### Even pace and negative split

As detailed in the previous chapter, marathon training combines slow cyclical running with bursts of speed and stop-and-start rhythm (intervals and fartlek), so the energy flow of marathon training is intentionally polyrhythmic. This is not so on race day, where a regular, linear, almost mechanical rhythm is recommended. Programmes and coaches strongly advise runners to discipline themselves to run an evenly paced race, that is, maintain the same *pace* (tempo) throughout the race. *Repetition and punctuality* are the key factors. The km splits should be identical *throughout* the race. Accordingly, for a sub-three-hour finish, one should keep a consistent '4:15 pace' (14.5 kph). This requires perfect harmony between the mechanical timing of the watch and a body that knows and feels at relative ease at this pace and is willing to be disciplined by the watch and its constant stream of data. Such runners are first and foremost running in recorded time. Alternatively, one can 'join' a suitable 'pacing balloon' and not worry about keeping an eye on the watch. Marathons offer popular 'pacing teams' led by experienced pacers – with visible signs or balloons with printed finish times – who have mastered the art of delivering a constant pace and guaranteed finish time (for instance, 2.59 or 3.59).

Some coaches' advice is to run in a 'negative split', which means running the second part slighter faster than the first. Nerurkar writes:

> Today's perceived wisdom about how best to run a marathon is to save your biggest effort for the end of the race. Run conservatively for the first half; treat the 20-mile point as 'halfway' in terms of effort; and race over the last six miles. If you follow this approach, you will have a better chance of maintaining an even pace for the entire 26-mile distance.
>
> *(2012, p. 163)*

Yet marathon racing ought to be evenly paced and eurhythmic. Sport science studies show that pacing strategy largely determines marathon performance, and 'maintaining a consistent marathon pace has been shown to be an effective race strategy to maximize performance' (March et al., 2011, p. 387; Renfree & Gibson, 2013).

An even or moderately negative pacing strategy has proved to be most 'economical'. It distributes runners' energy throughout the race and diminishes the risk of premature fatigue from muscle glycogen depletion, which may lead to hypoglycemia (low sugar levels) and hyperthermia (overheating) and a dramatic drop in pace in the final stages (March et al., 2011; Skorski & Abbiss, 2017; St Clair Gibson et al., 2006). This is associated with 'hitting the wall', which not only slows runners down but is also a highly painful and distressing sensation (Buman et al., 2008a, b, 2009; Zepp, 2016, p. 86). Moreover, such concomitant emotions cause increased heart rate and sweating, and may negatively impact one's running rhythm (Zepp, 2016, p. 88).

However, executing a negative split or maintaining a steady pace is notoriously difficult. It requires much discipline, experience, and peak fitness; it is difficult at the beginning of the race, when bodies are busting with energy, and at the end, when they are low in vigour. While studies show that many elite runners sustain a steady pace or negative split and seldom 'hit the wall' (Buman et al., 2008b; Morgan & Pollock, 1977; but see Santos-Lozano et al., 2014 for a different view), this chapter demonstrates that few ordinary runners are that skilled and fortunate. Indeed, we will see that many run directly into the infamous, malicious marathon wall and experience the drama of arrhythmia torture. The next section discusses the prevalence of this fear when people describe their race strategies.

## Race strategy

Almost all interviewees had a race strategy in terms of pace, including what to wear and how to hydrate. Being accustomed to training with watches, almost all run with GPS watches and some use heart rate monitors, believing that they will run too slow or fast without them, reflecting that time is invisible to the senses and can only be known through a watch: 'I'm a slave of the watch. ... I'm not good at sensing if I'm running too slow or fast ... I tend to run too fast compared to what I was supposed to run. So I'd rather look at the watch (Bente, personal communication, my translation). For all runners, whether chasing a new personal best or running for the experience, restricting oneself and adhering to one's specific pace is considered crucial. They are wary of starting too fast and running arrhythmically. As Torben said, 'I need to complete the race – that's the goal ... and running all the way, not being down and walking. ... I usually go pretty cold at 30 km. This year, I will do a different strategy and have learned to eat gels' (personal communication, my translation).

Many stressed the importance of simultaneously tracking their speed and heartbeat, and slowing down if it feels too fast.

> My mileage should be five minutes on average. Smooth and constant. I'm running with a watch. I follow the clock, but I will definitely slow down if my pulse feels too high. I know that you should not increase your heart rate too much before reaching 36 kilometres.
>
> *(Jurgen, personal communication, my translation)*

Reflecting on the nature of their marathon training (chapter 6), many are confident that they know their race pace. Claire planned for a negative split this year:

> During the first three miles, I warm up. In the first half, I go at the slower end of my pace. In the second half, I will start running at the faster end of my pace. ... I will hold back in the beginning, trying to create a negative split. It is less painful – hard-learned experience.
>
> *(Personal communication)*

Despite the prevalent advice to adopt an even pace or negative split, few of my interviewees were confident that they could do so in practice. They know what pace to start in and are convinced that they can sustain it for the first 30 kms, but they are unsure what will happen beyond that. In fact, against expert advice, many employ a 'positive split' strategy. They hope that by having 'minutes in the bank' when they run into that unpredictable territory beyond 30 km, they can afford to lose some minutes at the end and still triumph. My interviewees know that once the marathon commences, all preparations and game plans can be disrupted by unexpected events and by a body that is not performing well on the day. They cross their fingers, hoping that in the end they can sustain their pace, or at least not slow down too much, or that they have 'saved up' enough during the first 30 km.

While many of my interviewees run alone, others synchronise their pace and form groups with their training peers. They agree on a specific pace, start off together, and stick together as long as possible. For example, I interviewed two very fast runners, Klaus and Vincent, who had trained so much together that their running rhythms were synchronised. Their race blueprint is 3:45–46 pace. However, they are unsure what will happen once they reach the closing stages. They explained:

> The plan is laid, but whether it lasts is another issue. Between 3:45–46 for each kilometre. As long as it lasts. Then there is an open agreement that if someone falls behind or runs off, that's ok. However, preferably not before 30 kilometres. The strongest may well let go of the other at some point. ... If you have lost all energy or went cold, you do not wish to hold the other one back.
>
> *(Personal communication, my translation)*

While setting off and planning to run together, they are first and foremost running their own race; they will not slow if one of them struggles with the agreed pace or increase it after 30 km to pursue a negative split.

Groups are sometimes paced by faster runners who might carry gels and collect water and energy drinks at the nutrition stations. This is, for instance, the case within the NBRO where faster runners are expected to pace slower runners (some of the way) if they are not fully fit to run their own race. Jannick explained:

> In NBRO, running is very much a team sport. While you run for and with yourself, we have the motto 'if you don't race you pace or cheer', so if you are not cheering or attempting a personal record, you pace for those that aim for a personal record.

Jannick elaborates on the responsibility and pride of pacing NBRO friends:

> I think it's just as cool to pace as to race. Maybe even cooler. I'm more satisfied if I help someone to reach their goal. I'm also more nervous when I have to pace for others than when I have to run for myself. Then you are responsible for someone getting the time they need. If you mess up, they may burn out if you keep the pace too high. It's your responsibility.
>
> *(Personal communication, my translation)*

This is one example of how social capital within NBRO produces mutual obligations and 'coordinated actions' (Putnam, 1993, p. 137) amongst runners that might not know each other well prior to the event.

In summary, while marathon training is highly rational – an even pace is recommended and runners form pacing groups as a result – no one really knows how one's body will react to the gruelling work that awaits it. Below, I describe marathons to evoke how they are in fact a drama of rhythms with many rhythmic phases that evolve in the last weeks leading up to the race and as the race progresses, some eurhythmic, others arrhythmic, some repetitive, some irregular.

## The 'nervous' final preparation

Three weeks before the marathon, preparation devolves into the less intense training rhythms of so-called tapering to ensure fresh legs on race day. Runners are now running much less while tensions are building up. Runners fear that their prime form will be ruined by poor weather or sudden illness, or that those nagging injuries will intensify or cease to go away. Many debates with themselves about whether a current injury, or a past injury that upset their training, will impede their planned personal record attempt or their ability to participate. It is heartbreaking and almost impossible to admit to an injury, especially if one is otherwise in top form, the plane and the hotel are booked, or one has finally secured a 'starting bib' in the lottery for a notoriously oversubscribed marathon. They hope for a miracle. Self-doubt and 'running fever' bedevil most of my interviewees around this time, especially those aiming for, and having announced to others, an impressive time. They consult their Strava profile to find comfort and motivation in the tracked numbers. As Anton confessed:

> I always have a hard time during tapering. A lot of questions arise: Have you done enough? Have you done enough kilometres and fast enough? Will your body recover and be fresh? ... But looking at my diaries, I could see that I had trained better and more than ever before. I was a kilo lighter than last year at the Frankfurt Marathon and I had bought the new Nike shoes, and this is a faster route ... My resting heart rate had been very low lately.
>
> *(Personal communication, my translation)*

### Arrival: travel fever

Almost all my interviewees arrived a couple of days before running a marathon abroad in order to relax and because it is more convenient, to  collect their start numbers quietly and not worry about work and family. While some do light sightseeing, they mainly arrive early to secure requisite rest. This is how Jannick replied when I asked if one could arrive on Saturday afternoon for a Sunday race:

> You cannot do that if you have to run a marathon. One must have respect for the distance. You need to have at least one full day where you can eat and relax. Nap. Go to bed early. Everything else I think is disrespectful to the distance. It is something special. Different people have different rituals. As far as possible, I try

to spend the day using my legs as little as possible. Just sitting with my legs up a lot, eating a lot.

*(Personal communication, my translation)*

The last few days before the marathon involve individual preparatory rhythms of travelling, collecting one's start number, goodie bag and timing chip at the Expo, obtaining requisite food (so-called carbo-loading of carbohydrate-rich foods like pasta to maximise the storage of glycogen in the muscles and liver), hydrating and relaxing (Koehler, 2016). Runners are now wary of obtaining enough sleep and expending undue energy, although some do a gentle 'shake-out' run to keep the legs alive and calm the nerves. However, this preparation may go awry. A few out-of-town interviewees explained that too much socialising with friends, sightseeing or not sticking to their usual diet may impair their performance.

There is now an endless discussion about the final pacing strategy and predicted finish times, weather forecasts and how the forecasted brisk wind or heat might affect performance. People think about their race strategy, and they confirm with their running peers of exactly similar ability and ambition that they will run together at the agreed pace or discuss whether they should make minor last-minute adjustments. Runners always fear what the weather will be like this particular year, especially in fall and spring marathons. Moreover, although marathons take place the same time each year, weather is volatile and can differ dramatically from one year to the next. As Emery (2020) writes:

Fall and spring marathons are unpredictable, wondrous, and magnificent monsters. Chances of good or bad weather conditions are 50/50. Autumn races, like the New York City Marathon, are notoriously fickle: Will race day have the kind of weather you've been training in – hot? temperate? – or will early winter blindside you with frigid temps and biting wind?

For instance, the temperatures of the Boston Marathon have swung between 5.1°C and 25.2°C from one year to the next, while runners at the Chicago Marathon were freezing one year (1.7°C) and sweltering another year (25°C) (Larsen & Jensen, 2021, p. 73).

As discussed in previous chapters, runners are enmeshed in the weather, and 'weathering' is an acquired skill. The physiological literature suggests that seasoned marathon runners are skilled at dealing with adverse weather, whereas novice runners are more likely to suffer from it both corporeally and mentally:

a newcomer to marathon running may be unable to cope with extreme weather when confronted with it for the first time, whereas an experienced runner who has competed in all kinds of weather may well have developed effective coping strategies specific to the extreme conditions, such as focusing on the task at hand (e.g. running) and not on the weather, or motivating self-talk.

*(Zepp, 2016 p. 89)*

A common ritual the night before the race is preparing one's race outfit and supply of gels and charging one's watch. Many upload a photo of it, accompanied by a laconic text about the race and their ambitions. Now it is time to get to bed and get a good night's sleep. Unfortunately, the nerves cause widespread insomnia. Many 'twist and turn', panicking about how losing sleep will affect their performance tomorrow: is a bad night's sleep ruining half a year of training?

## Race nerves

Being morning events, marathons require an early rise. However, while getting a decent night's sleep escapes many, with adrenaline already pumping through the body, waking up is easy. We rush to the window and pray that the weather forecast is right or wrong, sighing with relief if there is no snow on the ground, burning sun, heavy rain or movement in the trees; or else we are confronted with what we feared, as one year in the Frankfurt Marathon:

> It is pitch dark outside. The road and the building are only occasionally lit up only by a tram with a warning light. The hotel's thick windows isolate me from the wind's ravine. Yet I can see how the leaves are thrown brutally around and the branches of the trees do not get a second's break. The blinking lights reveal that heavy rain is falling on the road. In the last few days, we have constantly talked about the weather and checked the weather forecast. We have feared the sight that now meets us through the window: rain and storm. A nightmare for a marathon runner. The sight alone makes me tired and cold. ... Like everyone else, I now hope the weather will show us some mercy over the next few hours.
>
> (Field notes, Larsen & Jensen, 2021, p. 75)

Such a sight is highly stressful, and there is real fear that this weathering of the course will impede the anticipated rhythms.

Now it is time for the final preparation. Marathon runners are advised to eat a light meal and drink plenty three hours before the race starts to fuel properly, but also allow for proper digestion and a visit or two to the toilet.

> All there is on my mind now is the final preparation for the run that starts in little less than three hours. The next hour is crucial: I need to drink and eat wisely, enough but not too much. And not least, I need to defecate. It is about sticking to the routines. I mix myself a 750 ml energy drink. Sweet, awful stuff. I know that I need to stop drinking two hours before the race to avoid a disastrous pee at the beginning. Because of the marathon, the breakfast is served early. Unsurprisingly, it is only runners and their families that make such an early morning start. I eat a small muesli bowl and a banana. Juice. Coffee. Oh yes, my 'stomach works'.
>
> (Field notes, Edensor & Larsen, 2018, pp. 738–739)

The fear of not being able 'to poop' before leaving one's home or hotel is a major concern for everybody. Upon leaving one's hotel new concerns take precedence: how to get to the start area (without disbursing too much energy), how to find the loo (or a bush), the bag deposit area and one's friends and assigned corral? However, there is always something magical about walking into a nippy and idle Sunday morning when other mobility rhythms are unusually dormant and the rest of the city – apart from the last 'night clubbers' and people walking their dogs – is sleeping. Walking and cycling runners dominate the drowsy streets, and we proceed in near silence to the start area.

Timing is crucial: early arrivers risk getting cold, while late arrivers may face long lines for toilets and packed corrals. An hour prior to the start, the start area is packed with excited and tense runners desperate to get going and yet fearing what awaits them. The final waiting time is particularly nerve-wracking for those needing the toilet. Many men (and some women) pee in public to avoid the long slow-moving lines for the toilet. Albert, a running partner of mine learned it the hard way:

> We are stuck in a slow-moving line for toilets and time is running out. The race will start soon. 'I will try another toilet', I yell to Albert. Further down the hall, I spot another queue, and it turns out that there are two toilets. It is my turn 15 minutes before the race commences.
>
> Rushing to race start, I spot my friend, distressed, and still stuck in the line. 'We are running out of time', I tell him. 'I know. I think I will be okay without the toilet, but it would have been nice.' He does not sound convinced.
>
> *(Field notes)*

At this small event (Odense Marathon), we were lucky that it was easy to get into our start corral. It would have been very different at one of the larger marathons. Some of my interviewees tell stories about how they arrived late and had to start way back in their corral. Scoot knew better the second time he ran the Valencia Marathon:

> Last year we barely got into our designated starting area as there was a huge crowd of people. We ended up in a crowd of people at the very back. … It was incredibly tight. … This year we knew the race and showed up early: we were among the first two to three runners in the starting corral. It would have been nice to wait in a warmer place, but it was perfect, as we got off to a seamless start.
>
> *(Personal communication, my translation)*

Waiting for the gunshot in one's minimal race outfit can be a teeth-chattering experience on a nippy, windy or raining morning. On chilly days, runners wearing t-shirts or singlets and tiny shorts are visibly shaking and freezing. Many try to keep warm by wearing plastic ponchos or an old jumper that they will discard once the race starts: 'It was raining and 4 degrees. So cold. Stood and waited and my lips were completely blue ... It was horrible' (Lone, personal communication, my translation). Others are – so it seems – more sensibly clothed. However, all this clothing will trouble them once their bodies warm up and the temperature rises later in the race. Experienced runners know that they should in fact be cold at this point. Experts advise runners to 'dress like it's 15 to 20 degrees warmer than it actually is', given the fact that 'no matter what the temperature says, your body is going to heat up as soon as you start moving' (*Runner's World* cited in Larsen & Jensen, 2021, p. 72). Freezing runners are not helped by the fact that it is not advisable to warm up (much) for a marathon (unlike shorter distances, where the pace is much higher). It is better to save energy, and all the pumping pre-race adrenaline will quickly make overexcited bodies race-ready once they get going (Moyna, 2019; Stöggl & Wunsch, 2016). While it is much nicer to wait for the start gun on a warm sunny day, this sensation is mixed with the fear that overheating might cause our bodies trouble once the sun gains full force and our bodies produce much surplus heat (Larsen & Jensen, 2021). Lone also told me about her experience at the London Marathon where she was chasing a new personal record:

> We were waiting for the start at 10, just frying in the sun. There I knew that it was probably not going to be the day. Okay, I decided to give it a shot until the half marathon point. How to deal with such weather? The wise people say that if the circumstances are not there, one must adjust. It was just too hot. But I had to try because I had been training for half a year. This pace just sits there, feels right.
>
> *(Personal communication, my translation)*

She is an experienced marathon runner and *knows* how such weather impacts negatively on her performances (Ely et al., 2007), that it is a likely suicide mission to run at a prospective personal best pace, but she cannot relinquish the attempt and lower the pace. This is a very common response to adverse weather conditions. In the heat of the moment, people forget that running is highly conditioned by the weather and that they are weather-sensitive bodies, not the indomitable machines that their training has programmed them to think. People have become so accustomed to a specific pace and the prospect of a new record is so mesmerising and motivating that few lower their ambitions even when they realise that the weather will work against them. Such ignorance and persistence only add to the drama of rhythms that is about to unfold.

## The start: disorder order

To prevent a chaotic arrhythmic start when very fast and very slow runners run together, runners are divided into corrals according to their intended speed (chapter 5). Marathons slide into rhythmic chaos and evade control if runners do not accede to this ordering. This coordination ensures isorhythmic rhythms where runners of roughly similar ability and intended speed are grouped together while they wait for the timed gun shot. Runners check their laces. Their hands are firmly placed on their watches, ready to press start the instant they run over the timing matts: marathons are run *in* time.

A Lefebvrian *spectator* analysis of the start of marathon reveals how the corrals organise and discipline runners, but also the uniquely polyrhythmic nature of marathons.
Spectators wait for the empty streets to come alive and watch with disbelief when the
first corral of young elite runners rushes ahead with their high prodigious speed, light
racing gear, long strides, aerodynamic running and super-thin bodies.

The other runners wait impatiently for their signal, then the next corrals of sub-elite
and serious runners and sub-three-hour pacing teams glide by in their minimal clothing: singlets, diminutive shorts, brightly coloured Vaporfly shoes or other fancy
models. While they also move fast and look almost equally skinny, their pace is slower
and strides are shorter – and they are older. There are many middle-aged men and
women in these corrals. The diversity of bodies becomes ever more evident as the last
waves of runners and pacer teams drift by (the last corral at the Tokyo Marathon starts
some 45 minutes after the elite runners). These bodies are not necessarily super-lean
and they tend to wear substantially more clothing (unless it is very hot); they see-
mingly dress for a comfortable warm start, risking 'overheating' later in the race. Still
others dress out in funny costumes (particularly common at the Tokyo Marathon) and
are busy waving to and interacting with the crowd (chapter 8).

The corrals bunch together large crowds of runners and produce a mass collective rhythm of synchronicity. Yet, in reality, as already touched upon, my interviewees often experience the start and the first kilometres as arrhythmic, nervous,
and claustrophobic. The corals are teeming with runners who almost rub shoulders
and obstruct each other. There is some elbowing, tense faces, rancid language and
near-accidents. It is difficult to reach one's pace, and there is much pushing and

FIGURE 7.1 Anticipation, Tokyo Marathon

**FIGURE 7.2** The blurry speed of the front runners, Tokyo Marathon

zigzagging from behind. People are eager to get further up in the corral, finding their particular pace straight away and running the painted 'ideal line'. Seasoned runners know that they need to get into their intended rhythm quickly and fear that bottlenecks and slower runners will slow them down and force them to spend undue energy on zigzagging and running extra metres.

**FIGURE 7.3** 'Slower' runners, Tokyo Marathon

**FIGURE 7.4** The optimal blue line, Berlin Marathon

Interviewees also emphasised the importance of holding back, not letting themselves get carried away and suffering later from an early sprightly gait. As these two experienced women, Beth and Jane, said:

JANE: From previous experiences, I can say that I start to go fast because I'm excited. I have told myself to go slower this time in the beginning.

BETH: It is hard in the beginning when the race starts, and you are in the middle of this crowd and everyone wants to go, and it is hard not to go out too fast. So, you really have to hold back.

*(Personal communications)*

Others expect and accept a sluggish start as part of their overall race strategy. They like to have the first couple of kilometres a little slower. They know from experience that the start is often very chaotic and that there is no guarantee that they can run in their race pace. They find that such a race strategy is less stressful. However, pacing oneself correctly or being lenient about bottlenecks is not easy when one's body is 'pumping'. From the beginning, the runner's 'physiological support systems … will immediately go into overdrive', the 'heart will pump three to four times the amount of blood around the body', and the heart rate and body temperature will increase (Moyna, 2019). With a body in 'overdrive', it is difficult not to get carried away by the atmosphere and the collective rhythm in the beginning, especially for novice runners. Despite the familiar warnings against starting too fast it remains a common occurrence, especially amongst novices. One study found that '33% of runners have their first 5 km segment as their single fastest race segment' (Smyth, 2018, p. 235), which is a striking figure given the often cramped condition and the lack of warm-up.

The feverish, somewhat arrhythmic first 5 km are succeeded by steadier, ordered rhythms over the next 10 km. The thick consistent flow of runners gradually disperses. The streets are less crowded and there is more space between the runners, who can follow the optimal line more easily and make razor-sharp turns. Runners settle into a regular rhythm, sometimes forming fluid groups with those at a similar pace and producing a collective eurhythmia for shorter or longer spells before drifting apart. Such groups are temporary gatherings, and few stick together for more than a couple of kilometres unless they decided to run together beforehand. However, individual runners may try to join or hang on to larger groups that can provide shelter from the wind, shade and a consistent pace.

By this point, runners will have accommodated themselves to the racecourse and the task at hand and found their rhythm; our bodies are properly heated and sweat runs down our faces and evaporates into the air to lower the temperature of our bodies (the heat produced by the body increase dramatically during a marathon, Moyna, 2019). Sounds of shoes beating against the asphalt and controlled breathing are consistent master sonic rhythms, together with occasional atmospheric reverberations from the crowd (chapter 8). Eurhythmic rhythms at this early stage can be disrupted by the need to pee, pile-ups at nutrition stations when runners reach out for or precipitously stop for drinks, or occasional slips and tumbles as spilled liquids make the roads slippery.

At this point, the legs need to feel light, and the pulse must be relatively low despite the high pace. Now the focused training reaps its rewards, allowing an anticipated and steady rhythm that seems fairly easy. Many report being like a machine at this point, flying over the asphalt, 'flowing' and fully absorbed by the task. They might feel 'groundless', as each landing does not leave much of an impact on their feet and legs. Their shoes are doing the required work. The body and brain still have plenty of fuel from breakfast and the carbo loading, so sugar depletion seems inconceivable. This confirms Leder's (1990) idea that a well-functioning body is absent. However, they should not be carried away. It is pivotal to save and take in new energy at the nutrition stations. My point is that the absent body needs to be in one's presence. Over the entire course of the marathon, runners will lose three to six litres of sweat, and they need to drink water and energy drinks (combined with energy gels) at each water station to replace the fluid and salt lost in sweat to avoid dehydration (Moyna, 2019; Noakes, 2003). Experienced runners know that it is vital to drink from the onset and throughout the race and not wait for thirst to set in. If they wait for a sensation, it is already too late. They grab a bottle or a cup 'on the go' and devour the content without slowing, while inexperienced runners often spill much of the water or make a full stop to ensure that they hydrate sufficiently. Seasoned runners also know that they need to fuel, save energy and run economically. They visually scan the course for energy-saving *information*. As Anton, a serious runner, says,

> In the first half of the race, when I have fresh legs, I think: 'Do I keep my times, remember to drink, remember to eat?' Whenever possible, I find somebody to shelter behind. If my group does not keep the pace, I go in front and set the tempo. But not if there is a direct headwind.
>
> *(Personal communication, my translation)*

Some scan the environment for their family members who will dispense energy gels and drinks, as well as emotional boosts, at agreed locations. As Paul explained:

> I appreciate [my wife's support]. It is good to know that I can get what I need or get rid of things. Water, salt tablets, gels, plaster. It is also good to know that there are points on the route where we meet. It is nice to say hi, get a kiss, and say 'see you in 8 km's time'.
>
> *(Personal communication, my translation)*

The kilometre signs and synchronised 'beep beep' sounds of watches with their 'split times' are also crucial, signalling progress and affording the opportunity to monitor one's time (and legs) against the target. The insistent rhythm of the current and overall pace is monitored incessantly; runners catch quick glances at their watches and fine-tune their pace if their split is too slow or fast, and they check in with their peers: 'we are three seconds ahead of pace, slow down a little'. The right pace is felt and displayed, a feeling and number. This is how Schmidt writes about his pace:

> I fall into a group that runs like me, and it is perfect. My legs have found the right speed and stride, and I am running precisely at my chosen pace: 3 minutes and 50 seconds per kilometre. I control every aspect of my body, and it fills me with joy, strength, and gratitude. I do not feel that I am using much energy, and the nerves are worn out at 10 km. I do not pay attention to the environment. I am concentrating on my rhythm.
>
> *(2018, p. 71, my translation)*

This illustrates how positive sensations of harmonic rhythmic flow stem from a biological and physiological sensation of being in control and mastering a very *specific* anticipated pace recorded by one's watch. Most runners-in-flow are highly 'time-conscious (in contrast to the idea of flow; Csikszentmihalyi, 1997); they check watches and heart rate monitors as much as their sensory organs to determine if they are really in flow or running too slow or fast' (Larsen, 2019b, p. 569). While racing is determined by the cyclical rhythms of the body, it is very much a *temporal* practice of linear, repetitive and anticipated rhythms. Race rhythms are always partly felt and partly recorded; there is no such thing as flow outside of recorded time when it comes to racing for the vast majority of runners. We should not make a false distinction between felt and recorded rhythms or see one as more authentic than the other. Rhythms are always measured, as Lefebvre (2004) wrote (chapter 2).

Finally, the above quote illustrates another analytical point. Paraphrasing Leder (1990), being in perfect flow and concentrating fully on one's rhythms and the unfolding course affordances make one absent to the wider aesthetic environment (and not only one's body). Runners that concentrate fully on their own race rhythm 'do not recognise the environment' for long spells (chapter 8). However, place matters – courses are *not* 'non-places' (Augé, 2008). Runners recognise and appreciate the material and non-representational affordances and sensations of *courses* (chapter 5) with few obstacles: running on super-fast smooth asphalt, broad and flat boulevards with no stop lights or impeding cars and walkers. This is the opposite of everyday running, an extraordinary *running* experience where the ecstasies of speed and flow rule.

## Second part: the hard work begins (15–30 kilometres)

There is now even more space between the runners. While the first 15 km should feel relatively easy, like light transport, at about 15–20 km the race gets hard. The occasional chattering between the runners is gagged and the atmosphere is taut.

A sudden need for the toilet or stomach problems caused by over-hydration and too many gels may produce arrhythmia, as happened with Maria, whom I paced:

'I need the loo. You two just continue.'
'I stick with you.'
'You are on your own, Henrik, Maria needs the loo.'
Two minutes later we hit the road again. We are still on time. Just about. But will this interruption undermine her? We find our rhythm again. But there are signs of agony on her face. And her breathing is heavier. She is behind me all the time now.

*(Field notes, Edensor & Larsen, 2018, pp. 741–742)*

It is also around this time that the body begins to feel the fatigue and dehydration from which people will learn if, for instance, overheating troubles their bodies and causes arrhythmia. This may be caused by a sudden increase in midday heat or the sun's radiation. Lone, who dreaded that the heat would kill her, was eventually defeated by the sun and 'heat island effects' produced by dense, tall buildings:

I hit Tower Bridge half-way through the marathon, and it was so hot. But I kept going. Then we came out on Canary Wharf where there were few spectators. The tall buildings that soaked up the sun made it feel like running into a sauna.

*(Personal communication, my translation)*

Alternatively, cold rain and temperatures may trouble runners, forcing them to run with plastic ponchos, or risk freezing, even suffering from hypothermia, if running in a normal race outfit, as happened to Scoot at the Chicago Marathon:

Everything went according to plan, except it was freezing, 6 degrees. But it felt like 3, and the wind started blowing vigorously during the race. I was wearing split shorts ... . After 5 km of headwinds, I couldn't feel my legs anymore. It had a strong impact, and I had difficulties with keeping the pace. My breathing, my heart rate, were fine... I'm very sensitive to the wind and cold temperatures and less to heat than so many others. Two days before, it was 20 degrees.

*(Personal communication, my translation)*

**FIGURE 7.5** Raining and plastic ponchos, Kyoto Marathon

Running is, as I have argued, contingent on weather. This example illustrates that there are individual biological limits to 'weather skills', and the weather is volatile and always shifting, sometimes dramatically during the race. That people run with and in this unpredictable matter adds drama to the overall choreography of marathons. Will the weather run with or against them at this critical stage?

At this part of the race, bodies start to 'appear' (Leder, 1990) and people begin realising if they have good or bad legs and their mind is ready to 'dig in' (Hockey & Allen-Collinson, 2015), endure pain, fight the war, today. It is here that runners are tested for the first time. Those who have not trained properly or taken the distance seriously risk hitting the wall prematurely. In particular, young men are now seen walking. Feeling fatigue this early is a bad sign, and semi-injured runners may now realise that their gamble has not paid off:

> I easily run past a NBRO runner who was injured prior to race. 'I'm too much in pain, I'm resigning.' A couple of kilometres further on I get in full contact with another running partner who started off slightly faster than agreed. We say hi and check in on each other, happy to be reunited. 'I'm beginning to feel the strain,' he says. I feel no strain and say nothing in return. This is too early, I think to myself. He is hanging on by the thread and is soon falling behind and out of sight. Around the 20 km sign he suddenly reappears, only to announce that he is quitting.
>
> *(Field notes)*

Scoot later told me that negative thoughts consumed him when the first signs of fatigue set in and his pace dropped below the target. Once people start losing their pace, they often start a negative thought process. This makes it even harder to catch up on the lost time and regain a good flow. Scoot lost this mental battle despite feeling relatively well and dropped out. He explained:

> It was primarily psychological. I felt I had a strong body. Fine heart rate and breathing. No issues with gels and carbohydrates. No problems in the heat. I thought it was brilliant weather. It is the head, the hunger, as I call it. I tried the same thing last year … but there it was an actual injury. … But the fact that you've dropped out of a marathon is a mental repetition that gets encoded in your brain. Suddenly, it's an option … you can better deal with the shame and explain why you did it. But it's also easier to do it, and that's the problem. … At first, it is a relief. The devil on the shoulders who whispers 'stop' finally gets peace. Then comes this bitter taste: should I have continued?
>
> *(Personal communication, my translation)*

Physically troubled runners are also fighting a tough mental battle and must dispense with negative thinking. It is crucial not to give in to the benevolent voices exhorting that it is a good idea and perfectly fine to put an end to the misery. This illustrates the body–mind integration (chapter 2) and that marathon running is also a mental act; runners in pain are easy victims of negative thinking and self-talk (Coyle, 2007; Samson et al., 2017; Sperlich, 2016).

Many non-elite runners, such as Scoot, employ the so-called 'dissociative cognitive strategy'. This involves turning attention away from one's troubled dysfunctional body towards things that have nothing to do with the job at hand (for instance, one's children) or to the crowd and the wider environment (chapter 8) (Morgan & Pollock, 1977; Zepp, 2016, p. 88). While this strategy may briefly reduce perceived pain (Baden et al., 2004) and exertion (Stanley et al., 2007), it is dangerous because runners no longer listen to or focus upon their bodies (what is called 'associative strategies') (Masters & Lambert, 1989; Morgan & Pollock, 1977).

Dropping out of the race as this stage is relatively common among achievement runners when they realise that a personal record has escaped them. They struggle to find the motivation to carry on, and perhaps McLoughlin is right when claiming that they would 'rather not finish than post a time they find shameful' (McLoughlin, 2010, p. 78). Yet others refuse to 'give up' and instead take pride in finishing on a bad day; for them, it would be shameful not to finish. They would hate losing character (Berking & Neckel, 1993) or face on a Goffmanian front stage (Goffman, 1978) and carrying a DNF stigma ('did not finish') (Reischer, 2001).

Now, when they cannot execute their original race strategy, it is time for Plan B. For instance, this was the case for Anton who around the 20 km sign suddenly felt cramping sensations. He quickly realised that his current pace was unrealistic. Many calculations went on his head. He figured that he could still meet his overall goal by marginally lowering the pace to a point where the pain was tolerable. Plan B motivated him through the pain barrier. At least for now. However, making further progress made him painfully aware that he was in trouble, but not without hope:

> Sometimes when you run, you suddenly feel some tenderness that you forget about 500 metres later because it is no longer there, and you are somewhere else. But this one sticks. What the hell am I doing? With 14 km remaining, my analysis is that I can't run with this. It's way too far to still go. So, I slow the pace and see if it will get better. At the same time, a small ... [group] that I know passes me by. They are running really well, I must admit... . I have plunged to pace 4:00. It also means that when I hit 30, it still looks reasonable ... for a sub-2:45 time. I have only dropped a few seconds of mileage time.
>
> *(Personal communication, my translation)*

Research shows that most non-elite runners' pace drops in the second part of the race, especially after 30 km; people start to fast and run out of energy (Ely et al., 2008; Haney & Mercer, 2011; March et al., 2011; Santos-Lozano et al., 2014). While many runners adopt a consistent pacing strategy, many fail in practice (Diaz et al., 2018). Results for 754,851 runners from 26 marathons show that only 13 per cent ran 'negative' (faster in the second half), while 87 per cent ran 'positive' (slower in the second part). Those who ran the first part in two hours were some ten minutes slower in the second part (Smyth, 2018, p. 6).

## Third part: emerging arrhythmia

> This is also what is so fascinating about marathons. Knowing that you are going to run 02:44:20 that day will take away much of the excitement of the race. That race, which is so awful when you are out there, and you feel completely wiped out, is also beautiful when you do succeed ... . It is typically between 32 and 37 km when everything is decided ...
>
> *(Anton, personal communication, my translation)*

> I was over the moon [when I crossed the finish line]. I had completed a marathon and run better than I had dared to hope for. It was so amazing. Such a great running expericience, not having a feeling of meeting the wall ... .
>
> *(Vera, personal communication, my translation).*

Training is repetitive, controlled and predictable, whereas a marathon 'by its nature, is a spontaneous, unpredictable, uncontrolled event, in which competitors have to make untold decisions that relate to their many bodily states' (Mills & Denison, 2013, p. 55). Running a marathon is always like running into a new territory where one's habitual pace might suddenly becomes different.

The last 12 km are particularly cruel and testing, and the race devolves into an (ar)rhythmic spectacle, with the synchronised eurhythmy of earlier stages collapsing. There is now more space between runners and the average pace is slowing (Rodriguez et al., 2014). This is the defining stage that makes marathons mythical, romantic, and dramatic – beyond planning and repetition. What Spinney terms a 'kinaesthetic burn' is a real danger now (2006, p. 712) and severe 'digging in' (Hockey & Allen-Collinson, 2015) is unavoidable. This moment exemplifies the culturally ingrained endurance ethos of 'pushing through' fatigue-induced pain and ignoring the burning desire to stop (Atkinson, 2008). Runners now consider themselves lucky if they are still running eurhythmically at their desired pace.

At this stage, various bodily disturbances can slow down runners as 'rhythms break apart, alter and bypass synchronization' (Lefebvre, 2004, p. 67). Fewer are flying over the asphalt, and each landing gives painful sensations in the bones, legs and tendons. They are heavier and stiffer, with a painful burning sensation, while the feet are aching. The legs now quiver with each impact, absorbing the violence of each collision with the asphalt. People now blame their shoes for not providing enough support, for insufficient cushioning, now when they land heavily. Their shoes, shorts or singlets may now be 'parasites' (Michael, 2000), triggering blisters, inner thigh chafing or bleeding nipples. The extra layers of clothing that warmed in the morning may now cause overheating and are dead weight wrapped around the stomach. Running is less dynamic and graceful and has shorter strides. People are dizzy and confused; their pulse is increasing and irregular, they are tired and suffer from dehydration, low sugar levels (hypoglycemia) and overheating (hyperthermia), or perhaps from being cold (hypothermia) if they have to walk now and then. Some struggling bodies are clearly freezing in the cold rain or heavy wind. People struggle to perform their finish-time calculations. Pain is etched on sweaty and tangled faces, with empty and dead eyes. People try to devour sports drinks or sugary gels to maintain normal blood glucose levels, but the sweet stuff is perhaps too sweet now. The brain and body have now used their supply of glucose (although sports drinks or sugary gels can maintain blood glucose levels to some extent). Running out of sugar (its favourite gasoline), the body is relying on burning fat, which is more inefficient (it provides much less energy per unit time than glucose) (Sperlich, 2016).

The combination of these physiological factors and the exertion might lead to dark thoughts and negative affective responses that will further haunt the already troubled runners (Ekkekakis, 2009). Runners are now so low on energy that will-power is decisive: a worn-out body begs one to stop or at least slow down. Most run the last 10 km at a slower pace than at the start of the race, and they constantly fear that their pace will drop any minute, or worse, that they will be the next victim of a sudden cramp. People are in pain, in dark places, and dreams are crashing to the ground while the world is watching. However, there is also excitement and determination written on people's faces. This is the rhythmic drama of marathon running at its most brutal. Who is the next to crash?

**FIGURE 7.6** Cramps 1, Tokyo Marathon

**FIGURE 7.7** Cramps 2, Kyoto Marathon

These physiological processes force many bodies to slow down. It is worst for those who hit the infamous and much-feared marathon wall, which is beyond normal fatigue. This unpleasant phenomenon 'is experienced by approximately half of all marathon runners' (Buman et al., 2008a, b; Morgan & Pollock, 1977), especially by first-timers, young runners, fast starters and male runners, less so by slow starters, women and experienced runners (Buman et al., 2008a; Deaner et al., 2015; Deaner et al., 2019; Smyth, 2018; Stevinson & Biddle, 1998).[2] Technologies are partly to blame. Vickers and Vertosick argue that the 'Riegel formula' (used in many race time calculators) predicts poorly for ordinary runners, providing over-ambitious finish times and therefore excessively fast paces: 'the predicted marathon times from Riegel are 10 min or more too fast for about half of all runners' (2016, p. 6).

Cramps, fatal dehydration or an overwhelming sensation of having no energy left is paramount when hitting the wall, where the pace drops massively in an instant and is likely to fall further as race the unfolds. Crashes may happen instantly, without much warning, or more gradually, as happened to me at the Valencia

Marathon in 2018. At the 32 km sign, I resigned. I worked harder, but my pace dropped slowly but gradually, despite my best intentions. I walked and jogged the last 9 km, with my head down. The experience was humiliating:

> The sound and sight of light feet and effortless bodies that pass by you is the worst thing about bonking. You are fighting alone with your own useless body. The other runners look like they are flying. You stop. It feels good for a short moment. The pain disappears. But then it starts to feel like shitting yourself. Now you're one of those sad quitters who do not have the will power to 'dig in' and endure the pain. They run. You walk. Your dreams evaporate and months of training feel wasted. Now there is 9 km to the finish line where self-hate is your only companion. I fake a smile to the crowd, which calls my name. This will take forever.
>
> *(Field notes)*

While relatively few runners end up walking, there are many troubled bodies, and 'crashing', stretching, stopping, resting, plodding ahead and toddling become increasingly common as the slower runners emerge.

The aforementioned Anton with cramps is now in serious pain:

> Thinking at 30 kilometres, if I run 4:00 until the finish line, I will run 2:45 something. It would still be pretty cool. After all, I've been training a lot. I figure out what can be done and find a new plan. I run a couple of km at a pace of 4.00 and it feels tolerable ... But soon after, the cramps get worse. As I hit 31–32, I'm down to 04:15 ... Now I'm at a point where people run past me. Those who are slower than me are the people who have *really* lost it. Every time I overtake someone, there are 10 others running past me. It's really brutal. There are so many that are running well. In pain, I manage to maintain that pace through until 35. ... Then I gradually lose more and more speed.
>
> *(Personal communication, my translation)*

Anton's pace drops dramatically and he loses many minutes over the last seven kilometres. He finishes with a body in pain and a broken heart. In a post-interview a couple of weeks later, he is still bitterly disappointed and struggles to understand why cramps struck when his form was excellent; he had so much experience and the rest of his body felt so strong. What went wrong? The answer was blowing in the wind.

A combination of fatigue and heavy wind may also cause a final collapse and kill jubilation, as happened to me at the Frankfurt Marathon:

> From the 28 km sign onward, I'm on fire, increasing my speed. A new PB is on the horizon. However, as we hit the 38 km sign and the wind-whipping skyscrapers, I learn the hard way that tailwinds have propelled me forward for the last eight kilometres. Now the tailwind is headlong, and I'm alone. At the 40 km sign I'm still ahead of my PB schedule by a couple of seconds, but the

brutal wind overwhelms my energy-depleted body and I lose more than 30 seconds over the next two kilometres, and agony is written all over my defeated, wind-swept face as I cross the finish line.

*(Field notes, Larsen & Jensen, 2021, p. 76)*

However, some runners never hit the wall, and they might even increase their speed and overtake suffering runners with ease, being energised by their pain. They move beyond those with whom they have shared a constant rhythm:

I was struggling. ... But then we came into a tailwind and then I could just feel that km after km, the energy just came back. I'm really good at running in tailwind and downhill. From the 32nd km, where my friends had a hard time ... I start to regain my strength.

*(Scoot, personal communication, my translation)*

This illustrates how the body can feel good, then bad, then good again (and so on) through the same race. Studies show that 'older, experienced runners are better maintaining a relatively constant running velocity as a result of their embodied memory of run speed from the previous races and less competitive attitude toward competing' (March et al., 2011, p. 387; Nikolaidis et al., 2019). Indeed, Young states that 'expert pacing skill is likely acquired via voluminous training across many years in the sport' (cited in March et al., 2011, p. 387).

In the final stages, the world elite male runners finish just after two hours. At this point, the slowest runners might only have run 15 km or less. Over the next two hours, 'serious' runners make it to the finish line. They sprint if they can mobilise any energy, and many raise their arms in jubilation. Others are visibly disappointed and distressed that they yet again fail to meet that targeted time and beat themselves. After this, the less purposive runners arrive, having been running (and walking) for five or six hours. Such runners are largely happy just to finish, measuring success not in time but in arriving (Cohen & Hanold, 2016; Rupprecht & Matkin, 2012). As Claire declared:

It is a great feeling that I'm able to run. ... All the training – it is really hard to get to the point where you can run a marathon ... the sense of work involved, the dedication and time, and being able to get to the finish line is what it is all about. And the fun part is, I did all this work, and now I get a reward for it. The reward is crossing the line – whatever the time.

*(Personal communication)*

Many 'walk the last stretch with their head down, but they are not ashamed or left behind. Their running may be painfully arrhythmic at this point, yet they are rhythmically aligned – part of a larger *isorhythmia* – with bodies of similar skills and shapes' (Larsen, 2019b, p. 574).

People are at near-collapse as they cross the line and stop moving and their watch in a single coordinated movement: they bend forward, support their hands on their legs or against a railing, or fall to the ground. Medics keep an eye on and care for those in need, while officials provide insulating ponchos and urge us to move forward as soon as we catch our breath to make space for incoming runners. We comply. However, our legs are protesting with cramps. When finishing, large doses of endorphins and adrenaline partially numb the muscles. However, it will not be long before the pain recurs, this time with spasmodic and biting strength, making it extremely unpleasant to walk, especially downstairs. Moreover, the fact that runners at this stage often begin to freeze in their minimal, sweaty race outfit only make this troubled walking extra painful.

As people cross the finish line, their embodied performances are boiled down to a definite 'time'. This number, relative to their previous results and age, largely determines success or failure for many. It awards prestigious new identities as sub-three-hour or sub-five-hour runners, while others fear that a poor result puts their identity as a fast runner at risk. Soon fellow runners and family members will ask, 'How did it go?', and how we fared is largely determined by our *time*. Those who triumphed are likely to be 'over the moon', and they will write a social media post where the improved time will be the main message, whereas those who fail are less vocal, if not silent. Disappointments seldom find their way to social media.

## Conclusion

This chapter has demonstrated and analysed the dramatical nature of marathon racing. 'Race rhythms' are simultaneously predictable and unpredictable, constituting a drama of rhythms. First, as discussed in chapter 5, this drama is conditioned by the staging of material *courses* where runners can chase records: effective corridors affording long-desired eurhythmic flows, predictable sensations of fast, smooth and linear movement. Second, marathons are scripted as cultural stages for breaking personal records. Runners have high aspirations and predict records, and therefore risk losing face if they fail to live up to their proclamations. Marathon runners are well drilled and expect their 'irrational bodies' (Lefebvre, 2004) to be rational machines by now. Much is at risk and runners are haunted by doubt. This Lefebvrian drama is also a Goffmanian (1978) public drama where faces and characters are both validated and lost.

This chapter has demonstrated how within the marathon's temporal and spatial framework, any individual runner's experience of rhythm may continuously change. I have shown that those who excel in marathons are those who sustain a largely eurhythmic race and deal readily with minor moments of arrhythmic disturbances. However, many fail. Despite extensive preparation, runners may experience eurythmia, arrhythmia or a mixture of both on the day itself. Runners realise that their bodies are, in fact, bodies. The marathon becomes a rhythmic drama because unpredictability lurks around every corner. Training for and running a marathon are two very different things.

I have discussed and argued that various contingencies that thwart a runner's extensive training, turning the experience into a personal drama and streets into spectacular theatres of excellence, celebration and suffering. Drama is thus provided by how well people sleep the night before the race, whether they manage to defecate, the volatile weather, the chaos at the start, how their bodies feel on the day, if they run into cramps, whether their shoes 'behave' or other bodily interruptions. For many, the race turns into an arrhythmic nightmare, while others manage to keep their pace going, although less gracefully. While a well-trained marathon body is resilient and almost 'machine like', it can burn out in the sun or under the strain of the workload. Stomach problems, cramps and dehydration trouble and slow down runners. Moreover, unlike machines, worn-out bodies break down mentally and negative thoughts consume the will to 'dig in'. Mind and body are inseparable. Athletes who are mentally fatigued reach exhaustion sooner than those with a positive fighting spirit.

Accordingly, I conclude that it is the contingent and unpredictable nature of marathon running that makes a new personal record – this new definite number – such a powerful and uplifting experience – and deeply frustrating for those who fail despite all their training. The marathon is a clash between two worlds: the world of the rational, prepared and predictive mind, the quantified self, and its irrational body and the chaos on the street and in the air. When we least expect it, our body strikes back and defeats us, with cramps, a bad stomach or fatigue, or the weather turns against us, or else our shoes or clothing become parasites, shattering our well-planned personal record aspirations.

This chapter has focused on race rhythms and time, which McLoughlin calls 'numbers'. However, it is erroneous to suggest that such numbering of the runner completely 'elides, supercedes, and obscures other affective, visceral, and social experiences of running, such as jouissance and play' (McLoughlin, 2010, p. 76). While time and pacing matters to all runners, many runners are attuned to jouissance and play, and there is more to marathon dramas than individual struggles, triumphs and seamless sporting excellence. The next chapter discusses how drama is also produced by the vibrant atmospheres of cheering, music, amusement and spectacular sights that literally transform drowsy Sunday streets into vibrant *places*.

## Notes

1 The chapter draws loosely on and extend ideas originally developed in Edensor and Larsen (2018).
2 A study of more than 1.7 million *recreational* runners' pace in the beginning of the race and at the end finds that an even pace leads to faster finish times because fast starters often 'hit the wall' and run the last five kilometres much slower than the first (Smyth, 2018). Starting too cautious is also a problem. Smyth also finds that 'fast finishes are also associated with slower finish-times, because they sometimes signal cautious pacing earlier in the race, as if runners are holding back for a final sprint' (Smyth, 2018, p. 230). Finally, Smyth's study documents that women are better pacers than men although they sometimes start too slow (Smyth, 2018, p. 230; see also Nikolaidis & Knechtle, 2017, 2018a, b).

# 8

# ATMOSPHERIC SENSATIONS AND PLACES

## Introduction

Whereas the previous chapter focused on the inward battle of 'racing' and the kinaesthetic sensations of flow and burn-out, this chapter explores how runners sense and appreciate the *wider* festive environment and associated atmospheres – of buildings, sights, spectators, sonic beats and cheering – in which they are emplaced during the race, for the running rhythms discussed in the previous chapter co-exist with the multiple rhythmic sounds and spectacles produced by crowds, dancers, performers and musicians. Rodaway (1994) notes that sensuous inputs such as sound and vision can comprise both 'information' and 'sensation'. Information, for instance, might be concerned with marching with others or dangers such as speeding cars, and sensation with pleasurable music. In the last chapter, we saw how racing achievement runners scanned bodies and courses for information (for instance, about kilometre signs and nutrition zones). I now discuss how marathon atmospheres and soundscapes are primarily 'sensational', a festive racket that replaces the usual sonic rhythms of traffic, work and shopping and adds affective beats and colour to this dramatic event. They transform the corridor courses discussed in the last chapter into vibrant places. This also means that runners experience marathons as a continuum of courses and places (or as 'land' and 'landscape', see chapter 6), of information and sensation, and the balance between the two very much depends upon their race strategy and form on the day.

Accordingly, this chapter explores how diverse atmospheres constitute marathons and how runners sense such sensations and their embodied rhythms of running are affected by them. It builds upon chapters 4 and 5, where it was argued that marathon courses are also designed as atmospheric places and many – especially experience runners – look forward to being engulfed by an exciting atmospheric and a striking visual environment that can carry their tired bodies forward and 'move them'. Indeed, marathons are evaluated not only according to their sport credentials but also in

DOI: 10.4324/9781003125068-8

relation to the degree to which the crowd turns them into exciting and noisy specta-cles. The interviewed runners and their families and friends repeatedly responded 'great atmosphere' when asked to articulate what they looked forward to on the race day. This included the aural sensations of loud music and cheering, as well as gazing upon the electric crowd and the many exciting features of the built environment consumed in passing.

Since racecourses are designed to be visually exciting and tourist travel is central to marathon running, I examine the multi-sensuous ways that marathon runners gaze upon and sense atmospheres and environments during different stages of the course. The visual in particular imbues practices with a unique character, and they become extraordinary and 'touristic' when conducted against a striking or unusual visual scene. However, gazing is always multi-sensuous, embodied, and mobile (Urry & Larsen, 2011), and it is unclear how tired racing bodies gaze at places and sense the atmospheres that engulf them.

While marathon atmospheres are staged 'from above' (chapter 5), I argue that this atmospheric production is co-produced by many different actors (and not by a central conductor or under one master beat). This concurs with an approach that explores how people take part in and co-produce atmospheres (Edensor, 2015; Hauge & Bille, forthcoming). Moreover, this co-produced atmosphere transforms courses into vibrant places. I also make the point that runners experience atmo-spheric shifts, and that the sensuous reception and attunement to atmospheric inputs depends on the shifting psychological and physiological sensations of running.

Such study requires an energetic rhythm analysist with observant eyes to see the spectacles that unfold during a marathon, but equally alert ears, as much of this atmo-sphere is transmitted by beats and sounds. As part of his 'balcony gaze', Lefebvre also listened to somatic rhythms made by humans and non-human agencies, claiming that a rhythm analyst is 'capable of listening to a house, street, a town as one listens to a symphony, an opera' (2004, p. 94). In his discussion of 'military drill', he noted how brass bands' repetitive somatic regulation ensured the rhythmic discipline of marching (Edensor, 2018). However, I argue that we need to be in the midst of it to fully appreciate, be energised by and contribute to it (chapter 3). Moreover, marathon music and cheering are a cacophony of sounds that hardly discipline runners, but rather surely incite them on in their own idiosyncratic ways and excite them at the same time. They add energy and excitement rather than discipline to this drama of rhythms.

I begin with a brief review of the literature on 'sport atmospheres', focusing in particular on match day atmospheres in and around football stadiums. I then compare the atmospheres between football stadiums and urban marathons to draw out the unique atmospheric and visual features of marathons. This is followed by an analytical discussion of the interviews. I explore the atmospheric and visual sensations that interviewees remember and long for. Next, I argue in detail how different forms of running enable different experiences, co-productions of and attunements to atmospheres. Then I examine the significant role of cheering and give the reader a taste of the atmospheric mayhem at Dronning Louises Bro

(Queen Louise's Bridge) in Copenhagen. I end with a post-marathon reflection on the rhythms and atmospheres that the Berlin Marathon transformed.

## Match day atmospheres

Edensor's (2015) study of match day atmospheres at Etihad Stadium, home of Manchester City, is a good starting point for discussing similarities and differences between how match day and race day atmospheres are experienced and co-produced. Edensor discusses how stadiums are designed to produce certain atmospheric qualities, for which purpose organisers pump up the atmosphere with cheerleaders, speakers, bands, mascots and stadium announcers (Edensor, 2015). This illustrates more broadly how architecture and infrastructure are not only a question of concrete matter or flesh but 'also about the production and circulation of affective energies and atmospheres whose materiality is distributed, vague, and felt' (Latham & McCormack, 2017, p. 374). Edensor also brings out how fan practices are always pre-formed and anticipated:

> the affective atmosphere during match day is always already staged, for fans arrive in the stadium affectively and emotionally primed to socialise, support their team and express themselves in distinctive ways, and the ground serves as a specifically designed stage for the performance of players, officials and managers, as well as fans.
>
> *(2015, p. 84)*

He focuses in particular on the role of competent and committed fans in generating the anticipated thick atmosphere. It is co-produced through packed stands, dense crowds, and bodies that sing, yell, chant, clap and scream their lungs out in support or complaint. Fans, he writes:

> engage in expressive chanting, they perform collective modes of celebration and despair, and share conviviality, humour and nostalgia. These codes of supporting, complaining and celebrating resonate with those of accompanying friends and family, as well as the familiar 90-minute companions that surround fans. Most share in singing and clapping, jumping in celebration, and slouching in disappointment.
>
> *(Edensor, 2015, p. 85)*

Waves of such affective and expressive support are infectious across the enclosed stadium, ebbing and flowing in response to events in the stands and on the pitch. Moreover, how people experience a particular atmosphere depends upon their mood. Edensor evokes joy of being part of such a collective body, where affective energies circulate in and between people and people share 'the moment with others' (Hauge & Bille, forthcoming, unpaginated).

While Edensor focuses on the effects that cheering practices have on the supporters themselves, he does hint at how players respond to being cheered at:

> Popular notions that supporters can affect the events that unfold during the game undergird the agency of fans in constituting a (good) atmosphere. Indeed, it is widely believed that the more fervent the support, the better will be the home team's performance for they will be inspired by the levels of noise and excitement. Conversely, there is a possibility, it is advanced, that a hostile atmosphere will intimidate the away side. There is a common sense understanding then, that fans can act as a '12th man' in influencing the outcome of the match, and this is often attributed as a key factor in accounting for the statistical fact that the home team is more likely to prevail across professional football.
>
> *(Edensor, 2015, p. 85)*

Atmospheric cheering has an invigorating effect that can lift one's team and intimidate the opponent. Moreover, as the COVID-19 lockdown has demonstrated, watching football matches with empty stands kills much of the joy of being a spectator (hence the use of recorded crowd noise in most TV productions).

## Race day atmospheres

There are obvious similarities between 'match day' and 'race day' atmospheres. First, as in football stadiums, the marathon atmosphere is in part staged 'from above'. Race organisers hire bands, DJs and performing artists that play and entertain people along the route with loud music and eye-catching performances. They may also distribute course maps that function as noisy 'clapping devices', 'horns' or 'microphones' to spectators. Some marathons have official 'cheering zones' where this atmosphere is particularly thick and intense – with people standing in close proximity, the music is loud and the street is covered with large banners and graffiti. This can be at busy corners or bridges where the visibility is good, and the 'soundscape' is somewhat contained in the otherwise open space. Moreover, the finish area is normally in an iconic and spectacular place (chapter 5), often decorated with flags, screens and commercial banners, and with acute commentators. When this is combined with effective sonic rhythms of rock or dance music and thousands of vocal spectators that incite the runners for the last stretch, finishing a marathon is normally highly symbolically charged and affective, an accomplishment where emotions run high.

Second, similar to stadiums, this atmosphere is also 'staged from below'. The numerous spectators who line the streets or watch from open windows or balconies play a crucial part in enacting and fulfilling the atmospheric potential of a marathon. They turn streets into 'standing stands' where locals, friends and family members are not just watching but also clapping; shooting confetti; displaying home-made posters with personal messages; shouting their lungs out, perhaps amplified by loud megaphones or crumpled maps that act as primitive megaphones; high-fiving runners; playing live music or loud bass-infused music from sound boxes on streets or massive speakers from balconies; and using whistles, cowbells, drums and other instruments. Techno, samba, brass, heavy rock and jazz blend with clapping, vocal exhortations and whistling, creating a dense 'soundscape' in certain places. Such beats resonate across streets, toning space and adding a sense of festivity and urgent rhythm. Such beating music is absorbed through bodies, encouraging runners to sustain their pace, to keep moving (Labelle, 2008, p. 190).

Running on muted streets is as uninspiring as playing for or watching matches with half-empty stands with subdued fans. Like dedicated football fans, my interviewees were articulate and reflexive about the atmospheric sensations they longed for and how they – as runners or spectators – play a part in animating and realising them. This illustrates that these atmospheres are largely produced by human practices. As Latham and McCormack note in their conceptual discussion of the *co-produced* affectual atmospheres at urban marathons:

> This affectual atmosphere is generated through all sorts of kinaesthetic involvements – the rhythm of the individual runner, the collective sound of thousands of feet striking asphalt, the in-out, in-out, in-out of the runners' breath, the shouts of the crowds, the rhythm of the bands that line the streets. So this is an affective atmosphere co-produced by both spectators and participants.
>
> *(Latham & McCormack, 2012, p. 66)*

What is unique about urban marathons' 'relational affective economy' (Latham & McCormack, 2012, p. 66) is that runners and spectators are on an equal footing and there is no rivalry between fans. Marathons are free events and spectators do not cheer on a specific team or boo at another, which potentially makes the atmosphere ardent and hostile in a football stadium. Such hostility is not present in marathons, where spectators cheer on friends and loved ones as well as 'strangers'. This one of the few events where ordinary athletes are treated as if they were professional football players or Tour de France riders, with many spectators sensing an obligation to vehemently applaud them and support the local running events (Larsen & Bærenholdt, 2019). While the atmosphere within the front corrals can be very serious and spirited (chapter 7), in the back corrals it is more relaxed and playful, with many runners waving and high-fiving spectators, some even wearing funny costumes.

In contrast to the enclosed stadium, where the action is spatially fixed on the pitch and the stands and the atmosphere is contained and transmitted relatively easily between the players and seated fans, the arena of the marathon is open, diffuse, changing and 'on the move', as it extends through stages throughout the city over a length of up to 42.195 km (chapter 7). Unlike the permanent and fixed nature of stadiums, the architecture of marathons is temporary as they override the usual rhythms of a place and sanction new rhythms that allow the street to be taken over and transformed by race organisers, runners, spectators, bands and performers.

The atmosphere is less thick and more volatile, and spectators need to be 'on the move' to see the different stages of the race. Hence, spectators are constantly seen navigating their way – on foot, bikes and trains – to the next spot on their race itinerary. The atmosphere is ebbing and flowing, and routes are normally composed of clusters of atmospheric noise and quiescence at different stages. There will always be stretches where few spectators congregate, and the most intense atmosphere will be concentrated in certain spots. By contrast, on quiet stretches where the sound of running feet dominates, perhaps punctuated by a few shouts, this leads to an inward, absorbed concentration (chapter 7). Atmospheres are fluid and ever-changing, dynamic and mutable (Edensor, 2015).

A final unique feature of marathon courses as against stadiums is that they are located in cities and are designed for 'tourist gazing'. This means that eyes are not only fixed on the ground or ball but also take in the surrounding environment. I argue that marathons have produced a new visual experience and way of seeing that I call 'the marathon gaze'. The 'tourist gaze' (Urry & Larsen, 2011) is historically tied up with leisurely walking and 'pauses' to photograph and inspect. When moving faster – for instance, with a sightseeing bus – a different visual experience unfolds, and the landscape becomes more 'cinematic' and the gaze turns into a glance (Larsen, 2001). While the marathon gaze also involves 'glancing', it provides a very different visual experience, as it is intimately linked with corporeal movement and endurance, as shown later.

## Anticipating and experiencing atmospheric and visual sensations

This section elaborates on the above by discussing how the interviewees verbalised and anticipated race day atmospheres, and how they feel and animate them. As Jenny stated:

> A city marathon without spectators will not make sense. A road race with no people in the streets would be meaningless. And the most boring one. There has to be either something beautiful to look at or spectator interaction.
>
> *(Personal communication)*

Indeed, running a marathon in a boring environment devoid of atmosphere appeals to few. I have discussed how much marathon training is somewhat uneventful, repetitive, lonesome and local (chapter 6), and any marathon must somehow reverse and be a contrast to this. This is also why marathon running died out during the COVID-19 lockdown when official city marathons were postponed. During the autumn of 2020, I tried to persuade my running friends to making our own marathon on our fast interval loop if the Valencia Marathon was postponed. I was in good form but also keen on running a marathon without a festive atmosphere for research purposes. What would that feel like? However, I failed. 'Come on, guys, let's try to organise our own little super-fast marathon with ten runners if the Valencia Marathon is cancelled. You know we can create a fast route around the park, we have done it with 5 km and 10 km races.' I had already tried a couple of times to stir up some excitement for the idea, but the reaction was once again lukewarm. As one said: 'You need a great atmosphere to run a marathon. This is not just something that you just train for and run in an indifferent environment'. Eventually I resigned myself to the fact that 2020 would be a strange year without marathons. I enrolled in some very low-key 10 km races, where the atmosphere is less vital, to keep my training on track and my motivation for running high.

For almost all my interviewees, it is vital that the racecourse be not only fast but also atmospheric, full of vibrant life, animating people, insistent beats and interesting sights. It needs to be a significant *place*, not just an indifferent course. Runners explain how they hear and sense all kinds of things – music, people on the street, dancing, noise, performers and running with others. Running a marathon is something extraordinary and highly demanding, and it demands a corresponding special scene for this testing experience to be memorable. The interviewees were clear that good marathons are not only closed-off streets but also attuned places with a festive atmosphere. The streets have a very different atmosphere on the days before and after the marathon, where one has to run on crowded pavements, where walkers may be annoyed by one's presence and cars and stoplights dominate the streets. Here people are likely to block off unpleasant noises and keep themselves entertained with music and podcasts (chapter 6). Extremely few runners run with music in their ears during races and few engage in conversations. They are sensuously absorbed by the atmospheric spectacles and move to the beats of others and music around them. Running on closed-off streets means that they can submit themselves fully to the atmosphere and to fellow runners rather than being observant of cars and lacing around pedestrians.

While all interviewees are concerned with the race itself and coping with its gruelling distance, many – especially those who are not chasing records – hope to experience something of the amazing street life and landmarks. They are simultaneously absorbed and focused on the job at hand and being immersed in the atmosphere.

The day before the Berlin Marathon I interviewed four middle-aged English runners, who I would classify as what I call 'experience runners' (see also chapter 4). They had previously participated in the London Marathon and spoke enthusiastically about how the London Marathon's massive sea of cheering people and co-runners produced an electrifying affective atmosphere that still sticks in their memory. They hoped that the Berlin Marathon would affect them in the same way:

RICHARD: I have done London three times and the atmosphere and whole event … is really, really good, and the number of people taking part … so I'm hoping that this is like what London is and that experience, the atmosphere and everybody around the race as well as people taking part in it. … Get around, enjoying the race and seeing a lot of people. And hopefully get past 4.30, if I can.

RAY: The atmosphere, we know, is going to be electric. We are really looking forward to doing it. You want to have a good race but also to enjoy the city. The atmosphere, the people. Seeing the city as you are running it.

*(Personal communication)*

Runners look forward to running in a noisy, carnivalesque scene, knowing that the bursting streets and vocal spectators will motivate them to push their tired minds and bodies forward. The atmosphere is energising: 'It bursts you on, gives you energy' (Claire, personal communication). As one woman, Helle, said:

> The atmosphere means absolutely everything. I am used to running alone. Running with a watch and a suiting pace. Here you get carried away. You are accompanied by others. Can find into a good pace with them. You can always see those you run at the same pace with.
>
> *(Personal communication, my translation)*

For Helle, the atmosphere is tied up with sociality; she expects to be carried away and forward by the atmosphere and the other runners rather than by her GPS watch. This testifies to the public character and 'camaraderie' that comes from running with others and being exposed to other city dwellers (Barnfield, 2018; Cidell, 2014). Marathon runners 'share the sharing and partake in an existential social exchange' (Hauge & Bille, forthcoming). The desired atmosphere is associated with collective engagement and the pleasures of being distracted as much as with performance enhancement. It is tied up with 'dissociative strategies' (see previous chapters), as the atmosphere energises but also distracts and arouses runners – for instance, making them run too fast when the atmosphere is thick and lose momentum when hitting quiet stretches. This explains why competitive runners are adamant about being carried away by the atmosphere. Yet this is less of a concern for 'experience runners', for whom marathon running is about experiencing the atmosphere and the city and not blocking out such stimuli (as with associative strategies). This indicates that runners' experiences of atmospheres and sights depend on how they run and their mood, to which they attune themselves, as now discussed.

## Attuning to atmospheres

It is thus important to recognise that how runners' sense and experience of a race atmosphere depend in part upon how fast they run and how hard they push themselves. This book has distinguished between 'achievement running' and 'experience running', and these modes of running produce different atmospheres, attune differently to atmospheres, and enable different experiences. This reflects that 'a space may attune our moods but is simultaneously "the extendedness" of our moods' (Böhme, 2002, p. 5). Atmospheres are intermediate phenomena, both internal and external – the atmosphere extends people's mood, which in turn feeds into the atmosphere (Böhme, 2002). People, as reflexive agents, can position themselves in the atmosphere in different ways: they may be fully swept away by it and contribute to it with open arms and supportive actions, or, alternatively, be disengaged or alienated from it (Hauge & Bille, forthcoming).

Several interviewees explained that *how* they run and *feel* during the race has a dramatic impact on how the race atmosphere affects them and how they in turn affect the atmosphere. This reflects the attention of atmosphere theory to moods. However, I suggest that peoples' bodily states also influence how they perceive and co-produce atmospheres. Drawing on the insight that gazing is conditioned upon movement, I argue that movement affects how atmospheres are felt and perceived. With reference to hill walking, Lund argues that 'the sense of vision and the mountaineer's gaze cannot be separated from examining the body that moves and touches the ground' (2005, p. 40). Gazing ought to be analysed 'in relation to the moving, multi-sensuous bodies because this provide us with a scope for looking at the body that senses – sees, touches, smells, hears and tastes – and how all these senses are integrated by the way in which the living body moves' (Lund, 2005, p. 41). As also touched upon in the previous chapters, this resonates with Ingold's argument that we do not perceive things 'from a fixed point but along what Gibson calls a "path of observation", a continuous itinerary of movement … . But if perception is thus a function of movement, then what we perceive must, at least in part, depend on how we move' (Ingold, 2004, p. 331).

To illustrate that movement and bodily states affect one's perception of atmospheres, I return to Richard and Ray, who were swept away by the atmosphere at the London Marathon. My point is that they were able to perceive and appreciate this positive atmosphere because their bodies were 'going well'. As Ray said:

> When we did London, then I was fitter … . We were chattering. We were able to enjoy it. See the scenery. The crowd were amazing. They were cheering, clapping, waving. Because we were in good shape. Are we here already? Like our bodies had been transporting us 13 miles. It was easy. Then, of course, it gets more difficult. If you're fit enough you can enjoy it. The miles fly by. You don't even realise it.
>
> *(Personal communication)*

Being in good shape meant that they had the energy to take in the atmosphere, at least in the early stages of the race where the required physical work is not too demanding (chapter 7). In the latter stages, it is more difficult with a tired and troubled body to appreciate the atmosphere and the scenery, as one's focus drifts when running with such a body. Peter was troubled by a niggling fear that his current day form was less impressive and that on Sunday he would run into pain and, equally disturbing, not be able to tune properly into the atmosphere and be positively affected by it. Or let us consider the couple I talked with at the Berlin Marathon. They were often taking it easy, in part to be able to tune into the atmosphere and see all the sights. However, they see less with tired legs, 'as the miles go on and on'. As they said:

DONALD: When you go 26 miles on foot you get to see a lot of a city. And if you go at the speed we go, you get to see a lot more than most. … You see less and less as the miles go along.

CLAIRE: I try really hard to stay in the moment because I really want to remember the experience, I don't want it to fly by. What was that race again? I really want to be in the moment.

*(Personal communication)*

This also means that the atmospheres change as the race progresses and one tires. However, the focus on seeing places and being 'in the moment' suggests that these runners first and foremost participate in marathons for the experience. I now discuss how the interviewees were aware that their specific race strategy and mindset largely determined how they experience the wider environment.

David made this clear in his reflections on two very different running experiences:

When I ran the Berlin Marathon the first time where I did not run to achieve anything, I saw and experienced so much. Caught a lot of atmosphere, bands, places. … When I ran it the second time and tried to get under three hours, I did not see a thing. You were so focused on your watch, eating gels, getting your drinks, how many miles, that you get some kind of tunnel vision. You do not see anything there. … There are no cars, there is a buzz, and the focus is towards the road.

*(Personal communication, my translation)*

While David ran the same marathon twice, each race was unique because he ran with different intentions and intensities, producing a different attunement to the atmospheres and sights. When racing hard, fully focused on his corporal state and rhythmic movement, all he sensed of the atmosphere and the wider environment was an indistinct 'buzz': he 'did not see a thing'. This is in direct contrast to his first Berlin Marathon when he did not 'did not run to achieve anything' and instead, as an experience runner, 'caught a lot of atmosphere, bands, places'. How people move through a landscape – their tempo, duration, intensity and mindset – thus influences their gaze and attunement to atmospheres. Those competitive souls who push their bodies to the maximum in the quest for a new personal best will often end up with tunnel vision. Their eyes are attuned to the task and the landscape is surveyed for information, not sensation: they are on the ground to coordinate proximity to other runners and avoid collisions, or on the horizon to assess what is coming, as discussed in chapter 7 (and in chapter 6 in relation to hard training). When running at a maximum, one hardly notices the environment, which passes by as a blurry, indistinct mess. They look *with* the landscape rather than *at* it (Nettleton, 2015), and their vision is rooted in their footwork (Larsen, 2019b, p. 571).

Take this English man in his thirties, an 'achievement runner' I interviewed at the Tokyo Marathon. Despite being a tourist in an exciting faraway city, based on previous experiences, Ben did not expect to see any landmarks or remember anything after the race except that crucial finish time:

If London and New York are anything to go by, then I will barely remember anything about the landmarks. I have done London three times and I couldn't tell you what it is like in the second part of the run except the part when you come to the Houses of Parliament and Big Ben. That's all I can remember, and I have run it three times, so probably not. It's a shame. I will run 26 miles tomorrow and not remember much about it other than the result.

*(Personal communication)*

Two other runners told me that they differentiate between 'experience marathons', where soaking up the atmosphere, having fun with the crowd, and seeing the city are key, and all-out marathons, where a fast time is the goal. They like to alternate between running such marathons. Lone distinguishes between being 'mindful' and having 'tunnel vision' and focusing on survival:

If I run after a PR, then it's almost tunnel vision. You keep control over your time. You are very focused on when drinks will come next. You spend a lot of time figuring out all sorts of things … I'm mindful when I do experience races. I look at where I am, experiencing sounds, people cheering. Reading t-shirts, signs. … Oncoming runners. The fast ones on their way out and the slow ones on their way home. When I run as fast as I can it is more survival.

*(Personal communication, my translation)*

Carsten also highlights the significance of the chosen 'mindset'. When racing, his vision is at the ground between his feet; but it is up when his purpose is enjoying the atmosphere:

You try as much as possible. It depends on your mindset for that particular race. If you go out and run all out, then you put your head down between your legs. But if your attitude is that you would like to get some fun out of it and experience the city, it is clear that you see much more of it. It was that attitude that I ran with in Tokyo, it was not a personal record attempt. I just had good legs. I think I saw much of the city.

*(Personal communication, my translation)*

This highlights how a low-paced run allows one to perform the tourist gaze, whereas fast-paced linear running with a high pulse and tunnel vision or the 'head down between the legs' largely prevents visual engagement with the landscape or appreciation of the atmosphere, although the latter role has an energising effect even unnoticed in the background (Larsen, 2019b, p. 571).

In an interview about the Tokyo Marathon, Lone explained that this race for her was all about having a good experience and absorbing the atmosphere rather than 'racing all out':

Because I had had two tough races … where I aimed for a PB, I just had to go over there and rediscover the fun and pleasure of running marathons. … A fantastic city, and all that with travelling. I had to go and feel that I had control over this distance rather than it controlling me. I have to smile and cheer people on, high-five the spectators and suck it all up instead of just running in this box where I have stomach pain and feel like vomiting.

*(Personal communication, my translation)*

For Lone, the Tokyo Marathon was about *re*discovering positive bodily sensations of marathon running after a few failed marathons attempting a personal best, including one when her body collapsed in a brutal heat at the London Marathon (chapter 7). In this case these positive sensations are tied up with indulging in and contributing to the atmosphere; indeed, she is actively and overtly co-producing the atmosphere. This was also the case for Oskar, who became a six-star finisher in the Tokyo Marathon:

> The race was great even before it started. I knew I would be a six-star finisher. So, the whole race should be something I would enjoy – all the way. I know that a marathon gets hard at some point, but you can enjoy it anyway. … In New York, I had a lovely, amazing race where I high-fived all the time and had time and energy to look around because … my objective was not an all-out race. … Going into the Tokyo race, I swore I'd keep an eye on all those cameras so I could remember to cheer, give high-fives and wave. And to watch the cheering and entertaining audience. I promised myself to keep an eye on that because time didn't matter today. So, I did. I must say that Tokyo is the perfect race for this because the atmosphere is crazy, and so many people are dressed up.
>
> *(Personal communication, my translation)*

This also illustrates how practitioners of achievement running and experience running typically co-produce the atmosphere in distinct ways. The 'achievement runners' will not interact much with the crowd, but nonetheless contribute by 'giving off' information through a clinched face, serious gesture and concentrated stare, interspersed with an intermittent wave to the crowd. They add seriousness to the atmosphere. However, the experience runner bestows play and reciprocity on the atmosphere, actively giving information by interacting directly with crowd (for instance by high-fiving and keeping eye contact), smiling and 'looking around'.

While Oskar was successful in taking in the sights and atmosphere, there is no guarantee that a slower pace will enable a positive experience. One year, at the sightseeing-friendly Kyoto Marathon, I deliberately aimed at enjoying the ride, taking in all the sights and soaking up the atmosphere. Accordingly, I chose to run at a moderate pace. However, the weather did not play its part in the early stages:

> My body temperature and the ambient temperature are still low, and combined with my moderate pace, my body, it feels, refuses to 'warm up' and my bone-frozen body overshadows other sensations during the first three or four kilometres. At one point, in panic, I grab a discarded poncho from a bin and

throw it around me, and it does not take long before my body heats up and runs smoothly, and my attention drifts away from the bad weather and what Leder calls my 'dys-appearing body'. … This in turn affords time and energy to indulge the senses in the sensations around me: the breathtaking scenery of snow-clad mountains on the horizon and the vibrant atmosphere and spectacles that enliven the streets for this day: enthusiastic high-fiving locals, bands, boisterous university cheer groups, geisha artists and martial arts practitioners.

(Larsen, 2021, p. 130)

Eventually, my well-functioning body allowed me to gaze eagerly on the astonishing shrines, temples, cheering monks, road signs, houses and locals that slid by: 'I'm flowing, absorbed in this sublime place rather than being burdened by the task at hand' (Larsen, 2021, p. 130). A well-paced marathon runner with fresh legs who is not time-obsessed can enjoy a mobile embodied marathon gaze that opens up the surrounding world. However, arrythmia can also hit easy-paced runners, as I painfully experienced at later stages in the Kyoto Marathon, when fatigue eventually clouded my vison and excitement for the surroundings:

When we pass the half-marathon mark, the course becomes flat and less spectacular. I also begin to feel the distance in my joints and muscles, which is a worrying sign so early in the race. … Yet the nice detour through the cherry trees blossoming in Kyoto Botanical Gardens and along the enchanting Kamo River provides enough distraction to keep my tourist gaze occupied. However, my pace is slowly dropping and my body is reappearing, feeling low on energy and with heavy legs, and I find it increasingly difficult to get excited by surroundings in the modern part of the city. While this part of the course is perhaps less intriguing to the 'tourist gaze', the point is rather that a troubled body is self-obsessed and oblivious to the wider environment unless it affects one's pace.

(Field notes, cited in Larsen, 2021, p. 130)

This illustrates how atmospheric intensities wax and wane during the race. Almost all marathons have boring parts where there is little to entertain the eyes and ears, where the atmosphere is muted, and spectators are passive or absent. Yet is also illustrates another analytical point: runners' visual and atmospheric experiences within a given place depend as much upon their shifting bodily states as upon the place itself. I found this stretch boring in part because I was drowsy and tired of running. I had little energy to enjoy the surroundings and different spectators. At this advanced stage of the course, I found it difficult to zoom in and appreciate what was passing by. On another day and with another body, I might have enjoyed the modern part of the city and mundane street life. This is important, as runners are not only exposed to landmarks and tourist bubbles. Racecourses also venture off the beaten tracks and give a unique possibility to experience local neighbourhoods where few tourists roam.

The next section examines the significant role of cheering by spectators and the acute affective emotional responses that such cheering can generate. It also addresses how experience runners in particular contribute to the co-production of the atmosphere, as touched upon in the two citations above.

## Cheering and emotional sensations

### Kyoto Marathon vignette

I'm standing at a small quiet corner in a sleepy traditional neighbourhood in the northern part of Kyoto watching runners moving towards me and making a turn. It is a chilly winter day. It is raining. Even the elite runners wear extra clothing. Despite the poor weather, many locals and out-of-town spectators have come out and are gathered, making this dormant corner unusually active.

This mundane urban space is transformed by the expectation and anticipation of the crowd, as well as by the runners who co-produce this altered atmosphere that will be gone in a few hours. I'm sipping coffee and taking in the sonic and visual atmosphere. As I experienced two years ago when I ran it, the countless Japanese volunteers are

FIGURE 8.1 Raining, Kyoto Marathon

**FIGURE 8.2** Cheering 1, Kyoto Marathon

atmosphere-makers as much as guardians – shouting support as much as controlling people. There is no official entertainment on this corner, but a group of young local baseball players are particularly active and vocal cheerers: they invite runners to high-five with them with outstretched arms, and many make a small detour to respond to this gesture, to which the boys respond with loud joyful chants. They are having a laugh, and few will fail to notice them or send a smile to them.

### Berlin Marathon vignette

Edensor and Larsen have this account:

> We are standing at the 38 km sign. Loud music is being played and cheerleaders do their dance stuff. Many runners are high-fiving spectators, laughing

**FIGURE 8.3** Cheering 2, Kyoto Marathon

and celebrating, looking round, hugging family members, and urging each other on in a less insistent rush towards the finish. Others dance along the finishing strait or stop to jive to the music on the spot, joining with the street dance troupe at the roadside (Sheehan, 2006). Others are visibly in pain, with wobbly legs, and seem oblivious to their surrounds. They can barely move their feet. Spectators call out (there are personalised names on the start number): 'Come on Sven, just another 1 km, you are almost there. You can do this'. They occasionally respond with a smile and a few lighter strides. Many cannot help being affected by, and, in turn, affecting the event by clapping along and shouting support to complete strangers.

*(2018, p. 743)*

The interviewees mention that the spectators create an electrifying atmosphere of exuberant support that gives them a much-needed boost, especially in the later stages when fatigue sets in and crushes one's willpower. The above vignettes illustrate how cheering can produce affective intensities and mutual interactions and gazes. Runners animate spectators to make noise and high-five, while spectators revitalise runners by yelling, dancing, shouting support, playing music and simply being present on the street, turning it into a temporary sport arena. Sheehan (2006, p. 259) remarks that 'participants' and spectators' repeated and ritualised performances create complex convivial situations of gazing and being gazed upon'. At play here is a 'relational affective economy in which there is a mutual and resonant feedback loop between the affects and emotions of the participants and those of the spectators. The spectators respond to the visible signs of affective intensity – sweat, grimace, smile – with their own gestures – waves, cheers, applause' (Latham & McCormack, 2012, p. 374). Carsten nicely illustrates this 'relationality' between runners and spectators:

> I'm a bit of an audience runner. I like to clap to the audience, and then they clap back … really nice feeling when you get applause. The hair rises, praise for one's work. I think they clap because they think it's impressive … I clap again. Clapping is a way to get them to clap back, which makes me happy, showing mutual respect. … If I have the energy, I always interact with the audience.
>
> *(Personal communication, my translation)*

Clapping and high-fiving are two ways that runners co-produce the anticipated atmosphere. They also stir up the atmosphere by roaring to the crowd and throwing their arms in the air when they encounter a silent crowd: 'Come on Copenhagen, make some noise!' Moreover, spectators are also animating each other, and when two or three people start to clap, others almost instantly join in with little hesitation. Engagement is transmitted to and resonates among the spectators, making it difficult not to be (at least a little) excited, touched and stirred by it, and many spectators – at least intermittently – become *active*, playing their part in creating a lively race atmosphere (as in football stadiums). Such generalised sociability bonds supporters and runners. It momentarily connects strangers (Wilks, 2013, p. 1) as spectators generously and indiscriminately cheer on those looking tired and needing a vocal boost (Larsen & Bærenholdt, 2019).

This sense of an atmospheric rhythmic community was deeply valued by the interviewees. It makes all the suffering seem extraordinary and eventful. Importantly, such cheering energises them. As Susan, a women in the forties, said about her previous experiences at the Berlin Marathon: 'The atmosphere is extreme. You will find that you are carried through. It is insane how many people call your name' (personal communication, my translation). People struggle with their own body, but they do so with others whose response lifts them. It is almost impossible not to be energised and emotionally affected. Richard and his friend Ray evoke how the electric crowd at the London Marathon overwhelmed Richard – made him cry:

> RICHARD: When we got to 15–16 miles, the crowd, the cheering, the cheering, I don't know what it was, but all of the sudden I felt like I was going to cry. All of a

sudden, tears were coming down my face while I'm running. I didn't know what it was. I was thinking to myself: pull yourself together. It lasted 3–4 minutes. I never had anything like that before. Never … .

RAY: I think it is a mixed feeling of the boost and support that you get from the supporters in the public and you are trying to deliver the expectations and that mixed feeling takes the emotional part of your body and overrides anything else in your mind and it shows, demonstrates, emotionally by tears coming out of your eyes.

*(Personal communication)*

I also interviewed several runners who said that seeing their supporting family members at certain pre-arranged spots on route sent a shiver through their bodies. Susan explained how being cheered on by one's loved ones is special and highly affecting: 'If you have family out there – they probably do not know – but as soon as you have passed them, the hairs stand up and you get a little extra energy. And then you wait to meet them again' (personal communication, my translation). Her family then began to explain how they will move along the different stages of the Berlin Marathon to support her – and all the Danish runners – in as many places as possible, combining moral support with handing out gels and drinks. They look forward to having great fun and love being vocal:

We meet her at 8, 18, 25, 27, and then at the finish line. As soon as they have passed, it is down to the subway, and then to the next place. … We try to cheer on all the Danes out there. … That is what is missing in Denmark: the atmosphere here in Germany – the courage to shout and scream.

*(Susan, personal communication, my translation)*

However, one place where 'shouting and screaming' is definitely not missing in Denmark is at the Dronning Louises Bro at the Copenhagen Marathon, where the atmosphere is particularly thick and vibrant.

## Dronning Louises Bro (Queen Louise's Bridge)

The Copenhagen Marathon has several 'cheering spots' that the organisers allocate to specific firms or running clubs and associations such as NBRO. They must in return stage a lively visual and sonic atmosphere. The Dronning Louises Bro is the heart of pro-cycling and 'liveable' Copenhagen, a popular hang-out place for young people. It is also the 'home ground' of NBRO (the meeting point is nearby). The last part of the NBRO motto is: 'if you don't pace you cheer', and the Copenhagen Marathon draws in a massive crowd of (often injured) NBRO runners who are keen and feel obligated to lift the spirits of their running friends by once again staging a sensuous mayhem at this bridge that will leave no one untouched, propel the runners forward and turn the cheering into a party in itself.

A party atmosphere does not simply materialise from thin air. Its realisation depends upon various material objects (chapter 5) and 'volunteering hands' that

**FIGURE 8.4** Dronning Louises Bro – the megaphone
Photo credit: Sofie Riisgaard.

'coordinate actions' and get things done, essentially social capital (chapter 4). The cheering committee and the many helpers arrive at the bridge a couple of hours before the first runners arrive. They carry a heavy arsenal of confetti, balloons, banners, graffiti paint, firework, stencils, long sticks with wooden signs with the NBRO logo engraved, powerful megaphones, foam hands, a professional DJ system with massive speakers, posters, cameras, soft drinks, beers and snacks.

**FIGURE 8.5** Dronning Louises Bro – the first NBRO runner
Photo credit: Sofie Riisgaard.

**FIGURE 8.6** Dronning Louises Bro – spectators
Photo credit: Sofie Riisgaard.

Alongside the official making of the route, the many NBRO volunteers – many dressed in the club jersey – are soon busy claiming the street by stencil graffiti-ing NBRO logos on the asphalt, hanging elevated banners across the street and setting up a DJ booth – in short, firing up a party mood. The bridge is soon packed with pumping music and hundreds of spectators waiting for the runners to arrive.

The scene bursts into life when the elite – mainly unknown African – runners arrive and people spur them on with much yelling, clapping and fireworks. However, the climax arrives when the first NBRO runners show up and a couple of NBRO spectators – with fireworks and flags in their hands – run alongside them to the bridge where the crowd have pushed into the street, leaving only a small densely packed corridor to run in. The bridge now resembles a mix between an Italian football stadium on fire and a densely packed Tour de France mountain stage where spectators almost rub shoulders with the riders and the passage is dangerously narrow. The noise is deafening, the fumes are overpowering, the air is red and it rains confetti.

It is a cacophony of sounds, sights and smells. Music, voices, liquids, firework, confetti, hands, utterings, clapping devices, megaphones and flags co-produce a sensuous overload that imprints itself physically and emotionally on spectators and the worn-out running bodies that play for the cameras and lift their arms in gratitude and celebration. This atmospheric moment is impossible to block out, and for a moment, runners – carried away – almost forget their tired bodies and speed up. Here it is, we may say, impossible to run with tunnel vision. Such sensations are hugely entertaining and energising, affective and emotional (especially for NBRO runners) at the same time. As one NBRO runner beautifully disclosed:

> Running over this bridge is like ... getting into a time pocket where everyone is running too fast, although one really should run slower as one would like to enjoy the moment as long as possible. You register a lot of things but at the same time nothing. I don't know how to explain it. It all happens so fast. One's hair rises, and you feel high. It is difficult to explain if you have not experienced that feeling of happiness yourself.
>
> *(Personal communication, my translation)*

This is one of few stretches where marathon runners hope that time would pass slower. And yet, despite the desire to stay in the moment, unreflexively, being overexcited, the pace increases a little. This also illustrates the analytical point that atmosphere is not only impressions and sensations but also raw energy.

Moreover, this co-produced atmosphere forms affective relationships and bonds social capital (within NBRO) and place identities. The making of this 'atmospheric bridge' provides this marathon course with a unique 'sense of place' that enables participants and especially NBRO runners to develop a 'topophilia' (Bale, 2004) or distinct sense of attachment to the bridge and event. Crossing that bridge will never be quite the same again. The bridge now ties the past and future together as people memorise past achievements and wonder how it will be the next time.

While the atmosphere dies out with the last runner, many running communities and clubs will generate new convivial atmospheres of drinking, socialising and dancing throughout the day in the finish area and later in bars, restaurants, and clubs, for NBRO – another of whose logos is 'run party repeat'– are part of the Bridge The Gap network of likeminded running communities across the world that come together at marathons to run and socialise in equal measure. Such associations *bridge* social capital *across* national borders (Larsen and Bærenholdt, 2019). They also inject this formerly tough and dead-serious event with a large dose of 'cool festivity' and looseness – although, as we have seen, many members are simultaneously competitive.

## Cycling and walking the route

I cycled the entire racecourse of the Berlin Marathon (Edensor & Larsen, 2018) and walked or ran parts of the other marathons to sense the rhythms and atmospheres that the event had transformed or would transform. In chapter 6 I discussed how densely packed pavements made running more or less impossible in Tokyo. When cycling through Berlin with sore legs the Monday after the race, I found the festive rhythms to be once again the usual, unapplauding rhythms of pedestrians, commuters, shoppers and tourists, the hums of cars, buses and trains, all coordinated by traffic signals. Most of the temporary architecture of fences, traffic signs and nutrition stations have been removed or are in the process of being moved. The streets are no longer covered with used plastic cups and gels. The tourist rhythms that move around Berlin's central attractions prevail again. Rather than forming the gateway to the race's finish, the Brandenburg Gate is the focus of tourist photography and guided tours. Open-air buses relay information to their passengers, and clusters of tourists are gathering around the Reichstag and Postdamer Platz and flow down Unter den Linden and around the Gendarmenmarkt, unimpeded by runners, barriers and security personnel. Similarly, hagglers, souvenir sellers and street performers are free once again to follow their customary routines and situate themselves in their usual stations.

I also learned that walking or even cycling – when combined with stops – affords visual experiences that often escaped me during the race. While designed to impress visually, I am always surprised by how difficult it is to remember and recognise the places on the routes. As argued, 'racing' in particular seems to prevent this sustained aesthetic engagement with places. Especially when walking, we seem to see much more of the landscape and its sensations. Perhaps this reflects, as Bale suggests that,

> it is 'the stroll', not a run, which provides a source of pleasure. One can take in the landscape and its variety more fully; one may pause and contemplate, even communicate. ... Solnit notes in her remarkable book on walking, 'a walker does not skip over much'. A runner, however, does.
>
> *(2004, pp. 75–76)*

Yet the difference between running and walking (or between achievement running and experience running) is only half the answer. Equally profoundly, I failed to notice these streets because they are *not* the same streets on race day and on any given Monday morning; they have different users, rhythms and atmospheres and therefore look, feel and sound poles apart. Runners, music, cheering, rows of spectators, fences, and 'running feet' on streets are replaced by noisy fuming cars and pedestrian movement on sidewalks. Running, say, Kurfürstendamm on the race day is one thing, but something completely different on a normal Sunday or a typical Monday after the race. Now the experience only exists as a memory.

## Conclusion

Drawing on theories about atmosphere and gazing, I have discussed racecourses as atmospheric places and focused on how runners sense and appreciate them, as well as the role of spectators in this dramaturgical production. Overall, this chapter demonstrates how atmospheres are contingently co-produced between many people, multiple things, and more or less 'coordinated actions'. Marathons are much more than just courses and runners, and spectators are 'emplaced' in and contribute to the production of this eventful place. Overall, I have established that marathons are highly atmospheric events that transform streets into lively sport environments where ordinary practitioners are treated like 'sport stars'. Marathons are not only eventful but also social and associational, connecting individual runners and spectators in a shared affective space of intense sociability.

The race atmosphere matters greatly to my interviewees, who vividly express their anticipation, memories and appreciations of the multi-sensuous atmosphere of the race. These vague impressions and interactions stick in their memory much more than do specific sights and neighbourhoods. They also know that 'racing hard' produces a 'tunnel vision'. However, a slower pace and less competitive approach does indeed enable the tourist marathon gaze and an immersion in the wider atmosphere. The sonic element is important to marathon runners, as the longed-for atmosphere is not just visual but, equally importantly, audible, produced through clapping, loud music, vocal support and other spectator acts. Marathon gazing is continually attuned by various shifting sounds of variable intensity, which create a particular visual and auditory atmosphere.

Lastly, the interviewees stress that atmospherics undoubtedly matter, lifting them in the moment and motivating them forward. However, I have argued that achievement running and experience running enable different 'moods' and co-produce different atmospheres. Cheering has the potential to animate and empower those engaged in sport to perform better. Atmospheric cheering energises running as an embodied rhythmic practice. However, this atmosphere is not only about improving performances; it is perhaps more importantly something deeply social and *touching*: it creates sociability, reciprocity, eventful places and place attachment, with people volunteering, running and cheering *together*. Marathons depend on this engagement to create what we might call 'atmospheric sociability'. This co-production also means that the atmospheric rhythms of marathons are ephemeral and vulnerable, which adds an extra element to marathon's drama of rhythms. If there is no common ethos and enthusiasm, the atmosphere dies out and the run collapses.

# CONCLUSION

I hope that this book has provided an interesting, lively and novel account of the places and embodied practices of marathons. This conclusion briefly summarises its contribution to the running and embodied-mobility literature. I have explored the intricate overlap between the ordinary and extraordinary nature of marathon running. This practice links everyday life and local places with exciting events, famous cities and tourist travel – unlike tourism, which is all about 'the extraordinary' (Urry & Larsen, 2011). While marathons are spectacular one-day events, marathon running is 'stretched out' across time and space; unlike many other urban events, marathons nourish specific skills as a part of everyday life. This book has therefore shifted between the mundane and special sensations of becoming and being a marathon runner. Marathon running is an idiosyncratic practice that deviates from most other mobile practices. The specific ways in which marathon running is different and transgressive can reveal interesting things about other urban mobilities.

This book is informed by the mobilities paradigm, practice theory, non-representational theory and carnal sociology. My interpretation of these theories has made it possible to take seriously the variegated embodied sensations, materialities, meanings and competences of marathon running. This book has explored, from an ethnographic perspective, how marathons take place and the embodied sensations and rhythms they invoke. I have run in marathons ('energising the rhythm analyst') and observed them, as well as interviewing other runners. The writing is intended to be accessible, lively and engaging, offering a tangible sense of what it feels like to run a marathon. The three main arguments developed in this book are summarised below.

First, I have argued that marathon running is a *rhythmic, embodied practice*. Although different sports are organised through particular rhythms, and various studies have discussed running as an embodied practice, little is known about the runner as 'a rhythmic figure' (Edensor et al., 2018, p. 111). While all mobilities are 'rhythmic', this book has demonstrated that marathon running is unique in being

DOI: 10.4324/9781003125068-9

organised around a core set of temporal rhythms that define it as an embodied practice. This book details the socially produced and learnt nature of *diverse* and historically specific marathon rhythms – and their dependence on specific objects, aspirations, places and measurements. These include the linear, 'mechanical' and timed rhythms of achievement running. They now also include the slower and more inclusive rhythms of jogging and what I call experience running, which 'democratised' running, ultimately 'slowing down' marathons and making them polyrhythmic (chapter 4). Rhythms imply measurement and running rhythms are both quantitative and qualitative, sensuously felt (for instance through ragged breathing and flow sensations), and measured and tracked through GPS watches and heart-rate monitors. The embodied rhythms of running – especially of 'achievement running'– are increasingly turned into 'numbers', while marathon dressage involves running in recorded time and circulating such data on social media (chapters 5–7).

The rhythmic core of marathon running is painstakingly detailed. There is an obsession with *even* pace *throughout* the race – preferably with a minimal increase ('negative split') at the end. This ensures an energy-saving run, which is essential for running as fast as possible (chapter 7), but also a eurhythmic run, allowing runners with healthy bodies to experience the scenery and atmosphere (chapter 8). To ensure such rhythmic competence, marathon training is overtly scripted and organised through varied, shifting rhythms; runners (learn to) adhere to and appreciate the long-established temporal rhythms of particular ways of running. Programmes, coaches and associations prescribe daily and weekly tasks that runners obediently carry out – week in, week out – when training for a marathon. This focus on repetition, 'mechanical', habitual rhythms and 'coaching' means that marathons resemble dressage. However, they represent a mild form of dressage. Many runners appreciate expert guidance, while others use such knowledge reflexively to construct their own programmes and routines in an informed way, synchronising them with domestic obligations and social relations. The rhythms of running are also about making time for running and deprioritising other temporal demands (chapter 6). The rhythms of training provide structure in everyday life, adding meaning and a sense of accomplishment to leisure time.

To become a competent, well-schooled runner is to experience the ecstasies, highs and flows of running rhythmically. The runner realises that his or her previously unfit, or old and decaying body can suddenly run long distances at unimagined speeds. Such pleasures are intensified when all of these volatile sensations become a number – a personal best time – that proves one has beaten oneself again and excelled in this demanding sport. These 'embodied ecstasies' must be understood in relation to the reduced physicality of much modern movement, leisure and work, as well as to the new societal value placed on 'achievements' – we are what we 'achieve'. I hope this book will inspire future work on the differences and similarities between various forms of movement and sport, in particular by conducting the form of energised rhythmanalysis that I have proposed. Hopefully, many mobility scholars will be animated to write lively, engaging and dramatical accounts about various form of mundane or eventful mobile life, based upon their own *and* not least other peoples' movement.

Second, I have argued and demonstrated that marathons are unique, fascinating and transformative places. Marathons are more than just running. They afford distinctive experiences of moving through and gazing upon some of the world's most exciting cities. Marathons are an outgrowth of the boom in city tourism, which began in the 1990s, when cities began to regain their past glory (Urry & Larsen, 2011). 'Bundling' marathons with tourist travel and exciting cities makes them particularly attractive.

I have argued that runners have particular needs and material relationships with the features and volumes of places and weather worlds. They have an open relationship with the environment, mediated by specialised clothing and shoes. Runners are very sensitive to the flat worlds they run on and the horizontal weather they run in and with. When training, their desired flows and linear rhythms are interrupted by stoplights and blocked by the slow and irregular rhythms of pedestrians, some of whom might find wheezing runners excessive and deviant. Busy roads with hard tarmac, cyclists, pedestrians and many stoplights are not ideal places for running. Nonetheless, we have seen how runners are skilled at reworking urban affordances and carving out appropriate what I have termed 'training grounds', which they slowly learn to live with and regard with affection (chapter 6). However, runners always cast an envious eye on those not-for-us-streets, with their smooth asphalt and ample space. The fact that serious running is still somewhat transgressive and 'out of place' in this everyday milieu explains why marathons are so exciting. They turn everything on its head, appropriating and reconfiguring streets into perfect rhythmic order as running environments, and replacing the usual rhythms that pervade cities and frustrate runners.

This book have proposeed the concept of 'course-places' to highlight the fact that marathons simultaneously provide fast, generic routes and distinctive, exciting places. Courses connote speed and seamless movement on smooth asphalt, broad streets and few corners (chapter 7). Places connote local features, (tourist) experiences, atmospheres and marathon gazing (chapter 8). The best marathons combine these two elements seamlessly. Courses and places co-*exist* and runners experience them both and as course-places (although they are analysed separately). However, achievement runners are more attuned to course-related features than to place-related ones. As demonstrated, racing very hard produces tunnel vision, attention to 'information' and blocked ears, which make it harder to experience places. Nevertheless, achievement runners are fully connected to the racecourse by their groundwork, weather work and scanning practices; they enjoy running freely and fast on a perfect racetrack, always noticing how they weather affects their embodied movement. Courses are *not* 'non-places'.

From a *place*-oriented perspective, marathons turn streets into highly affective, atmospheric places that create excitement, sociability and marathon tourist gazing – that is, experience running. Marathons exemplify the contemporary eventification and touristification of place. These place-related qualities make marathons truly doable and memorable. If marathons ever stop staging exciting, atmospheric places and provide mere courses instead, they will die out immediately, unable to attract practitioners.

As 'experimental urban labs', marathon running demonstrate the multifaceted and contingent ways that runners engage with, make sense of, and make material, social and cultural places. Moreover, marathons demonstrate that car-free streets can enliven embodied mobility and create lively streets, where people come together and communities flourish. They also illustrate the complex nature of pavements and the need to design them for everyday running, just as bike lanes and skate parks empower cyclists and skaters (Latham & Layton, 2020). Although there is much discussion of 'walkability' in urban design, there is little talk of 'runability'. This reflects that sport plays an inferior role in mobilities studies and urban studies where the focus is on commuting and leisurely walking, not serious sport. My hope is that this book has demonstrated ways in which sport could play a substantial role in future urban mobilities research.

Third, marathon running is a multifaceted drama of rhythms, involving unpredictability, struggles, pain and success. As discussed, these things occur because marathons are painstakingly planned to be predictable, ordered events, with isorhythmic rhythms that impose a temporary but rigid social order on time and space. This approach forces highly ordered rhythms upon the event, as well as normative meanings, efficient delivery and smooth running (chapter 5). For their part, runners undertake a great deal of rationalised and scientific-based training, running short test races and taking tests to determine their *exact* pace and *predicted* finish time (chapter 6). Thus, the drama is not about how the race will turn out, but whether it will fulfil expectations honed through everyday drilling and various calculations. A marathon is a success if the runner meets his or her expectations.

Yet things can go awry; anticipated rhythms can be transmuted, and runners lose face on Goffmanian front stages. Marathon running is never overwhelmed by rationality or preparatory calibrations, as shown in chapters 7 and 8. The vigilant ordering is easily ruined by poor planning, inclement weather, terror attacks or pandemics. Courses become slow. Marathons are cancelled. Runners realise that their bodies are irrational, embodied, prone to cramps, heat stroke and shoe-induced blisters – not well-oiled, carefully engineered machines. The minds of runners can overwhelm them with negative thoughts, impeding their progress. Their pace can drop and become arrhythmic. They can experience pain, while others whizz by, on the road to a new record. They may lose face, while others excel – this time! Next time it will be different. In this way, marathon running ties together the past and future through memories of failed attempts, personal records and dreams about the next time. This fusion of temporal schemes is at the heart of marathon running. The grandeur of a race hinges on the bodily attunement and expectations forged months and weeks in advance. In fact, marathons attract so many practitioners because they are rational and irrational at the same time.

Future studies may investigate other urban practices or events where dramas of eurhythmia and arrhythmia emerge and unfold. This drama of rhythms is not confined to marathons, but an integrated aspect of our everyday rhythms. Predictable, yet always producing surprises. Why did I fail? Next year, things will be different.

# REFERENCES

Abbas, A. (2004). The embodiment of class, gender and age through leisure: a realist analysis of long-distance running. *Leisure Studies*, 23(2), 159–175.

Adam, B. (1995). *Timewatch: The Social Analysis of Time*. Cambridge: Polity.

Adey, P. (2014). Security atmospheres or the crystallisation of worlds. *Environment and Planning D: Society and Space*, 32, 834–851.

Agger, B. (2011). *Body Problems: Running and Living Long in Fast-food Society*. London: Routledge.

Allen, K. (no year). How marathon race time works. *How Stuff Works*. https://adventure.howstuffworks.com/outdoor-activities/running/events/marathon-race-timing.htm

Allen, V. J., Yasso, B., & Burfoot, A. (2012). *The Runner's World Big Book of Marathon and Half-Marathon Training*. New York: Rodale.

Allen-Collinson, J. (2003). Running into injury time: distance running and temporality. *Sociology of Sport Journal*, 20, 331–350.

Allen-Collinson, J. (2008). Running the routes together: corunning and knowledge in action. *Journal of Contemporary Ethnography*, 37(1), 38–61.

Allen-Collinson, J. (2009). Sporting embodiment: sports studies and the (continuing) promise of phenomenology. *Qualitative Research in Sport and Exercise*, 1(3), 279–296.

Allen-Collinson, J. (2018). 'Weather work': embodiment and weather learning in a national outdoor exercise programme. *Qualitative Research in Sport, Exercise and Health*, 10(1), 63–74.

Allen-Collinson, J., & Hockey, J. (2005). Autoethnography: Self-indulgence or rigorous methodology. In M. McNamee (ed.), *Philosophy and the Sciences of Exercise, Health and Sport: Critical Perspectives on Research Methods*. London: Routledge, 187–202.

Allen Collinson, J., & Hockey, J. (2007). 'Working out' identity: distance runners and the management of disrupted identity. *Leisure Studies*, 26(4), 381–398.

Allen-Collinson, J., & Hockey, J. (2011). Feeling the way: notes toward a haptic phenomenology of distance running and scuba diving. *International Review for the Sociology of Sport*, 46(3), 330–345.

Allen-Collinson, J., & Hockey, J. (2015). From a certain point of view: sensory phenomenological envisionings of running space and place. *Journal of Contemporary Ethnography*, 44 (1), 63–83.

Allen-Collinson, J., Jennings, G., Vaittinen, A., & Owton, H. (2019). Weather-wise? Sporting embodiment, weather work and weather learning in running and triathlon. *International Review for the Sociology of Sport*, 54(7), 777–792.

Allen-Collinson, J., & Leledaki, A. (2015). Sensing the outdoors: a visual and haptic phenomenology of outdoor exercise embodiment. *Leisure Studies*, 34(4): 457–470.

Allen-Collinson, J., & Owton, H. (2015). Intense embodiment: senses of heat in women's running and boxing. *Body & Society*, 21(2), 245–268.

Allen-Collinson, J., Vaittinen, A., Jennings, G., & Owton, H. (2018). Exploring lived heat, "temperature work," and embodiment: novel auto/ethnographic insights from physical cultures. *Journal of Contemporary Ethnography*, 47(3), 283–305.

Amit, V., & Salazar, N. B. (eds). (2020). *Pacing Mobilities: Timing, Intensity, Tempo and Duration of Human Movements*. London: Berghahn Books.

Andersen, J. J. (2021). Marathon Statistics 2019 Worldwide (Research). *RunRepeat*, 2 March. https://runrepeat.com/research-marathon-performance-across-nations

Anderson, L. (2006). Analytical autoethnography. *Journal of Contemporary Ethnography*, 35, 373–395.

Andrews, G. J. (2017). From post-game to play-by-play: animating sports movement-space. *Progress in Human Geography*, 41(6), 766–794.

Andrews, G. J. (2018). *Non-Representational Theory & Health: The Health in Life in Space-Time Revealing*. London: Routledge.

Askwith, R. (2015). *Running Free. A Runner's back to Nature*. London: Yellow Jersey Press.

Atkinson, M. (2008). Triathlon, suffering and exciting significance. *Leisure Studies*, 27(2), 165–180.

Atkinson, M. (2015). The suffering and loneliness of the fell runner: an ethnographic foray. In G. Molnár & L. Purdy (eds), *Ethnographies in Sport and Exercise Research*. London: Routledge, pp. 110–124.

Atkinson, G., & Drust, B. (2005). Seasonal rhythms and exercise. *Clinics in Sports Medicine*, 24(2), 25–34.

Augé, M. (2008). *Non-Places: An Introduction to Supermodernity*. New York: Verso.

Austen, I. (2001). You clocked what? For marathon runners, it's gun vs. chip. *New York Times*, 1 Nov. www.nytimes.com/2001/11/01/technology/you-clocked-what-for-marathon-runners-it-s-gun-vs-chip.html

Axelsen, M., & Robinson, R. N. (2009). Race around the world: identifying a research agenda for the distance runner. *Annals of Leisure Research*, 12(2), 236–257.

Baden, D. A., Warwick-Evans, L., & Lakomy, J. (2004). Am I nearly there? The effect of anticipated running distance on perceived exertion and attentional focus. *Journal of Sport and Exercise Psychology*, 26(2), 215–231.

Balch, O. (2019). Why are middle-aged marathon runners faster than twentysomethings? *Guardian*, 2 April. www.theguardian.com/lifeandstyle/shortcuts/2019/apr/22/why-are-middle-aged-marathon-runners-faster-than-twentysomethings

Bale, J. (1996). Space, place and body culture: Yi-Fu Tuan and a geography of sport. *Geografiska Annaler: Series B, Human Geography*, 78(3), 163–171.

Bale, J. (2000). Human geography and the study of sport. In J. Coakley & E. Dunning (eds), *Handbook of Sports Studies*. London: Sage, pp. 171–186.

Bale, J. (2004). *Running Cultures: Racing in Time and Space*. London: Routledge.

Barnfield, A. (2016). Grasping physical exercise through recreational running and non-representational theory: a case study from Sofia, Bulgaria. *Sociology of Health & Illness*, 38 (7), 1121–1136.

Barnfield, A. (2018). 'Autonomous geographies of recreational running in Sofia', Bulgaria. *International Review for the Sociology of Sport*, 53(8), 944–959.

Barratt, P. (2017). Healthy competition: A qualitative study investigating persuasive technologies and the gamification of cycling. *Health & Place*, 46, 328–336.

Barry, K., Borovnik, M., & Edensor, T. (eds). (2021). *Weather: Spaces, Mobilities and Affects*. London: Routledge.

Bauman, Z. (2001). 'Consuming life'. *Journal of Consumer Culture*, 1(1), 9–29.

Becker, H. S. (1953). Becoming a marihuana user. *American Journal of Sociology*, 59(3), 235–242.

Berking, H., & Neckel, S. (1993). Urban marathon: the staging of individuality as an urban event. *Theory, Culture & Society*, 10(4), 63–78.

Bille, M., Bjerregaard, P., & Sørensen, T. F. (2015). Staging atmospheres: materiality, culture, and the texture of the in-between. *Emotion, Space and Society*, 15, 31–38.

Bille, M., & Simonsen, K. (2019). Atmospheric practices: on affecting and being affected. *Space and Culture*, doi:1206331218819711.

Bissell, D. (2008). Comfortable bodies: sedentary affects. *Environment and Planning A*, 40(7), 1697–1712.

Bloom, M. (2015). What is the best surface to run on to avoid getting injured? Not all running surfaces are created equal – we've rated the top 10, from asphalt to woodland. *Runner's World*, 1 Jan. www.runnersworld.com/uk/health/injury/a760152/top-10-running-surfaces/

Blue, S. (2017). Maintaining physical exercise as a matter of synchronising practices: experiences and observations from training in mixed martial arts. *Health & Place*, 46, 344–350.

Böhme, G. (2002). The space of bodily presence and space as a medium of representation. In M. Hård et al. (eds), *Transforming Spaces: The Topological Turn in Technology Studies*. www.ifs.tudarmstadt.de/fileadmin/gradkoll/Konferenzen/SpacesBoshmePaper.html

Bourdieu, P. (1984). *Distinction*. London: Routledge & Kegan Paul.

Boyle, P. & Haggerty, K. (2009). Spectacular security: mega-events and the security complex. *International Political Sociology*, 3, 257–274.

Breedveld, K., Scheerder, J., & Borgers, J. (2015). Running across Europe: The way forward. In *Running across Europe*. London: Palgrave Macmillan, pp. 241–264.

Bridel, W., Markula, P., & Denison, J. (eds). (2016). *Endurance Running: A Socio-cultural Examination*. London: Routledge.

Brohm, J. M. (1978). *Sport, a Prison of Measured Time: Essays*. London: Ink Links.

Brown, K. M. (2017). The haptic pleasures of ground-feel: the role of textured terrain in motivating regular exercise. *Health & Place*, 46, 307–314.

Bryant, J. (2006). *The London Marathon*. London: Random House.

Buman, M. P., Brewer, B. W., & Cornelius, A. E. (2009). A discrete-time hazard model of hitting the wall in recreational marathon runners. *Psychology of Sport and Exercise*, 10(6), 662–666.

Buman, M. P., Brewer, B. W., Cornelius, A. E., Van Raalte, J. L., & Petitpas, A. J. (2008b). Hitting the wall in the marathon: phenomenological characteristics and associations with expectancy, gender, and running history. *Psychology of Sport and Exercise*, 9(2), 177–190.

Buman, M.P., Omli, J. W., GiacobbiJr, P. R., & Brewer, B. W. (2008a). Experiences and coping responses of "hitting the wall" for recreational marathon runners. *Journal of Applied Sport Psychology*, 20(3), 282–300.

Burns, G. T. & Tam, N. (2020). Is it the shoes? A simple proposal for regulating footwear in road running. *British Journal of Sports Medicine*, 54(8), 439–440.

Carlén, U., & Maivorsdotter, N. (2017). Exploring the role of digital tools in running: the meaning-making of user-generated data in a social networking site. *Qualitative Research in Sport, Exercise and Health*, 9(1), 18–32.

Carolan, M. S. (2008). More-than-representational knowledge/s of the countryside: how we think as bodies. *Sociologia Ruralis*, 48(4), 408–422.

Carter, T. F. (2011). Interrogating athletic urbanism: on examining the politics of the city underpinning the production of the spectacle. *International Review of the Sociology of Sport*, 46(2), 131–139.

Carter, T. F. (2018). *On Running and Becoming Human: An Anthropological Perspective*. Cham: Springer.

Chalip, L. & J. McGuirty (2004). Bundling sport events with the host destination, *Journal of Sport & Tourism*, 9(3), 267–282.

Chalkley, B., & Essex, S. (1999). Urban development through hosting international events: a history of the Olympic games. *Planning Perspectives*, 14(4), 369–394.

Chase, L. F. (2015). Beyond Boston and Kathrine Switzer. In W. Bridel, P. Markula, & J. Denison (eds), *Endurance Running: A Socio-Cultural Examination*. London: Routledge, pp. 61–77.

Cheuvront, S. N., & Haymes, E. M. (2001). Thermoregulation and marathon running. *Sports Medicine*, 31(10), 743–762.

Chiampas, G., & Jaworski, C. A. (2009). Preparing for the surge: perspectives on marathon medical preparedness. *Current Sports Medicine Reports*, 8(3), 131–135.

Cidell, J. (2014). Running road races as transgressive event mobilities. *Social and Cultural Geography*, 15, 571–583.

Cidell, J. (2016). Time and space to run. In K. Hannam, M. Mostafanezhad, & J. Rickley (eds), *Event Mobilities: Politics, Place and Performance*. London: Routledge, pp. 82–94.

Classen, C. (1997). Foundations for an anthropology of the senses. *International Social Science Journal*, 49(153), 401–412.

Cohen, D. T., & Hanold, M. T. (2016). Finish lines, not finish times: making meaning of the "marathon maniacs". *Sociology of Sport Journal*, 33(4), 347–356.

Cook, M., & Edensor, T. (2017). Cycling through dark space: apprehending landscape otherwise. *Mobilities*, 12(1), 1–19.

Cook, N. (2015). *Marathon Training*. London: Robert Hale.

Cook, S., Shaw, J., & Simpson, P. (2016). Jography: exploring meanings, experiences and spatialities of recreational road-running. *Mobilities*, 11(5), 744–769.

Cooper, P. L. (1992). The "visible hand" on the footrace: Fred Lebow and the marketing of the marathon. *Journal of Sport History*, 19(3), 244–256.

Cooper, P. L. (1998). *The American Marathon*. Syracuse: Syracuse University Press.

Coppieters, B. (2012). The organisation of marathons in divided cities: Brussels, Belfast, Beirut and Jerusalem. *The International Journal of the History of Sport*, 29(11), 1553–1576.

Coyle, E. F. (2007). Physiological regulation of marathon performance. *Sports Medicine*, 37 (4–5), 306–311.

Crang, M. (2001). Rhythms of the city. In J. May and N. Thrift (eds), *Timespace*. London: Routledge, pp. 187–207.

Cresswell, T. (2006). *On the Move: Mobility in the Modern Western World*. London: Routledge.

Cresswell, T. (2010). Towards a politics of mobility. *Environment and Planning D: Society and Space*, 28(1), 17–31.

Crossley, N. (1995). Merleau-Ponty, the elusive body and carnal sociology. *Body & Society*, 1 (1), 43–63.

Crossley, N. (2006). In the gym: motives, meaning and moral careers. *Body & Society*, 12(3), 23–50.

Csikszentmihalyi, M. (1997). *Finding Flow: The Psychology of Engagement with Everyday Life*. New York: Basic Books.

de Certeau, M. (1998). *The Practice of Everyday Life*. Minnesota: University of Minnesota Press.

Deaner, R. O., Addona, V., & Hanley, B. (2019). Risk taking runners slow more in the marathon. *Frontiers in Psychology*, 10, 333.

Deaner, R. O., Carter, R. E., Joyner, M. J., & Hunter, S. K. (2015). Men are more likely than women to slow in the marathon. *Medicine and Science in Sports and Exercise*, 47(3), 607.

Dempsey, N. P. (2008). Hook-ups and train wrecks: Contextual parameters and the coordination of jazz interactions. *Symbolic Interaction*, 31(1), 57–75.

Denison, J. (2006). The way we ran: reimagining research and the self. *Journal of Sport and Social Issues*, 30(4), 333–339.

Denison, J., & Markula, P. (2003). Introduction: moving writing. In J. Denison & P. Markula (eds), *Moving Writing: Crafting Movement in Sport Research*. New York: Peter Lang, pp. 1–24.

Denison, J., & Mills, J. P. (2014). Planning for distance running: coaching with Foucault. *Sports Coaching Review*, 3(1), 1–16.

Díaz, J. J., Fernández-Ozcorta, E. J., & Santos-Concejero, J. (2018). The influence of pacing strategy on marathon world records. *European Journal of Sport Science*, 18(6), 781–786.

Drummond, M. (2010). The natural: an autoethnography of a masculinized body in sport. *Men and Masculinities*, 12(3), 374–389.

Duffy, M., Waitt, G., Gorman-Murray, A. & Gibson, C. (2011). Bodily rhythms: corporeal capacities to engage with festival spaces. *Emotion, Space and Society*, 4(1), 17–24.

Edensor, T. (2003). Defamiliarizing the mundane roadscape. *Space and Culture*, 6(2), 151–168.

Edensor, T. (2010). Walking in rhythms: place, regulation, style and the flow of experience. *Visual Studies*, 25(1), 69–79.

Edensor, T. (2012). Introduction: thinking about rhythms. In T. Edensor (ed.), *Geographies of Rhythm: Nature, Place, Mobilities and Bodies*. Aldershot: Ashgate, pp. 1–19.

Edensor, T. (2015). Producing atmospheres at the match: fan cultures, commercialisation and mood management in English football. *Emotion, Space and Society*, 15, 82–89.

Edensor, T. (2018). The sonic rhythms of place. In M. Bull (ed.), *The Routledge Companion to Sound Studies*. London: Routledge, pp. 190–197.

Edensor, T., & Holloway, J. (2008). Rhythmanalysing the coach tour: the Ring of Kerry, Ireland. *Transactions of the Institute of British Geographers*, 33(4), 483–501.

Edensor, T., Kärrholm, M., & Wirdelöv, J. (2018). Rhythmanalysing the urban runner: Pildammsparken, Malmö. *Applied Mobilities*, 3(2), 97–114.

Edensor, T., & Larsen, J. (2018). Rhythmanalysing marathon running: 'a drama of rhythms'. *Environment and Planning A: Economy and Space*, 50(3), 730–746.

Edensor, T., & Sumartojo, S. (2015). Designing atmospheres: introduction to special issue. *Visual Communication*, 14(3), 251–265.

Ehn, B., & Löfgren, O. (2010). *The Secret World of doing Nothing*. Berkeley: University of California Press.

Ekkekakis, P. (2009). The dual-mode theory of affective responses to exercise in metatheoretical context: II. Bodiless heads, ethereal cognitive schemata, and other improbable dualistic creatures, exercising. *International Review of Sport and Exercise Psychology*, 2(2), 139–160.

Elden, S. (2004). Rhythmanalysis: an introduction. *Rhythmanalysis: Space, Time and Everyday Life*. London: Continuum, pp. vii–xv.

Elkington, S., & Stebbins, R. A. (2014). *The Serious Leisure Perspective: An Introduction*. London: Routledge.

Elliott, A., & Urry, J. (2010). *Mobile Lives*. London: Routledge.

Ellis, C. (2004). *The Ethnographic I: A Methodological Novel about Autoethnography*. Walnut Creek, CA: AltaMira Press.

Ellis, C., Adams, T. E., & Bochner, A. P. (2010). Autoethnography: an overview. *Historical Social Research/Historische Sozialforschung*. https://nbn-resolving.org/urn:nbn:de:0168-ssoar-363237.

Elmose-Østerlund, K., & van der Roest, J.W. (2017). Understanding social capital in sports clubs: participation, duration and social trust. *European Journal for Sport and Society*, 14(4), 366–386.

Ely, M. R., Cheuvront, S. N., Roberts, W. O., & Montain, S. J. (2007). Impact of weather on marathon-running performance. *Medicine and Science in Sports and Exercise*, 39(3), 487–493.

Ely, M. R., Martin, D. E., Cheuvront, S. N., & Montain, S. J. (2008). Effect of ambient temperature on marathon pacing is dependent on runner ability. *Medical and Science in Sports and Exercise*, 40(9), 1675–1680.

Emery, L. (2020). The best gear for virtual marathon training this fall. *RunnersWorld*, 26 Aug. www.runnersworld.com/training/a20820878/what-to-wear-for-cool-weathermarathons/.

Esmonde, K. (2019). Training, tracking, and traversing: digital materiality and the production of bodies and/in space in runners' fitness tracking practices. *Leisure Studies*, 38(6), 804–817.

Ettema, D. (2015). Runnable cities: how does the running environment influence perceived attractiveness, restorativeness, and running frequency? *Environment and Behaviour*, 48, 1127–1147.

Ettorre, E. (2016). *Culture, Bodies and the Sociology of Health*. London: Routledge.

Ewert, G. D. (2007). Marathon race medical administration. *Sports Medicine*, 37(4/5), 428–430.

Fine, G. A. (2004). *Body and Soul: Notebooks of an Apprentice Boxer* by Loïc Wacquant. *American Journal of Sociology*, 110(2), 505–507.

Finn, A. (2012). *Running with the Kenyans: Discovering the Secrets of the Fastest People on Earth*. London: Faber & Faber.

Finn, A. (2015). *The Way of the Runner: A Journey into the Obsessive World of Japanese Running*. London: Faber & Faber.

Fisette, J. L. (2015). The marathon journey of my body-self and performing identity. *Sociology of Sport Journal*, 32(1), 68–88.

Forsberg, P. (2014). Segmentation of Danish runners. In J. Scheerder, K. Breedveld & J. Borgers (eds), *Running across Europe: The Rise and Size of One of the Largest Sport Markets*. New York: Palgrave, pp. 59–72.

Forsyth, A. (2015). What is a walkable place? The walkability debate in urban design. *Urban Design International*, 20(4), 274–292.

Franck, K. A., & Stevens, Q. (2007). Tying down loose space. In K. Franck & Q. Stevens (eds), *Loose Space: Possibility and Diversity in Urban Life*. London: Routledge, 1–33.

Freund, P., & Martin, G. (2004). Walking and motoring: fitness and the social organisation of movement. *Sociology of Health & Illness*, 26(3), 273–286.

Gaffney, C. (2014). Geography of sport. In J. Maguire (ed.), *Social Sciences in Sport*. Leeds: Human Kinetics, pp. 109–134.

García-Vallejo, A. M., Albahari, A., Añó-Sanz, V., & Garrido-Moreno, A. (2020). What's behind a marathon? Process management in sports running events. *Sustainability*, 12(15), 6000.

Getz, D., & Andersson, T. D. (2010). The event-tourist career trajectory: A study of high-involvement amateur distance runners. *Scandinavian Journal of Hospitality and Tourism*, 10 (4), 468–491.

Getz, D., & McConnell, A. (2011). Serious sport tourism and event travel careers. *Journal of Sport Management*, 25(4), 326–338.

Gibson, J. J. (1977). The concept of affordances. In R. Shaw & J. Bransford (eds), *Perceiving, Acting, and Knowing*. London: John Wiley.

Giddens, A. (1991). *Modernity and Self-identity: Self and Society in the Late Modern Age*. Stanford: Stanford University Press.

Gimlin, D. (2010). Uncivil attention and the public runner. *Sociology of Sport Journal*, 27(3), 268–284.

Goffman, E. (1978). *The Presentation of Self in Everyday Life*. London: Harmondsworth.

Goodridge, J. (1999). *Rhythm and Timing of Movement in Performance: Drama, Dance and Ceremony*. London: Jessica Kingsley.

Goodsell, T. L., & Harris, B. D. (2011). Family life and marathon running: constraint, cooperation, and gender in a leisure activity. *Journal of Leisure Research*, 43(1), 80–109.

Goodsell, T. L., Harris, B. D. & Bailey, B. W. (2013). Family status and motivations to run: a qualitative study of marathon runners. *Leisure Sciences*, 35(4), 337–352.

Gotaas, T. (2009). *Running: A Global History*. London: Reaktion Books.

Gratton, C., & Henry, I. (eds). (2002). *Sport in the City: The Role of Sport in Economic and Social Regeneration*. London: Routledge.

Green, B. C., & Jones, I. (2005). Serious leisure, social identity and sport tourism. *Sport in Society*, 8(2), 164–181.

Groth, S., & Krahn, Y. (2017). Sensing athletes: sensory dimensions of recreational endurance sports. *Journal of Ethnology and Folkloristics*, 11(2), 3–23.

Hall, S. A., Manning, R. D., Keiper, M., Jenny, S. E. & Allen, B. (2019). Stakeholders' reception of critical risks and challenges hosting marathon events: an exploratory study. *Journal of Contemporary Athletics*, 13(1), 11–22.

Haney, T., & Mercer, J. (2011). A description of variability of pacing in marathon distance running. *International Journal of Exercise Science*, 4(1), 133–140.

Hauge, B., & Bille, M. (forthcoming). Atmospheres between being and becoming in public squares in Copenhagen. *Urban Studies*.

Havens, T. R. (2015). *Marathon Japan: Distance Racing and Civic Culture*. Honolulu: University of Hawai'i Press.

Hewitt, P. (2012). *Keep on Running: The Highs and Lows of a Marathon Addict*. Chichester: Summersdale.

Higdon, H. (2011). *Marathon: The Ultimate Guide*. New York: Rodale.

Highmore, B. (2004). Homework: routine, social aesthetics and the ambiguity of everyday life. *Cultural Studies*, 18(2–3), 306–327.

Hilditch, G. (2014). *Marathon and Half Marathon. A Training Guide*. Marlborough: Crowood.

Hindley, D. (2020). 'More than just a run in the park': an exploration of parkrun as a shared leisure space. *Leisure Sciences*, 42(1), 85–105.

Hitchings, R., & Latham, A. (2016). Indoor versus outdoor running: understanding how recreational exercise comes to inhabit environments through practitioner talk. *Transactions of the Institute of British Geographers*, 41(4), 503–514.

Hitchings, R., & Latham, A. (2017a). How 'social' is recreational running? Findings from a qualitative study in London and implications for public health promotion. *Health & Place*, 46(July), 337–343.

Hitchings, R., & Latham, A. (2017b). Exercise and environment: new qualitative work to link popular practice and public health. *Health & Place*, 46, 300–306.

Hockey, J. (2006). Sensing the run: the senses and distance running. *Senses and Society*, 1, 183–201.

Hockey, J. (2009). Mundane ritual practices and distance running training. *Journal of Ritual Studies*, 23(2), 77–88.

Hockey, J. (2013). Knowing the 'going': the sensory evaluation of distance running. *Qualitative Research in Sport, Exercise and Health*, 5(1), 127–141.

Hockey, J., & Allen-Collinson, J. (2006). Seeing the way: visual sociology and the distance runner's perspective. *Visual Studies*, 21(1), 70–81.

Hockey, J., & Allen-Collinson, J. (2007). Grasping the phenomenology of sporting bodies. *International Review for the Sociology of Sport*, 42(2), 115–131.

Hockey, J., & Allen-Collinson, J. (2016). Digging in. In W. Bridel, P. Markula & J. Denison (eds), *Endurance Running: A Socio-Cultural Examination*. London: Routledge, pp. 227–242.

Hockey, J., & Allen-Collinson, J. (2017). Running a temperature. In A. Sparkes (ed.), *Seeking the Senses in Physical Culture: Sensuous Scholarship in Action*. London: Routledge, pp. 42–62.

Hockey, J., & Allen-Collinson, J. (2019). Distance runners as thermal objects: temperature work, somatic learning and thermal attunement. *Culture Machine*, 17, 1–18.

Hockey, J., Dilley, R., Robinson, V., & Sherlock, A. (2015). 'There's not just trainers or non-trainers, there's like degrees of trainers': commoditisation, singularisation and identity. *Journal of Material Culture*, 20(1), 21–42.

Howe, P. D., & Morris, C. (2009). An exploration of the co-production of performance running bodies and natures within 'running taskscapes'. *Journal of Sport and Social Issues*, 33 (3), 308–330.

Ingle, S (2020a). Controversial Nike Vaporflys to escape ban but running shoe rules will tighten, *Guardian*, 31 Jan. www.theguardian.com/sport/2020/jan/28/controversial-nike-vaporflys-escape-ban.

Ingle, S (2020b). Nike stirs the pot with 'gamechanger' running shoe in step with new rules. *Guardian*, 5 Feb.www.theguardian.com/sport/2020/feb/05/nike-air-zoom-alphafly-next-shoe

Ingle, S (2021). World Athletics gives seal of approval for controversial Nike Vaporfly shoes. *Guardian*, 31 Jan. www.theguardian.com/sport/2020/jan/31/world-athletics-seal-approval-controversial-nike-vaporfly-shoes-athletics

Ingold, T. (2002). *The Perception of the Environment: Essays on Livelihood, Dwelling and Skill*. London: Routledge.

Ingold, T. (2004). Culture on the ground: the world perceived through the feet. *Journal of Material Culture*, 9(3), 315–340.

Ingold, T. (2007). Earth, sky, wind, and weather. *Journal of the Royal Anthropological Institute*, 13(1), 19–38.

Ingold, T. (2010). Footprints through the weather-world: walking, breathing, knowing. *Journal of the Royal Anthropological Institute*, 16(1), 121–139.

Ingold, T. (2011). *Being Alive: Essays on Movement, Knowledge and Description*. London: Routledge.

Ingold, T., & Kurttila, T. (2000). Perceiving the environment in Finnish Lapland. *Body & Society*, 6(3/4), 183–196.

Jensen, O. B. (2013). *Staging Mobilities*. London: Routledge.

Jensen, O. B. (2016). Of 'other' materialities: why (mobilities) design is central to the future of mobilities research, *Mobilities*, 11(4), 587–597.

Jensen, O. B. (2021). Pandemic disruption, extended bodies, and elastic situations: reflections on COVID-19 and mobilities. *Mobilities*, 16(1), 1–15.

Jensen, O. B., Lanng, D. B., & Wind, S. (2016). Mobilities design: towards a research agenda for applied mobilities research. *Applied Mobilities*, 1(1), 26–42.

Jones, C. (2017). How can I run in the 2018 London Marathon? *Guardian*, 23 April. www.theguardian.com/voluntary-sector-network/2017/apr/23/how-can-i-run-in-the-2018-london-marathon-charity.

Jones, P. (2012). Sensory indiscipline and affect: a study of commuter cycling. *Social & Cultural Geography*, 13(6), 645–658.

Jones, P. (2017). Mobile bodies. In M. Silk, L. Andrews & H. Thorpe (eds), *Routledge Handbook of Physical Cultural Studies*. London: Routledge, pp. 304–312.

Kärrholm, M. (2009). To the rhythm of shopping: on synchronisation in urban landscapes of consumption. *Social & Cultural Geography*, 10(4), 421–440.

Keh, A. (2019). Eliud Kipchoge breaks two-hour marathon barrier. *New York Times*, 10 Dec. www.nytimes.com/2019/10/12/sports/eliud-kipchoge-marathon-record.html

Kelly, M. (2019). The fastest year of marathoning in a decade. *Canadian Running*, 16 Dec. https://runningmagazine.ca/the-scene/2019-the-fastest-year-of-marathoning-in-a-decade/

Kelly, L. A., Lichtwark, G. A., Farris, D. J., & Cresswell, A. (2016). Shoes alter the spring-like function of the human foot during running. *Journal of The Royal Society Interface*, 13 (119), doi:20160174.

Kerr, R. (2014). From Foucault to Latour: gymnastics training as a socio-technical network. *Sociology of Sport Journal*, 31(1), 85–101.

Klauser, F. (2012). Sport megaevents and the city. *Environment and Planning C*, 30, 1–2.

Koch, N. (2017). Introduction: critical geographies of sport in global perspective. In N. Koch (ed.), *Critical Geographies of Sport: Space, Power and Sport in Global Perspective*. London: Routledge, pp. 1–11.

Koch, N. (2018). Sports and the city. *Geography Compass*, 12(3), 12:e12360.

Koehler, K. (2016). Nutrition for marathon running. In C. Zinner & Sperlich, B. (eds), *Marathon Running: Physiology, Psychology, Nutrition and Training Aspects*. Cham: Springer, pp. 47–67.

Kornum, N., Gyrd-Jones, R., Al Zagir, N., & Brandis, K. A. (2017). Interplay between intended brand identity and identities in a Nike related brand community: co-existing synergies and tensions in a nested system. *Journal of Business Research*, 70, 432–440.

Labelle, B. (2008). Pump up the bass: rhythm, cars and auditory scaffolding. *Senses and Society*, 3(2), 187–204.

Lara, B., Salinero, J. J., & Del Coso, J. (2014). The relationship between age and running time in elite marathoners is U shaped. *Age*, 36(2), 1003–1008.

Larsen, J. (2001). Tourism mobilities and the travel glance: experiences of being on the move. *Scandinavian Journal of Hospitality and Tourism*, 1(2), 80–98.

Larsen, J. (2008). De-exoticizing tourist travel: Everyday life and sociality on the move. *Leisure Studies*, 27(1), 21–34.

Larsen, J. (2014). (Auto)Ethnography and cycling. *International Journal of Social Research Methodology*, 17(1), 59–71.

Larsen, J. (2017). The making of a pro-cycling city: social practices and bicycle mobilities. *Environment and Planning A*, 49(4), 876–892.

Larsen, J. (2018a). Commuting, exercise and sport: an ethnography of long-distance bike commuting. *Social & Cultural Geography*, 19(1), 39–58.

Larsen, J. (2018b). Autoetnografi: kropslig mobilitet og sport. In M. Jacobsen & H. L. Jensen (eds), *Etnografier*. København: Hans Rietzels, pp. 151–170.

Larsen, J. (2019a). Running and tourism: A practice approach. In L. James, C. Ren & H. Halkier (eds), *Theories of Practice in Tourism*. London: Routledge, pp. 41–57.

Larsen, J. (2019b). 'Running on sandcastles': energising the rhythmanalyst through non-representational ethnography of a running event. *Mobilities*, 14(5), 561–577.

Larsen, J. (2020). Ups and downs with urban cycling. In O. B. Jensen, C. Lassen, V. Kaufmann, M. Freudendal-Pedersen & I. Lange (eds), *Handbook of Urban Mobilities*. London: Routledge, 127–136.

Larsen, J. (2021). Marathon mobilities. In H. Endo (ed.), *Understanding Tourism Mobilities in Japan*. London: Routledge, pp. 124–137.

Larsen, J., & Bærenholdt, J. O. (2019). Running together: the social capitals of a tourism running event. *Annals of Tourism Research*, 79, 102788.

Larsen, J., & Jensen, O. B. (2021). Marathon running in the 'weather'. In K. Barry, M. Borovnik & T. Edensor (eds), *Weather: Spaces, Mobilities and Affect*. London: Routledge, pp. 67–80.

Larsen, J., Urry, J., & Axhausen, K. W. (2007). Networks and tourism: mobile social life. *Annals of Tourism Research*, 34(1), 244–262.

Larsen, J., Urry, J., & Axhausen, K. (2008). Coordinating face-to-face meetings in mobile network societies. *Information, Communication & Society*, 11(5), 640–658.

Lash, S., & Urry, J. (1993). *Economies of Signs and Space*. London: Sage.

Latham, A. (2015). The history of a habit: jogging as a palliative to sedentariness in 1960s America. *Cultural Geographies*, 22(1), 103–126.

Latham, A., & Layton, J. (2020). Kinaesthetic cities: Studying the worlds of amateur sports and fitness in contemporary urban environments. *Progress in Human Geography*, 44(5), 852–876.

Latham, A., & McCormack, D. P. (2012). Globalizations big and small. In I. Farías & T. Bender (eds), *Urban Assemblages: How Actor-network Theory Changes Urban Studies*. London: Routledge, pp. 53–72.

Latham, A., & McCormack, D. P. (2017). Affective cities. In M. L. Silk, D. L. Andrews & H. Thorpe (eds), *Routledge Handbook of Physical Cultural Studies*. London: Routledge, pp. 369–377.

Laub, T. B. (2011). *Danskernes Motions- og Sportsvaner*. København: Idrættens Analyseinstitut.

Laurier, E. (1999). That sinking feeling: elitism, working leisure and yachting. In D. Crouch (ed.), *Leisure Practices and Geographical Knowledge*. London: Routledge, pp. 195–213.

Laurier, E. (2010). Participant observation. In N. Clifford, S. French & G. Valentine (eds), *Key Methods in Geography*. London: Sage, pp. 116–130.

Leder, D. (1990). *The Absent Body*. Chicago: University of Chicago Press.

Lefebvre, H. (2004). *Rhythmanalysis: Space, Time and Everyday Life*. London: Continuum.

Lev, A. (2019). Becoming a long-distance runner: deriving pleasure and contentment in times of pain and bodily distress. *Leisure Studies*, 38(6), 790–803.

Lev, A., & Zach, S. (2020). Running between the raindrops: running marathons and the potential to put marriage in jeopardy. *International Review for the Sociology of Sport*, 55(5), 509–525.

Lieberman, D. E., & Bramble, D. M. (2007). The evolution of marathon running. *Sports Medicine*, 37(4–5), 288–290.

Lindsey, J. (2019). The race to build the world's fastest running shoe. *Runnersworld*, 5 Dec. www.runnersworld.com/gear/a28709248/fastest-running-shoes/

Lomborg, S., & Frandsen, K. (2016). Self-tracking as communication. *Information, Communication & Society*, 19(7), 1015–1027.

Lorimer, H. (2005). Cultural geography: the busyness of being more-than-representational. *Progress in Human Geography*, 29(1), 83–94.

Lorimer, H. (2012). Surfaces and slopes. *Performance Research*, 17(2), 83–86.

Lund, K. (2005). Seeing in motion and the touching eye: walking over Scotland's mountains. *Etnofoor*, 18(1), 27–42.

Lupton, D. (2015). Data assemblages, sentient schools and digitized health and physical education (response to Gard). *Sport, Education & Society*, 20(1), 122–132.

Lupton, D. (2016). Foreword: lively devices, lively data and lively leisure studies. *Leisure Studies*, 35(6), 709–711.

Lupton, D., Pink, S., LaBond, C. H., & Sumartojo, S. (2018). Digital traces in context: personal data contexts, data sense and self-tracking cycling. *International Journal of Communication*, 12, 647–665.

Lyon, D. (2018). *What is Rhythmanalysis?* London: Bloomsbury.

MacNaughton, P., & Urry, J. (2001). Bodies of nature: introduction. In P. MacNaughton & J. Urry (eds), *Bodies of Nature*. London: Sage, pp. 1–11.

Maffesoli, M. (1995). *The Time of the Tribes: The Decline of Individualism in Mass Society*. London: Sage.

Maller, C., Nicholls, L. & Strengers, Y. (2016). Understanding the materiality of neighbourhoods in 'healthy practices': outdoor exercise practices in a new master-planned estate. *Urban Policy and Research*, 34(1), 55–72.

March, D. S., Vanderburgh, P. M., Titlebaum, P. J., & Hoops, M. L. (2011). Age, sex, and finish time as determinants of pacing in the marathon. *Journal of Strength & Conditioning Research*, 25(2), 386–391.

Markula, P. (ed.). (2003). *Moving Writing: Crafting Movement in Sport Research.* New York: Peter Lang.

Markula, P., & Pringle, R. (2006). *Foucault, Sport and Exercise: Power, Knowledge and Transforming the Self.* London: Routledge.

Masters, K. S., & Lambert, M. J. (1989). The relations between cognitive coping strategies, reasons for running, injury, and performance of marathon runners. *Journal Sport Exercise Psychology*, 11, 161–170.

Masters, K. S., & Ogles, B. M. (1995). An investigation of the different motivations of marathon runners with varying degrees of experience. *Journal of Sport Behavior*, 18(1), 69–79.

McDougall, C. (2010). *Born to Run: The Hidden Tribe, the Ultra-runners, and the Greatest Race the World has Never seen.* London: Profile Books.

McGehee, N. G., Yoon, Y., & Cardenas, D. (2003). Involvement and travel for recreational runners in North Carolina. *Journal of Sport Management*, 17(3), 305–324.

McGillivray, D., & Frew, M. (2015). From fan parks to live sites: mega events and the territorialisation of urban space. *Urban Studies*, 52(14), 2649–2663.

McLoughlin, C. (2010). Playing with numbers. *Anthropological Theory*, 10(1/2), 75–80.

McMahon, J., & Thompson, M. (2011). Body work—regulation of a swimmer body: an autoethnography from an Australian elite swimmer. *Sport, Education and Society*, 16(1), 35–50.

McQuire, J. (2018). 414,168 people enter the 2019 London Marathon, making it the most popular marathon on the planet. *Runner's World*, 10 May. www.runnersworld.com/uk/news/a776151/london-marathon-most-popular-marathon-on-the-planet/

Merriman, P. (2014). Rethinking mobile methods. *Mobilities*, 9(2), 167–187.

Metzler, B. (2019). *Kicksology: The Hype, Science, Culture & Cool of Running Shoes.* Boulder: Velopress.

Michael, M. (2000). These boots are made for walking …: mundane technology, the body and human-environment relations. *Body & Society*, 6(3–4), 107–126.

Middleton, J. (2010). Sense and the city: exploring the embodied geographies of urban walking. *Social and Cultural Geography*, 11, 575–596.

Mills, J. P., & Denison, J. (2013). Coach Foucault: problematizing endurance running coaches' practices. *Sports Coaching Review*, 2(2), 136–150.

Mills, J. P., & Denison, J. (2015). Charting the development of contemporary endurance running training theory. In W. Bridel, P. Markula & J. Denison (eds), *Endurance Running: A Socio-Cultural Examination.* London: Routledge, pp. 50–60.

Mills, N. J. (2003). Running shoe materials. In A. Subic (ed.), *Materials in Sports Equipment.* Sawston: Woodhead Publishing, pp. 65–73.

Mitchell, (2001). Race timing: how it works. *Marathon Guide.* www.marathonguide.com/features/Articles/RaceTiming.cfm

Morgan, W. P., & Pollock, M. L. (1977). Psychologic characterization of the elite distance runner. *Annals of the New York Academy of Sciences*, 301(1), 382–403.

Moyna, N. (2019). What happens to your body when you run a marathon? *Brainstorm*, 17 Dec. www.rte.ie/brainstorm/2017/1024/914860-what-happens-to-your-body-when-you-run-a-marathon/

Munch, P. (2013). Danmark er verdens største maratonnation. *Politiken*, 26 Sept. https://politiken.dk/forbrugogliv/motion/art5472657/Danmark-er-verdens-største-maratonnation

Murakami, H. (2007). *What I Talk About When I Talk About Running.* New York: Vintage Books.

Nash, M. (2017). Gender on the ropes: an autoethnographic account of boxing in Tasmania, Australia. *International Review for the Sociology of Sport*, 52(6), 734–750.

Nerurkar, R. (2012). *Marathon Running: From Beginner to Elite.* London: Bloomsbury.

Nettleton, S. (2015). Fell runners and walking walls: towards a sociology of living landscapes and aesthetic atmospheres as an alternative to a Lakeland picturesque. *The British Journal of Sociology*, 66(4), 759–778.

Nettleton, S., & Hardey, M. (2006). Running away with health: the urban marathon and the construction of 'charitable bodies'. *Health*, 10(4), 441–460.

Newman, J., & Falcous, M. (2012). Moorings and movements: the paradox of sporting mobilities. *Sites*, 9(1), 38–58.

Nikolaidis, P. T., Alvero-Cruz, J. R., Villiger, E., Rosemann, T., & Knechtle, B. (2019). The age-related performance decline in marathon running: the paradigm of the Berlin Marathon. *International Journal of Environmental Research and Public Health*, 16(11), 2022.

Nikolaidis, P. T., & Knechtle, B. (2017). Effect of age and performance on pacing of marathon runners. *Open Access Journal of Sports Medicine*, 21(8), 171–180.

Nikolaidis, P. T., & Knechtle, B. (2018a). Pacing in age group marathoners in the 'New York City Marathon'. *Research in Sports Medicine*, 26(1), 86–99.

Nikolaidis, P. T., & Knechtle, B. (2018b). Pacing strategies in the 'Athens Classic Marathon': physiological and psychological aspects. *Frontiers in Physiology*, 9.

Nixon, D. V. (2012). A sense of momentum: mobility practices and dis/embodied landscapes of energy use. *Environment and Planning A*, 44, 1661–1678.

Noakes, T. (2003). Fluid replacement during marathon running. *Clinical Journal of Sport Medicine*, 13(5), 309–318.

Ogles, B. M., & Masters, K. S. (2003). A typology of marathon runners based on cluster analysis of motivations. *Journal of Sport Behaviour*, 26(1), 69–85.

Pantzar, M. & Shove, E. (2010). Understanding innovation in practice: a discussion of the production and re-production of Nordic Walking. *Technology Analysis & Strategic Management*, 22, 447–461.

Pedersen, H., Kremmer Pedersen, L., & Thing, L. F. (2018). 'Liquid running communities': an analysis of serious runners' communities. *European Journal for Sport and Society*, 15(3), 234–249.

Pedoe, D. S. T. (2007). Marathon medical support historical perspectives. *Sports Medicine*, 37 (4/5), 291–293.

Petersen, A. (2016). *Præstationssamfundet*. København: Hans Reitzels.

Picciotto, B. (2016). From the ground to the clouds: minimalist and maximalist footwear in the sport of running. *Explorations in Media Ecology*, 15(3–4), 331–342.

Pink, S. (2009). *Doing Sensory Ethnography*. London: Sage.

Pink, S. (2011). From embodiment to emplacement: re-thinking competing bodies, senses and spatialities. *Sport, Education and Society*, 16(3), 343–355.

Pink, S. (2012). *Situating Everyday Life: Practices and Places*. London: Sage.

Pink, S., & Fors, V. (2017). Being in a mediated world: self-tracking and the mind–body–environment. *Cultural Geographies*, 24(3), 375–388.

Pink, S., Leder Mackley, K., & Moroşanu, R. (2015). Researching in atmospheres: video and the 'feel' of the mundane. *Visual Communication*, 14(3), 351–369.

Pink, S., Ruckenstein, M., Willim, R., & Duque, M. (2018). Broken data: conceptualising data in an emerging world. *Big Data & Society*, Jan/June, 1–13.

Plymire, D. C. (2004). Positive addiction: running and human potential in the 1970s. *Journal of Sport History*, 31(3), 297–315.

Purdy, L., Potrac, P., & Jones, R. (2008). Power, consent and resistance: an auto-ethnography of competitive rowing. *Sport, Education and Society*, 13(3), 319–336.

Putnam, R.D. (1993). *Making Democracy Work: Civic Traditions in Modern Italy*. Princeton: Princeton University Press.

Putnam, R.D. (2000). *Bowling Alone*. New York: Simon & Schuster.

Quealy, K., & Kats, J. (2019). Nike's fastest shoes may give runners an even bigger advantage than we thought. *New York Times*, 13 Dec. www.nytimes.com/interactive/2019/12/13/upshot/nike-vaporfly-next-percent-shoe-estimates.html?smid=nytcore-ios-share

Qviström, M. (2013). Landscapes with a heartbeat: tracing a portable landscape for jogging in Sweden (1958–1971). *Environment and Planning A*, 45, 312–328.

Qviström, M. (2017). Competing geographies of recreational running: the case of the 'jogging wave' in Sweden in the late 1970s. *Health & Place*, 46, July, 351–357.

Rantala, O., Valtonen, A., & Markuksela, V. (2011). Materializing tourist weather: ethnography on weather-wise wilderness guiding practices. *Journal of Material Culture*, 16(3), 285–300.

Reckwitz, A. (2002). Toward a theory of social practices: a development in culturalist theorizing. *European Journal of Social Theory*, 5, 243–263.

Reischer, E. L. (2001). Running to the moon: the articulation and construction of self in marathon runners. *Anthropology of Consciousness*, 12(2), 19–34.

Renfree, A., & Gibson, A. S. C. (2013). Influence of different performance levels on pacing strategy during the Women's World Championship marathon race. *International Journal of Sports Physiology and Performance*, 8(3), 279–285.

Rhodes, M (2017). Nike says this shoe will propel runners to a sub-two-hour marathon. *Wired*, 3 July. www.wired.com/2017/03/nike-zoom-vaporfly-elite/.

Richards, G., De Brito, M., & Wilks, L. (2013). *Exploring the Social Impacts of Events*. London: Routledge.

Richards, G., & Wilson, J. (2005). Social capital, cultural festivals and tourism in Catalunya. *Anuario Turismo y Sociedad*, 4, 170–181.

Rigauer, B. (1981). *Sport and Work*. New York: Columbia University Press.

Roberts, I. (2010). *The Energy Glut: The Politics of Fatness in an Overheating World*. London: Zed Books.

Robinson, R., Patterson, I., & Axelsen, M. (2014). The 'loneliness of the long-distance runner' no more: marathons and social worlds. *Journal of Leisure Research*, 46, 375–388.

Roche, M. (2003). Mega-events, time and modernity: on time structures in global society. *Time and Society*, 12, 99–126.

Rodaway, P. (1994). *Sensuous Geographies: Body, Sense and Place*. London: Routledge.

Rodriguez, E., Espinosa-Paredes, G., & Alvarez-Ramirez, J. (2014). Convection–diffusion effects in marathon race dynamics. *Physica A: Statistical Mechanics and its Applications*, 393, 498–507.

Ross, J. (2018). The women who crashed the Boston Marathon. *JSTOR Daily*, 18 March. https://daily.jstor.org/the-woman-who-crashed-the-boston-marathon/

RunnerClick (no year). World's largest and most recent marathon study. https://runnerclick.com/marathon-finishing-times-study-and-statistics/

Rupprecht, P. M., & Matkin, G. S. (2012). Finishing the race: Exploring the meaning of marathons for women who run multiple races. *Journal of Leisure Research*, 44(3), 308–331.

Sailors, P. R. (2009). More than a pair of shoes: Running and technology. *Journal of the Philosophy of Sport*, 36(2), 207–216.

Sailors, P. R. (2019). Chips and showmanship: running and technology. *Philosophies*, 4(2), 30.

Salazar, N. B. (2020). The ambigious role of pacemakers in the paradoxical quest for a proper pace of life. In V. Amit & N. B. Salazar (eds), *Pacing Mobilities: Timing, Intensity, Tempo and Duration of Human Movements*. London: Berghahn Books, pp. 19–35.

Salazar, N. B., & Amit, V. (2020). Introduction: Why and how does the pacing of mobilities matter? In V. Amit & N. B. Salazar (eds), *Pacing Mobilities: Timing, Intensity, Tempo and Duration of Human Movements*. London: Berghahn Books, pp. 1–18.

Sallis, J. F., Frank, L. D., Saelens, B. E., & Kraft, M. K. (2004). Active transportation and physical activity: opportunities for collaboration on transportation and public health research. *Transportation Research Part A*, 38(4), 249–268.

Samson, A., Simpson, D., Kamphoff, C., & Langlier, A. (2017). Think aloud: an examination of distance runners' thought processes. *International Journal of Sport and Exercise Psychology*, 15(2), 176–189.

Santos-Lozano, A., Collado, P. S., Foster, C., Lucia, A., & Garatachea, N. (2014). Influence of sex and level on marathon pacing strategy: insights from the New York City Race. *International Journal of Sports Medicine*, 35(11), 933–938.

Schatzki, T. (2001) *Social Practices*. Cambridge: Cambridge University Press.

Scheerder, J., Breedveld, K., & Borgers, J. (2015). Who is doing a run with the running boom? In J. Scheerder, K. Breedveld & J. Borgers (eds), *Running across Europe*. London: Palgrave Macmillan, pp. 1–27.

Schmidt, A. L. (2015). *Politiken*, 26 Dec.https://politiken.dk/debat/art5633956/Anders-Legarth-Schmidt-Min-bedste-artikel-handler-om-min-datters-sygdom-og-død

Schmidt, A. L. (2018). *Jeg løber*. Copenhagen: Politiken.

Schultz, J. (2019). Breaking into the marathon: Women's distance running as political activism. *Frontiers: A Journal of Women Studies*, 40(2), 1–26.

Serravallo, V. (2000). Class and gender in recreational marathon running. *Race, Gender & Class*, 7(2),96–121.

Sheehan, R. (2006). Running in place. *Tourist Studies*, 6(3), 245–265.

Sheller, M., & Urry, J. (2000). The city and the car. *International Journal of Urban and Regional Research*, 24(4), 737–757.

Sheller, M., & Urry, J. (2006). The new mobilities paradigm. *Environment and Planning A*, 38 (2), 207–226.

Shilling, C. (2012). *The Body and Social Theory*. London: Sage.

Shipway, R., & Holloway, I. (2016). Health and the running body: notes from an ethnography. *International Review for the Sociology of Sport*, 51(1), 78–96.

Shipway, R., Holloway, I., & Jones, I. (2013). Organisations, practices, actors, and events: exploring inside the distance running social world. *International Review for the Sociology of Sport*, 48(3), 259–276.

Shipway, R., & Jones, I. (2007). Running away from home: understanding visitor experiences and behaviour at sport tourism events. *International Journal of Tourism Research*, 9(5), 373–383.

Shipway, R., & Jones, I. (2008). The great suburban Everest: An 'insiders' perspective on experiences at the 2007 Flora London Marathon. *Journal of Sport & Tourism*, 13(1), 61–77.

Shove, E., & Pantzar, M. (2005). Consumers, producers and practices: understanding the invention and reinvention of Nordic walking. *Journal of Consumer Culture*, 5(1), 43–64.

Shove, E., & Pantzar, M. (2007). Recruitment and reproduction: the careers and carriers of digital photography and floorball. *Human Affairs*, 17, 154–167.

Shove, E., Pantzar, M., & Watson, M. (2012). *The Dynamics of Social Practice: Everyday Life and How It Changes*. London: Sage.

Sikes, P. J. (ed.). (2013). *Auto-ethnography*. London: Routledge.

Simpson, P. (2008). Chronic everyday life: rhythmanalysing street performance. *Social and Cultural Geography*, 9(7) 807–829.

Simpson, P. (2019). Elemental mobilities: atmospheres, matter and cycling amid the weather-world. *Social and Cultural Geography*, 20(8), 1050–1069.

Skorski, S., & Abbiss, C. R. (2017). The manipulation of pace within endurance sport. *Frontiers in Physiology*, 8, 102.

Smith, A. (2016). *Events in the City: Using Public Spaces as Event Venues*. London: Routledge.

Smith, G. (2002). Racing against time? Aspects of the temporal organization of the runner's world. *Symbolic Interaction*, 25, 343–362.

Smith, S. L. (1998). Athletes, runners, and joggers: Participant-group dynamics in a sport of 'individuals'. *Sociology of Sport Journal*, 15(2), 174–192.

Smith, S. L. (2000). British nonelite road running and masculinity: a case of 'running repairs'? *Men and Masculinities*, 3(2), 187–208.

Smyth, B. (2018). Fast starters and slow finishers: a large-scale data analysis of pacing at the beginning and end of the marathon for recreational runners. *Journal of Sports Analytics*, 4(3), 229–242.

Soei, A. (2016). *Forsoning*. Copenhagen: Tiderne Skifter.

Southerton, D. (2003). 'Squeezing time': allocating practices, coordinating networks and scheduling society. *Time & Society*, 12(1), 5–25.

Sparkes, A. C. (1996). The fatal flaw: a narrative of the fragile body-self. *Qualitative Inquiry*, 2 (4), 463–494.

Sparkes, A. C. (2000). Autoethnography and narratives of self: reflections on criteria in action. *Sociology of Sport Journal*, 17(1), 21–43.

Sparkes, A. C. (2002a). *Telling Tales in Sport and Physical Activity: A Qualitative Journey*. London: Human Kinetics Publishers.

Sparkes, A. C. (2002b). Autoethnography: self-indulgence or something more. In P. Bochner & C. Ellis (eds), *Ethnographically Speaking: Autoethnography, Literature, and Aesthetics*. Lanham: Rowman Altamira, pp. 209–232.

Sparkes, A. C. (ed.). (2017). *Seeking the Senses in Physical Culture: Sensuous Scholarship in Action*. London: Routledge.

Spellman, G. (1996). Marathon running: an all-weather sport? *Weather*, 51(4), 118–125.

Sperlich, B. (2016). Physiological aspects of marathon running. In C. Zinner & B. Sperlich (eds), *Marathon Running: Physiology, Psychology, Nutrition and Training Aspects*. Cham: Springer, pp. 1–12.

Spinney, J. (2006). A place of sense: a kinaesthetic ethnography of cyclists on Mont Ventoux. *Environment and Planning D: Society and Space*, 24, 709–732.

Spinney, J. (2008). Cycling between the traffic: mobility, identity and space. *Urban Design Journal*, 108(Autumn), 28–30.

Spinney, J. (2010). Improvising rhythms: re-reading urban time and space through everyday practices of cycling. In T. Edensor (ed.), *Geographies of Rhythm: Nature, Place, Mobilities and Bodies*. Basingstoke: Ashgate, pp. 113–128.

Spinney, J. (2011). A chance to catch a breath: using mobile video ethnography in cycling research. *Mobilities*, 6(2), 161–182.

Spotswood, F., Shankar, A., & Piwek, L. (2020). Changing emotional engagement with running through communal self-tracking: the implications of 'teleoaffective shaping' for public health. *Sociology of Health & Illness*, 42(4), 772–788.

Spry, T. (2001). Performing autoethnography: an embodied methodological praxis. *Qualitative Inquiry*, 7, 706–732.

St Clair Gibson, A., Lambert, E. V., Rauch, L. H., Tucker, R., Baden, D. A., Foster, C., & Noakes, T. D. (2006). The role of information processing between the brain and peripheral physiological systems in pacing and perception of effort. *Sports Medicine*, 36(8), 705–722.

Stanley, C. T., Pargman, D., & Tenenbaum, G. (2007). The effect of attentional coping strategies on perceived exertion in a cycling task. *Journal of Applied Sport Psychology*, 19(3), 352–363.

Stebbins, R. A. (1992). *Amateurs, Professionals, and Serious Leisure*. Vancouver: McGill-Queen's Press.

Stebbins, R. A. (2007). *A Perspective for Our Time*. New Brunswick: Transaction Publishers.

Stevinson, C. D., & Biddle, S. J. (1998). Cognitive orientations in marathon running and 'hitting the wall'. *British Journal of Sports Medicine*, 32(3), 229–234.

Stone, B. (2009). Running man. *Qualitative Research in Sport and Exercise*, 1(1), 67–71.

Stöggl, T., & Wunsch, T. (2016). Biomechanics of marathon running. In C. Zinner & B. Sperlich (eds), *Marathon Running: Physiology, Psychology, Nutrition and Training Aspects*. Cham: Springer, pp. 13–45.

Sudnow, D. (1993). *Ways of the Hand*. Cambridge, MA: MIT Press.

Sumartojo, S., Pink, S., Lupton, D., & LaBond, C. H. (2016). The affective intensities of datafied space. *Emotion, Space and Society*, 21, 33–40.

Suozzo, A. (2006). *The Chicago Marathon*. Illinois: University of Illinois Press.

Sutton, C. (2016). Embodying a healthy running body in a British non-elite road running community. In E. Ettorre (ed.), *Culture, Bodies and the Sociology of Health*. London: Routledge, pp. 71–90.

Thorpe, H. (2014). Moving bodies beyond the social/biological divide: toward theoretical and transdisciplinary adventures. *Sport, Education and Society*, 19(5), 666–686.

Thorpe, H. (2015). 'My hormones were all messed up'. In W. Bridel, P. Markula & J. Denison (eds), *Endurance Running: A Socio-Cultural Examination*. London: Routledge, pp. 63–180.

Thorpe, H., & Rinehart, R. (2010). Alternative sport and affect: non-representational theory examined. *Sport in Society*, 13(7–8), 1268–1291.

Thrift, N. (2008). *Non-representational Theory: Space, Politics, Affect*. London: Routledge.

Tillmann-Healy, L. M. (1996). A secret life in a culture of thinness. In C. Ellis & A. P. Bochner (eds), *Composing Ethnography: Alternative forms of Qualitative Writing*. Lanham: Rowman & Littlefield, pp. 76–108.

Tomlinson, A. (2004). Pierre Bourdieu and the sociological study of sport: habitus, capital and field. In R. Giulianotti (ed.), *Sport and Modern Social Theorists*. London: Palgrave Macmillan, pp. 161–172.

Tulle, E. (2007). Running to run: embodiment, structure and agency amongst veteran elite runners. *Sociology*, 41(2), 329–346.

Urry, J. (2000). *Sociology beyond Societies: Mobilities for the Twenty-first Century*. London: Routledge.

Urry, J. (2007). *Mobilities*. Cambridge: Polity Press.

Urry, J., & Larsen, J. (2011). *The Tourist Gaze 3.0*. London: Sage.

Van Maanen, J. (1988). *Tales from the Field: On Writing Ethnography*. Chicago: University of Chicago Press.

Vannini, P. (2015a). Non-representational ethnography: new ways of animating lifeworlds. *Cultural Geographies*, 22(2), 317–327.

Vannini, P. (2015b). Non-representational research methodologies. In P. Vannini (ed.), *Non-Representational Methodologies: Re-envisioning Research*. London: Routledge, pp. 50–77.

Vannini, P. (2017). Making sense of the primal scream. In A. Sparkes (ed.), *Seeking the Senses in Physical Culture: Sensuous Scholarship in Action*. London: Routledge, pp. 25–41.

Vannini, P., Waskul, D., & Gottschalk, S. (2013). *The Senses in Self, Society, and Culture: A Sociology of the Senses*. London: Routledge.

Vannini, P., Waskul, D., Gottschalk, S., & Ellis-Newstead, T. (2012). Making sense of the weather: dwelling and weathering on Canada's Rain Coast. *Space and Culture*, 15(4), 361–380.

Veblen, T. (2005). *Conspicuous Consumption*. London: Penguin.

Vergunst, J. (2010). Rhythms of walking: history and presence in a city street. *Space and Culture*, 13, 376–388.

Vickers, A. J., & Vertosick, E. A. (2016). An empirical study of race times in recreational endurance runners. *BMC Sports Science, Medicine and Rehabilitation*, 8(1), 26.

Vihma, T. (2010). Effects of weather on the performance of marathon runners. *International Journal of Biometeorology*, 54(3), 297–306.

Vorm, T. (2017). *Sidste Tog til Boston: Marathonløbets Historie*. Copenhagen: People's Press.

Vugts, H. F. (1997). The influence of the weather on marathon results. *Weather*, 52(4), 102–107.

Wacquant, L. (2004). *Body & Soul*. Oxford: Oxford University Press.

Wacquant, L. (2005). Carnal connections: on embodiment, apprenticeship, and membership. *Qualitative Sociology*, 28(4), 445–474.

Wacquant, L. (2015). For a sociology of flesh and blood. *Qualitative Sociology*, 38(1), 1–11.

Wainwright, S. P., & Turner, B. S. (2006). 'Just crumbling to bits'? An exploration of the body, ageing, injury and career in classical ballet dancers. *Sociology*, 40(2), 237–255.

Waitt, G. R. (2017). 'Natural', intimate and sensory landscapes. In L. Silk, L. Andrews & H. Thorpe (eds), *Routledge Handbook of Physical Cultural Studies*. London: Routledge, pp. 323–332.

Warde, A. (2005). Consumption and theories of practice. *Journal of Consumer Culture*, 5(2), 131–153.

Waterton, E. (2013). Non-representational theories. In P. Howard, I. Thompson & E. Waterton (eds), *The Routledge Companion to Landscape Studies*. London: Routledge, pp. 66–75.

Watson (2021). Average marathon times, sorted by demographics [+ half marathons]. *Marathon Handbook*. https://marathonhandbook.com/average-marathon-time/

Weed, M. (2009). Progress in sports tourism research? A meta-review and exploration of futures. *Tourism Management*, 30(5), 615–628.

West, L. R. (2015). Strava: challenge yourself to greater heights in physical activity/cycling and running. *British Journal Sports Medicine*, 49(15), 1024–1024.

Whelan, G. (2012). Running through a field: performance and humanness. *Performance Research*, 17(2), 110–120.

Wicker, P., Hallmann, K., & Zhang, J. J. (2012). What is influencing consumer expenditure and intention to revisit? An investigation of marathon events. *Journal of Sport & Tourism*, 17(3), 165–182.

Wilks, L. (2013). Introduction. In M. de Brito, G. Richards and L. Wilks (eds), *Exploring the Social Impacts of Events*. London: Routledge, pp. 1–12.

Wunderlich, M (2008). Walking and rhythmicity: sensing urban space. *Journal of Urban Design*, 13, 125–139.

Zepp, C. (2016). Coping with stress during a marathon. In C. Zinner & B. Sperlich (eds), *Marathon Running: Physiology, Psychology, Nutrition and Training Aspects*. Cham: Springer, pp. 83–105.

Zinner, C. (2016). Training aspects of marathon running. In *Marathon Running: Physiology, Psychology, Nutrition and Training Aspects*. Cham: Springer, pp. 153–171.

# INDEX

Page numbers in *italics* refer to figures.

Lightning Source UK Ltd.
Milton Keynes UK
UKHW021819271222
414250UK00024B/512